Girocho

Tech Sergeant John Henry Poncio, U.S. Air Force, 1945

Girocho

A GI's Story of Bataan and Beyond

JOHN HENRY PONCIO *and* MARLIN YOUNG

LOUISIANA STATE UNIVERSITY PRESS   BATON ROUGE

Copyright © 2003 by Louisiana State University Press
All rights reserved
Manufactured in the United States of America
First printing
12 11 10 09 08 07 06 05 04 03
5 4 3 2 1

Designer: Laura Roubique Gleason
Typeface: Minion text with Impact display
Printer and binder: Thomson-Shore, Inc.

Library of Congress Cataloging-in-Publication Data:

Poncio, John Henry, 1918–
    Girocho : a GI's story of Bataan and beyond / John Henry Poncio and Marlin Young.
        p. cm.
    ISBN 0-8071-2851-1 (cloth : alk. paper)
    1. Poncio, John Henry, 1918– 2. World War, 1939–1945—Personal narratives,
American. 3. World War, 1939–1945—Prisoners and prisons, Japanese. 4. Prisoners
of war—Philippines—Biography. 5. World War, 1939–1945—Concentration camps—
Philippines. 6. Bataan, Battle of, Philippines, 1942. I. Young, Marlin, 1936– II. Title.
    D811.P6185 A3 2003
    940.54'7252'092—dc21

                                                        2002152940

This account of what happened on Bataan, and later in prison camps in the Philippines and Japan, is dedicated to the men and women who served with valor. Some were incredibly brave, some were not so brave, but all were heroes in their own way.

It is also dedicated to those who did not survive, those who were buried naked and left this world as they entered it, with no possessions, no identity—but, I assure you, heroes all.

—John Henry Poncio

Contents

Illustrations

Preface

In September 1946, one year after the end of World War II, my mother's sister, Inez Pierron, introduced me to her new husband, John Henry Poncio. He was tall, slightly gray, and seemed to have a great sense of humor. I liked my new uncle right away.

Although many members of our family served with honor in various branches of the military during the war, I considered John Henry extra-special: the first real live hero that this ten-year-old girl had ever met.

I remember how my family and I sat around the kitchen table in our old country house near New Iberia, Louisiana, and listened in amazement to John's terrible ordeal at the hands of the enemy. After four months of intense fighting in MacArthur's Luzon Force in the Philippines, John was captured by the Japanese on April 9, 1942, survived the infamous Bataan Death March, and spent the remainder of the war in concentration camps.

John, who was twenty-eight, had just reenlisted in the air force. After their marriage, he and Inez moved from base to base: first to Chennault Air Force Base in Lake Charles, Louisiana, then to Biggs Air Force Base in El Paso, Texas, then on to Barksdale Air Force Base in Shreveport, Louisiana, then Langley Air Force Base in Newport News, Virginia, and finally to Louisiana Polytechnic Institute (now Louisiana Tech University) in Ruston, where he was an ROTC rifle coach and instructor.

In 1953, he received orders for reassignment to Hunter Air Force Base (formerly Savannah Army Airfield) in Georgia. When he got word, through a friend, that his outfit was shipping out to Korea, John marched into the office of his commanding officer and resigned. No way was he going to risk being captured again, this time by the Communists. The CO gave him the usual spiel about staying in the air force, but his heart wasn't in it. He thought John's decision was wise.

With his fourteen years of active service, credit for years spent in the Louisiana National Guard, and his POW status, John retired from the air force and moved back to his hometown of Morgan City, Louisiana. He worked with the city's engineer and later as deputy tax assessor in St. Mary Parish. In 1970, he ran for tax assessor and lost by only a few hundred votes. After the election, he retired from the parish but remained active in local and state politics.

All through those years he was a frequent lecturer to various civic and public associations and school groups. Many who heard him talk about his POW experiences urged him to write a book. After he retired, he tried. "I built an office behind the house, furnished it with a desk, a chair, and a typewriter," he said. "I put a sheet of paper into the machine and just sat there. Although I wrote poetry in high school and once a three-act play, it didn't take me long to figure out I couldn't do this." Instead he got a tape recorder and, whenever the mood would strike, talked about the past. It took a few months, but when he finished he had nine hours of tape. Inez transcribed the tapes for him, verbatim. But his story was still not in literary form.

In 1981 my husband was seconded to a Japanese trading firm from Arkel International, Baton Rouge, and we moved to Indonesia so that he could work in the sugar industry. During the next three years we traveled throughout the Orient and came to know many Japanese people, their customs, and a little of their language. (My husband had lived with a Japanese family while serving in the navy in Japan in the mid-1950s, and he helped me gain insight into much of their philosophy.)

In 1990, having moved back to Louisiana, I asked John to lend me his manuscript. Although I had listened to the tapes years before, reading the transcription made me realize that John's story had all the elements of a good book: suspense, danger, tragedy, and even humor. I also realized that, to do it justice, further research was necessary. Dates, times, and other facts had to be accurate—or as accurate as human memory of events experienced under duress could make them—and they had to jibe with the history books.

I did my research at the National Archives in Washington, D.C., specifically in the Military Reference Branch of the Philippine Archives. I found affidavits given to the International Red Cross and the Provost Marshal's Office by many POWs, both in the Philippines and in Japan. Some reported on conditions aboard the "hell ships." Records from sub-camp Hirohata in Japan were there, along with the affidavits of the warrant officer and the camp doctor. Books about MacArthur's strategy and campaigns in the Pacific, as well as one written from the Japanese military viewpoint, were helpful in relating John's experience to the "big picture." In addition, I conducted long interviews with John Henry, in telephone conversations that lasted for hours and during visits in which we closeted ourselves while he relived every aspect of the war.

As I began setting John's story down on paper, I tried to see it all through his eyes. Listening to his tapes and the inflections in his voice were invaluable. Later, when I read him episodes I had written, he would look at me and ask, "Vas you *dere*, Charlie?" In the end, he said that I had done an excellent job of telling it like it was, and he was proud of our combined effort.

Throughout our joint project, John was frequently ill. Stricken with cancer in 1983, he once more beat the odds. The night of his surgery, his prayer was typical of his simple faith. "Lord," he said, "your boy's in trouble again." His last years were painful. Already blind in his left eye from the effects of malnutrition during his imprisonment, he developed a form of aplastic anemia and suffered from mysterious fevers and deteriorating joints—long-term effects of beriberi contracted in the camps. Early in 1998, his doctors discovered a massive brain tumor. Through it all, he maintained his sense of humor and a strong love for God and country. John Henry died on October 25, 1998, at the age of eighty.

During his lifetime, John was recognized for his wartime role. His experiences in the Philippines were profiled in the *New Orleans Times-Picayune* on April 9, 1992, the fiftieth anniversary of the Bataan Death

March. He was mentioned in Margaret Utinsky's book *"Miss U"* (published in 1948) as one of her "boys," a member of her underground organization in the Philippines. His military decorations included the Purple Heart and the Bronze Star. On May 9, 1992, fifty years after the surrender of Corregidor, he and his fellow Louisiana POWs were honored by the Veterans of Foreign Wars and awarded a certificate of recognition and a specially struck medal "for remarkable perseverance, indomitable courage and heroic devotion."

John was a professional soldier and a unique individual who could appreciate the irony of his situation. His story is a straightforward and honest tale of ordinary men doing extraordinary things, with no apologies, condemnations, or animosity. While some events helped him see things from the enemy's standpoint, and he was befriended by a few Japanese people along the way, that didn't stop him from sabotaging their war effort every chance he got.

Marlin Young

Acknowledgments

I wish to thank several people for their assistance in making this book a reality. My husband, Seab, helped in many areas, from How To Turn On The Computer to the technical aspects of getting the book ready for publication. He also listened for hours to what I had written, and his objective criticism was always constructive.

My daughter Lauren Pursley's unique ability to capture certain moments in her illustrations, when words were not sufficient to tell the full story, is truly a gift, and I'm grateful to her.

I would also like to express my appreciation to Dr. Joseph Dawson of Texas A&M University, whose encouragement and detailed suggestions for changes helped to make the book much better.

Special thanks go to LSU Press's Sylvia Frank Rodrigue and the anonymous outside reader who liked the manuscript and felt it could be used as collateral reading in history courses. They have made a dream come true.

Lastly, I'd like to pay tribute to my uncle, the late John Henry Poncio, for being the special man he was. His story can teach us many things about life and endurance, but his greatest lesson is the ability to forgive.

Girocho

1 Lightning Strikes Twice

For weeks, a dreary, smoky shroud had hung over our Japanese prison camp, blotting out the sun and doing nothing to alleviate the all-pervading, gloomy atmosphere. Finally, the east wind began to clear it away. Patches of blue appeared here and there. But the air held something else—you could feel it. Maybe an end to the misery we called life, maybe not. God knows we had waited long enough. Normally, I would have been chomping at the bit to get on with it. But today I just wanted to go back to bed. In the past four years, I'd lived a lifetime. I looked eighty; I felt a hundred.

I eased my body onto the hard wooden bench built along the outside of the barracks and closed my eyes. Going "Asiatic"—the old trick of the mind that helped me escape reality so many times before—came easily to me. Before I knew it, the dreamlike state transported me back in time to the Philippines and to May 1942.

Facing the enemy, in torn and ragged coveralls, I stood at attention with twelve other American prisoners in front of the Filipino schoolhouse. Greenbottle flies buzzed my shaved head, nose-diving into the sweat trickling down my face. The terrific heat generated by a relentless sun sapped what little strength we had left; most of us could barely stand.

Only a few weeks before, our American-Filipino forces had surrendered to the Japanese after four months of brutal fighting on empty stomachs in the jungles of Bataan. The forced march that followed was a living nightmare. Wounded by a sniper the day of the surrender and still suffering crippling bouts of diarrhea from the polluted drinking water, by some miracle I had made it to this point, but this twenty-three-year-old Sicilian was hungry and mad as hell!

Several of the Japanese officers, dressed in khakis, peaked caps and leggings looked on from the shade of the porch as their interpreter addressed us. "Because your Amelican names are difficurt to pronounce, you will be renamed," he said in a singsong voice. Stepping up to me, he pinned a ribbon inscribed in *kana,* or Japanese characters, to the frayed edges of my collar. "From this day forward, you will be called Girocho, after famous samurai in folklore who stole from rich and gave to poor."

I almost laughed in his face. *Well, I'll be damned,* I thought. *Just call me Robin Hood.* Looking straight into his almond-shaped eyes, I silently told him, *Frankly, you son of a bitch, I don't care what you call me as long as you feed me.*

My buddy was next. "You are velly tall, with hairy chest, so you will be Girocho's number-one man, Omasa." I could only guess what Laurence was thinking.

The emperor's man went down the line, stopping to pin a name on each man's collar. The little impromptu ceremony caused a lot of snickering and jabbering among the onlookers; no doubt it was their idea of a joke.

A sudden commotion in the camp's compound put an end to my trance, propelling me into the present. Reluctantly, I opened my eyes. For the last year and a half I'd been held in a POW camp situated outside the small village of Hirohata, a few miles from the Inland Sea of Japan. But in the past few weeks the picture kept changing so fast that it was getting harder and harder to keep up.

I could see the guys gravitating toward the gate. It irritated me. I wanted to stay with the dream. Believe it or not, that brief period I spent known as "Girocho" hadn't been too bad. Sadly, it was all downhill after that. *Curiosity kills cats,* I reminded myself. No doubt, the itch to see what lay on the other side of the hill, colliding with world events, had almost done this cat in. But, I could never stand suspense.

Dragging my mind back from the past, I limped over to the fence, urged on by something I couldn't name. As I elbowed my way through the unresisting crowd, the stunned look on my comrades' faces made me uneasy. Then, I got a load of the poor bastards choking the road in front of the camp. "My God!" I said.

For months, literally thousands of American B-29s had flown over our area day and night. Huge Superfortresses, flying in parallel formations like flocks of geese heading south, carried out their missions in wave after wave, dropping tons of incendiaries on the cities and towns below.

When the bombs struck the immediate vicinity of our camp and the village of Hirohata, friends and family members of the local guards began to die in the raids. Nasty to begin with, the guards stepped up their brutal treatment of the prisoners. "Amelicans, no good!" they would scream, knocking those of us within range across the shoulders or over the head with their clubs. "Takusan no bakugeki ga kuru. Soshite, takusan no nihonjin ga shinu" (Many bombers come. Many Japanese die). "Okuno kokumin ga shinu daro" (Many people in country die). In their grief, they beat us, inflicting their unique brand of punishment without mercy.

The night our bombers struck the nearby city of Himeji, all of us were dead asleep when the door of the barracks crashed open and the Jap guard switched on the light. Sick, barely alive, we groaned and tried to shield our eyes from the glare. The enraged guard stood in the middle of the aisle, swinging his bat, threatening to kill everyone in the barracks. "Tenko [reveille]," he yelled. "Speedo, speedo!" Most of us couldn't move fast enough to suit him, so he clubbed us or kicked us with his hobnail boots. His friends joined in the fun, shoving us, punching us, sending some of us sprawling into the courtyard as we filed out of the building to witness the spectacle.

A column of fire, easily five miles in diameter, resembled a blast from hell, shooting up into the clouds and maybe heaven itself. It gave off an eerie orange glow, lighting up the faces of the men around me.

Like the sound of an immense fiery tornado destroying everything in its path, the roar of the flames filled the air as they engulfed the city. The scene was indescribable. We just stood there, gaping at the holocaust, unable to speak.

Shortly after that, the planes stopped flying over. Days went by, but the skies remained empty. What could it mean? *Is the war over?* we wondered. If so, who won?

Rumors flew. Unbelievable rumors. We heard something about a "lightning bomb." "Pika don, pika don," the guards screamed at us. A bomb so powerful it completely wiped out cities. We heard about astronomical death tolls in places where hardly anyone survived. We didn't buy it. But now the terrible sight of hundreds of dazed and zombielike refugees streaming by the camp finally convinced us that something terrible must have happened.

It seemed impossible that only a few months before we had watched another procession come down this same road. On that beautiful fall day in 1944, happy and carefree Japanese men and women paraded in their finery in front of our camp, singing and dancing to the music of pipes and drums. The sound of the noisy, laughing crowd, celebrating the festival of their rice god, carried for miles on the crystal-clear air. But on this day, the air carried the unmistakable odor of burned flesh and the peculiar sound made by scores of *geta* (wooden shoes) crunching on gravel. Now and then a child whimpered.

We stared in horror at the people whose scorched strips of clothing hung like ribbons from their bodies—in many cases, the fabric was fused to their skin. They looked as if they had been very badly sunburned. The shock on their faces and the pain and misery reflected in their eyes aroused genuine sympathy in the silent men who watched. But the sight of them also filled me with dread as the full realization of our predicament began to set in. The camp authorities repeatedly warned us that if America invaded Japan, they would execute all prisoners without fail. The way they said it made your flesh crawl.

I also remembered all the times I saw civilians practice with burned and sharpened bamboo sticks: trained from childhood to attack us in suicidal hand-to-hand combat, if it came to that. The thought made sleep impossible.

During the entire period of my imprisonment, eagle-eyed Japs kept close watch over us. We felt their presence even while we slept. But several days later, on August 15, the compound was mysteriously empty. We found our jailers, army soldiers and civilian guards alike, standing inside headquarters, heads bowed, listening to the radio. A couple of the prisoners who spoke fluent Japanese eased over and eavesdropped outside the window. They heard the emperor of Japan addressing the Japanese people, telling them the war was over, Japan had lost, and he had surrendered to the United States. He praised his subjects, saying they had done their best, but he warned them not to retaliate or hold out in any way.

We had won the war! But we could take no comfort in the fact. The day we had waited for so long meant almost nothing. Even the smallest gesture on our part, a smile or a V for victory sign, might bring them down on our heads. Instead of a victory celebration, the universal question on everybody's mind seemed to be: What stops them from lining us up against a wall and shooting us—or worse yet, chopping off our heads (threats made by the more sadistic guards)?

Cynical men—some bitter, some hopeless, others seemingly hardened beyond redemption—now just sounded scared. They whispered to each other in endless conversations: "What do you think's gonna happen? Will they torture us before they finally kill us?"

Someone asked me what I thought. It didn't pay to tell him, so I just shrugged. To myself I said, *Hey, John, you old so and so, some luck you got. You've spent all this time using every trick you knew to stay alive for just one more lousy day, only to wind up dead after we've won the war!*

The situation looked bad. I couldn't count the times we had witnessed the enemy's arrogance and been the object of their senseless cruelty—an arrogance stemming from the fanatical pride in their race and their devout worship of country.

The next twenty-four hours would be a living hell for everyone in camp. Knowing from experience that their rigidly obeyed Bushido Code could roughly be translated as, "We'd rather lose ass than face," each man prepared himself the best way he could and waited for the end.

2   The Beginning of the End

Rumor had it that the code name for military operations in the Philippines read PLUM. For once, the scuttlebutt proved right. PLUM stood for Philippines, Luzon, Manila. But after the first few weeks on Bataan—"at government expense"—we decided we had been sent "PLUM straight to hell!"

In retrospect, none of what happened after we left the West Coast in the fall of 1941 should have come as a great surprise. The signs were all there. In a short time, the future I had mapped out suddenly took a left turn. As every GI knows, snafu (situation normal, all fouled up) is standard military issue. For me, it was becoming a way of life.

When Hitler marched into Poland in 1939, I was twenty-one years old and an aeronautical-engineering student at Louisiana State University in Baton Rouge. I had spent three years in the National Guard (I lied about my age and joined at seventeen), was an expert marksman, and had risen to the position of assistant coach of the ROTC Rifle Team in my second year in that program at LSU. On September 1, 1939, when we got word of the invasion, the team was competing in the National Rifle Matches at Camp Perry, Ohio.

Many of us predicted that before it was all over, America would become involved in the war in Europe. Within a month I decided to quit school and enlist in the Army Air Corps—a total force of about twenty-two hundred men at the time.

I was fortunate to be assigned to the 13th Bombardment Squadron at Barksdale Field in Shreveport, Louisiana, only a few hours from my hometown of Morgan City. I also went through boot camp at Barksdale. Three months later I got promoted to mechanic. Raise in pay: $6.00 a month.

By the fall of 1940, Europe was under siege by the Germans. Paris had fallen, and the battle of Britain was launched, with London under aerial attack. It became increasingly apparent that America would be drawn into the war.

About that time, my commanding officer selected me as a candidate for bombardier, to be trained in the use of the new, top-secret Norden bombsight. This was not a volunteer assignment; all the men in the program were hand-picked and their backgrounds checked out by the army before they were sent to Savannah Army Airfield in Georgia for training.

Before leaving for Savannah, I went home to visit my paternal grandparents, who had immigrated to this country from Italy in the 1880s. Although they spoke English with a heavy accent, they owned and operated a small grocery store in Morgan City.

My father died in the 1918–19 flu epidemic that swept this country. Since I was the only grandson and "figlio la gaddina bianca"—an old Sicilian saying that means "the child of the white chicken"—I spent long periods of time with Grandma and Grandpa from an early age and finished high school while living with them. They doted on me, brought me up as a son, gave me a strong sense of identity, and tried to endow me with some of their faith and courage—strengths I would need again and again in the months and years to come.

A few days before my furlough ended, I got a haircut. The barber, who was also the town's chief of police, asked me if I liked the air corps.

"Yeah, sure," I answered.

"Tell me the truth, now—are you in trouble, or something?" he continued.

"Not that I know of. Why?"

"A couple of FBI men have been snooping around, asking questions. They wanted to know about your character, your habits and the like. I hear they even talked to your grandparents."

"Oh, Lord, I'm in trouble now," I said, laughing.

"Don't worry, boy," he said with a chuckle. "I didn't tell 'em everything I know!"

Although background checks were routine for these top-secret assignments, I guess they wanted to make certain that, with the name Poncio and having been raised by Italian grandparents, I was a loyal American and not a Mussolini sympathizer.

Opportunities to make a good living and achieve some level of success were scarce during the Great Depression, especially in our sleepy southern town. Fishing was Morgan City's main source of income; there was very little in the way of industry or business. Later, shipbuilding and the oil boom would change all that. But at the time, I felt the military offered me a chance to make something of myself. I planned to make it my career.

I enjoyed army life and the feeling of camaraderie in our squadron. Being bound by oath to keep everything we heard or learned in the classroom a secret helped forge an esprit de corps among the men. As time went by, not only did we become a team, we became good friends. I found the work interesting and challenging. We figured that when we got into the war with Germany, we'd give 'em hell!

Eager to get into the fray, I jumped at the first opportunity to fly to North Africa with a detachment to instruct the British in low-level bombing. But the day before they left, I slipped off the wing of my plane during refueling and fell, hurting my back.

The doctor examined me and said, "It's the hospital for you, Sergeant."

"C'mon, Doc," I pleaded with him, seeing my big chance about to slip away. "I'll be okay."

"No," he insisted. "We'd better keep you for a few days. This kind of injury could come back to haunt you."

No appeal could sway him. I tried every argument in the book, but no soap!

The night before the men left, my pal Red dropped by the hospital ward to say goodbye. The grin on his face belied his words of sympathy. "Hey, John. Tough break, man! I know how you must feel. But I just got the word. Guess I'll be going in your place."

Before dawn the next morning, I lay in my hospital bed listening to the transport take off, sorrier than hell I couldn't go with them.

Up for promotion to staff sergeant, with a pay raise, in October 1941, and prompted by my girl's ultimatum—"Either a new car or a new girl, John. I'm developing muscles in all the wrong places from pushing this jalopy up the hills"—I decided to replace my old Ford wreck with a beauty of an automobile, a 1939 LaSalle—an even snazzier car than the base commander's!

But just a few days before my promotion, I was shanghaied into the 91st Bombardment Squadron. The duties of this new armament unit, formed by picking several men from each air corps squadron, would consist of arming the dive-bombers and equipping the planes with machine guns.

All my training as a bombardier would be useless. In one fell swoop, I lost not only my flight pay and the raise due a staff sergeant, but the opportunity to become an officer later when the air force commissioned all bombardiers.

I had to sell my car for half the cost. Even worse, the 13th went back to Barksdale in Shreveport, while I shipped out to the West Coast with a bunch of strangers, bound for God knows where.

On or around October 20, 1941, we arrived at Fort McDowell on Angel Island in San Francisco Bay to be processed for overseas duty. It was a long, uncomfortable journey. Traveling by train from Savannah up the coast to Richmond, we then headed for Chicago. By the time the trip was over, we had snaked our way all through the West.

Waiting around Fort McDowell for our ship to sail, we got word that our personal baggage lay at the bottom of San Francisco Bay. During the transfer of two boxcars to barges before loading the cars onto a freighter in the harbor, the dock's ramp broke, dumping both cars into about fifty or sixty feet of water. After the cars were raised, a quartermaster claims officer took us to identify our things. As I stood on the dock in San Francisco in the chilly morning air, gloomily surveying the soggy mess that was everything I owned in the world, I began to wonder if Somebody was trying to tell me something. Apparently I wouldn't need the new wool civvies on a tropical island. My leather jacket, a birthday gift from a special friend, was dead, and my red wool bathrobe had dyed my white dress shirts pink.

The quartermaster claims officer told us he would file a claim for damages and that we would be paid in the future. "Yeah, sure," was the disgusted response. Since we were sailing for the Philippines in a day or two, we figured we could kiss our stuff, and the money, goodbye.

We boarded the SS *President Coolidge,* a luxury liner leased by the government shortly before the war. There was a shortage of troop transports at the time, and leasing ocean liners gave the military time to either build new ships or reactivate old ones.

Built to sail between San Francisco and the Orient, the *President Coolidge* had plush interiors, paneled in rare woods, and beautiful stained-glass skylights. No conversion was made to the ship, other than stacking bunks five high on the decks to accommodate the large numbers of men. The officers got the staterooms.

The trip allowed us to relax and have a good time. They served us great chow, and an orchestra entertained us. We danced with the hostesses on board and played the slot machines, just like on a regular cruise. We reached Honolulu in about a week and docked there for a few hours.

We went ashore to look around, followed everywhere by little Hawaiian and Japanese kids who kept asking, "Mister, Mister, when is the war going to start?"

"What war?" we asked.

Maybe we were badly informed or just plain stupid, but although many of us had been in the military for quite some time, the general focus for most of the GIs was on Europe; I don't think we realized that war in the Pacific was imminent. We knew we weren't on the friendliest of terms with Japan, but being average Joes, we had no understanding of the Japanese and what they were capable of doing. I guess we all thought—if we thought at all—that Japan was just a second-rate country. Before long, we would discover the extent of their determination to conquer all of Asia and to become the dominant force in that part of the world.

The next day we left for Manila. Except for one engineer company, the majority of the 3,500 men on board were from the air corps—reinforcements for the men already stationed in the Philippines. After fishing one guy out of the harbor, who decided at the last minute he preferred Hawaii to the Philippines, we got under way and soon joined up with a troop transport, the USS *Hugh L. Scott*, and a heavy cruiser, the USS *Louisville*, our escorts on the last leg of the trip.

As though we expected trouble, we set a zigzag course all across the Pacific. Every time another ship showed up on the horizon, the *Louisville* steamed over to investigate the situation. At night, blackout conditions applied. It took us about two weeks to reach the Philippines, but other than these few precautions it was an uneventful cruise.

We arrived in Manila on Thanksgiving Day and had turkey and all the trimmings on board the ship. Later, we moved to Fort McKinley, a Philippine Army fort in Manila, to wait for our planes and equipment to come in from the States.

The last time I saw our A-24s, low-level attack bombers (or DB-7s, as the Brits called them), they were being ferried across San Francisco Bay on barges to be loaded onto a ship bound for the Philippines. We expected them in the next two weeks, after which our duties would consist of building airstrips throughout the island of Luzon. With nothing much to do until then, we were given leave to go downtown a few times.

Manila, an interesting and exciting city, fascinated us. Young and inexperienced, from small towns or farms back home, most of the men had never been out of the States. We could stand on one corner of the Escolta (the main street) and see every make of automobile in the world and practically every race on earth go by—Chinese, Japanese, and Indians, just to name a few—in their colorful native dress.

Our first taxi ride was traumatic. The driver's seat was on the right side of the car, and he drove on the left side of the road. I hopped into the front seat next to him, while the rest of the bunch settled in the back. As we took off down the narrow, congested streets at top speed, I kept stomping on the floorboard, applying brakes that weren't there.

"Look out," I yelled, gripping the door handle with white-knuckled fingers as the driver narrowly missed a pedestrian crossing the road.

"No problem, Joe," he said with a broad grin as he leaned on his horn while plowing through traffic, his foot rooted to the gas pedal. I guess the people were used to it; they just parted like the water in front of a speeding boat. But all of us fly-boys emerged from the joy ride weak-kneed and slightly pale.

The movie theaters in Manila operated a little differently from those in the States. The seats in the balcony cost more than the seats on the ground floor. That made sense, though, because the people in the balcony threw trash and bottles and flicked their lit cigarettes over the railing—they even urinated on the floor—all of which was hazardous to the people sitting below.

One night we saw *Blood and Sand,* making it the fourth time for me. It was a good movie, but after seeing it once in Savannah and twice on the ship coming over, I could quote some of Tyrone Power's lines verbatim.

I enjoyed the food in the Philippines. As a Louisiana boy, I already loved rice and seafood, so I fit right in with the natives. Although we enjoyed most of the dishes, the Filipinos had one favorite that we found hard to swallow. They liked baluts, unhatched duck eggs, which they ate by breaking a hole in the shell and sucking out the unborn duckling. To them it was a delicacy; to us it stunk! Even later, when things got so bad we were starving to death, I personally knew of no American who could stomach it.

The Filipina women we met were usually very friendly, and many were quite beautiful. Much to our surprise, they spoke excellent English, so we had no trouble communicating. Several huge dance halls with plenty of amiable hostesses dotted the city; at a dime a dance, a GI could have a good time for very little money.

The Filipinos had devised ways to cope with potentially embarrassing situations caused by their crowded conditions and lack of privacy. The average American soldier found some of these customs confusing at times. In the rural areas, men and women bathed together in streams or rivers, but they carefully avoided looking at each other. Likewise, when women stepping into or out of the calesas (two-wheeled, horse-drawn carriages) raised their skirts above their ankles, the Filipino men averted their eyes. The GIs always stared in frank admiration, and some even whistled. We got a lot of dirty looks and quite a few comments about our bad manners.

Killing time on a street corner one day, I heard the sound of running water. Looking all around, I realized that an old woman, standing next to me in a long dress, was urinating on the sidewalk. I failed to turn away in time, and she saw the shock on my face. She got extremely agitated and upset with me for noticing and gave me one hell of a tongue-lashing in her native Tagalog. Her privacy had been invaded, and it was all my fault. It didn't make the slightest bit of difference to her that my shoes were getting wet.

3 Escape to Corregidor

In the early morning hours of Monday, December 8, 1941—Philippine time—most of the men were asleep in the temporary tent city that had been set up for us at Fort McKinley. Some of the men in my unit were lying in their bunks, listening to the radio, when the announcer suddenly broke in to say that the Japanese had bombed Pearl Harbor.

"We're at war!" the men yelled, waking the rest of the guys with the news. "The sonuvabitches have bombed the Islands!"

Others, coming back from a night on the town, heard the broadcast on car radios and rushed in to tell their friends, "It's finally happened!" Accounts of the strike soon spread like wildfire throughout the base.

Back in the hospital (again) for a minor injury the day before, I didn't get the word until dawn. At first, I had a hard time believing it. By this time, war rumors were a dime a dozen. Besides, the brass figured the Japs would attack in the spring; certainly no one pegged Hawaii for the first strike.

When the rumor was officially confirmed, Iba, Clark, and Nichols Fields, the air bases on Luzon, went on full alert. At Fort McKinley, we prepared to move out of the tents into a ravine at the edge of the field, giving us more protection in case of attack. Elsewhere, men in other squadrons and companies began digging foxholes and trenches, setting up sandbagging operations to fortify their positions, and constructing bunkers and first-aid stations.

The regulars in the army and the air corps, already stationed in the Philippines, had their assignments, but we had no permanent station. Our squadron just stood around waiting for something to happen. We didn't have long to wait. Nine hours after the Japs bombed Pearl Harbor, as part of their coordinated plan to attack Allied bases in the Pacific, they flew in from Formosa and started pounding us.

"Oh God! I see 'em! Here they come!" men hollered as they ran for cover. Waves of enemy planes roared in from the sea. They came in low, bombing and strafing all the major fields in the Philippines. We tried shooting back, but our Enfields and Springfields were no match for the hordes of Zeroes and dive-bombers. We had no choice but to seek cover and literally take it lying down.

"This is no damn way to fight a war!" men groused, impatient and frustrated. "Where the hell are our planes?"

"Yeah. What I wouldn't give for a chance to meet the Japs in the air!"

None of us knew that right after the strike on Pearl, the ship with our fifty-two DB-7s had made a left turn and headed for Australia. We would never see those planes again.

The Far Eastern Air Force in the Philippines, woefully inadequate for total war, had some old Filipino training planes, about thirty-five Flying Fortresses, or B-17s, and a hundred or so P-40s. That day all the shiny Flying Fortresses, lined up in a row at Clark Field, provided an easy target for the Japs. The decision to fly some of the P-40s off the field came too late, and a wave of incoming Zeroes blasted most of them, and all but three of the B-17s, out of existence. Several of the fighter pilots managed to give chase, but the Zeroes quickly knocked out two.

Someone got the bright idea that if we borrowed one of three aging B-18s belonging to some other outfit at nearby Nichols Field, we could raid the island of Formosa. I would be lead bombardier. Excited by the chance to finally do something positive, several of us went looking for our bombing tables and other gear we'd need for a strike.

While we were digging into our equipment down at the docks, the Japs attacked the field, blowing to bits the B-18 that was loaded and ready for takeoff. The other two B-18s, parked close by, went up in flames. We heard the loud explosions and saw the orange flames and oily black smoke from the port. That ended our idea of raiding Formosa.

With so many Jap planes pitted against us, we didn't stand a chance in hell of getting off the ground. But that never occurred to us. We felt we had to do something, no matter what the cost. But with the destruction of those bombers, along with the detour of the DB-7s to Australia, our squadron's chances of fighting the enemy in the air died.

Unwilling to give up entirely, our badly outnumbered pilots went up each day to meet the Japs with the pitifully few P-40s left intact. Even so, we gave them a rough time—especially the Filipino aces in their training planes.

The Japanese Mitsubishis were good planes but no match in combat tactics for the agile little biplanes. Much faster than the trainers, which could easily pull out of the way, a Zero had to fly two or three miles before the pilot could turn it around. By that time, the little Stearman was either on him or running. We always said that all the damned Zeroes up there just got in each other's way.

Later, on Corregidor, I would get to see Captain Villamor, a Filipino ace, and thirteen of his pilots in action. They went up and attacked a hundred Zeroes. It might have been foolhardy, but that didn't stop Villamor, who did an outstanding job of it. I don't think the Japs knocked any of his planes down that day, but he got five or six of theirs.

Without planes, and with Japanese invasion of the island imminent, our forces were fast running out of time, so headquarters decided to turn us into infantrymen.

All four squadrons in the 27th Bombardment Group became the 27th Provisional Infantry Battalion. The 91st had good mechanics, radiomen, pilots, cooks, electricians, bombardiers, and gunners. But only three of us knew anything about infantry training—Bill Williams and I from our service in the National Guard before the war, plus one old-timer from the U.S. Cavalry. Everyone else was strictly air corps.

Starting from scratch, the troops marched out to a cleared area and received some fundamental instructions in handling a rifle, how to advance and infiltrate—generally the type of training a dogface got. That only lasted a few hours, for the Japanese, strongly supported by planes and ships, landed at Vigan and Aparri in northern Luzon on December 10. Two days later, they came ashore at Legazpi in the south. The third week in December, troop transports carrying 150,000 men, again backed by the Japanese air force (now based on the northern and northwestern coasts of Luzon) and their warships, landed at Lingayen Gulf. The squeeze was on.

In the meantime, I joined men from other squadrons and moved out to an area near the town of San Fernando in Pampanga Province to begin building an airfield for the planes that would be coming in "any day now."

It was harvest time in the Philippines, and the native workers under our supervision leveled the rice paddies. We started work on gun emplacements, concealed inside a tepeelike framework of bamboo. When covered with the sheaves, they resembled shocks of rice drying in the sun. But the daily raids on Luzon by the unopposed Japanese air force made it difficult to finish the job.

During the days and weeks following the initial attack, the Japanese continually bombed and strafed the Philippines. By the third week in December, the city of Manila was threatened by ground troops advancing from six different beachheads on Luzon.

Although air raids became routine in Manila, the daily attacks were usually confined to military and strategic targets in and around the city. On Christmas Day, the sirens competed with the ringing of church bells as bombers struck the port area. Cavite Naval Base, six miles south of the city, took a direct hit, blowing up the huge reserves of gasoline and ammunition stored there.

Unfortunately, civilian casualties mounted with each new attack. After evacuating some of the population to safety zones in the provinces, General MacArthur declared Manila an open city on December 26, in the hope of saving it from total destruction. Even though American and Philippine forces were withdrawn and Manila's defenses crippled by dismounting the anti-aircraft batteries and removing or destroying the military stores, the Japs ignored MacArthur's decree and bombed the business district of Manila for the first time on the day of the declaration.

Knowing there might not be enough troops to defend the island of

Luzon in the event of war, the Filipino army, in cooperation with the United States military, had devised a plan years before known as War Plan Orange, or WPO-3. The plan called for the combined forces to defend the island by backing into the Bataan Peninsula, which jutted out into the South China Sea and into the opening of Manila Bay. There they were to make their stand against the enemy, backed up by Fort Corregidor, Fort Drum, and Fort Hughes, small islands that formed a defensive system across the mouth of the bay.

At first, MacArthur insisted on defending Luzon on the beaches, but his plans were soon scrapped due to a lack of reinforcements. The last week of December, he reluctantly gave orders to implement WPO-3. The withdrawal of our eighty thousand Filipino-American forces to Bataan, along with supplies and matériel to sustain us for an indeterminate period, began. Forced to abandon the airstrip, we joined the general exodus from Pampanga into Bataan. A place had been set up for the men of the 91st in the reserve line, south of Abucay, just below the Bagac and Orion road, approximately sixty miles from Manila. For about a week, we helped dig the trenches and mount the gun emplacements, preparing for the battle to come.

Meanwhile, scuttlebutt had it that we might be getting our bombers soon. Our squadron commander pulled me aside and said, "Sergeant, if and when those planes arrive, we'll need our bombing equipment. Take the jeep and three men, get down to the port, and retrieve our gear."

"Yes sir!" I said, eager to be in the air corps again.

Bataan was nothing short of mass confusion. As the Americans moved in, thousands of Filipinos, fleeing the imminent invasion by the Japanese, also joined the throng going into the peninsula. Pedestrians leading their wagons, pulled by carabao (water buffalo) and loaded with children and possessions, together with others riding bicycles or driving old cars, jammed the left side of the road. A long, slow procession of military trucks, tanks, and automobiles, accompanied by thousands of troops, effectively blocked the right side of the narrow highway. Choking clouds of dust coated everything in sight.

It was difficult to see ahead without pulling out of line. Impatient to get ahead of the slow-moving traffic, we pulled out once too often and got clobbered by an oncoming tank. It hit the left rear wheel of the jeep, flipping us over, and we landed upside down in the middle of a rice paddy. Fortunately, the soft mud saved us.

No one bothered to stop and help us. We turned the vehicle upright without much trouble, but pushing it back onto the road took some doing. After we scraped the mud off the seats (and our clothes) we climbed in. It started up on the third try but refused to budge. We piled out to assess the damage. The drive shaft, the shackle, and one wheel were busted.

"The wheel's no problem," I said. "We've got a spare. But what about the rest?"

One of the guys, a mechanical genius, just grinned and said, "Give me a minute. I've got an idea."

I watched him paw through the toolbox, fish out a rattail file, and use it to replace the shackle bolt. He started the jeep once more, this time putting it in front-wheel drive. She moved! Laughing, we changed the tire, got in, and drove the damn thing all the way into Manila. As far as I know, it was driven all over Bataan in the same condition.

In the city, we scrounged around, found the bombing equipment we needed, loaded it up, and realized we had room to spare. "You see what I see?" our mechanic said, spying piles of cargo sitting out in a square across from the port.

"Man, it looks like food and supplies," I said. "I think I even see cartons of cigarettes! All of it's just lying out there in the open."

"Yeah, looks like someone offloaded one of those inter-island steamers and just abandoned everything in a panic," he said. "We might as well take as much of this stuff back as possible. Before this is over, we'll need it and a helluva lot more."

By the time we had commandeered three trucks and loaded them with everything under the sun, including machinery, it was too late to start the run back to Bataan. We spent the night in a closed-down dance hall. But nobody slept. An entire army on the march makes a lot of noise. The constant rumble of trucks, big guns, and troops streaming in from the south, passing through the city, and going north kept us awake most of the night. At dawn, red-eyed and irritable, we joined the pitiful throngs of refugees heading in the same direction.

When the CO saw all the food, cigarettes, and other supplies, he asked, "Is there any more of this stuff down there?"

"There's a whole city square full of it," I told him. "Say the word and we'll go back tomorrow."

He gave us the okay, and the next day we picked up another truck and made the long trek back to the city. This time, we concentrated on taking back as much food as we could carry.

The whole time we spent transporting supplies to our unit from the port, we had to dodge the bombing and strafing that went on several times a day. On one trip, a Jap pilot took aim and dropped his bomb right behind the truck I was driving. "Son of a bitch!" I shook my fist and yelled at the pilot, convinced from the noise and the impact that I'd taken a direct hit. But I had to laugh when it started raining syrup and I got pummeled with bits of peaches, pears, and cherries from exploding cans. Bomb fragments apparently tore through a case of fruit cocktail stacked on top of the supplies, plastering the windshield and the cab of the truck with fruit and soaking the rest of the boxes in the back.

I couldn't stop to wash it off. I just turned on the wipers to clear the windscreen and kept going. As the retreating masses slowed us to a walk, the sweet, sticky mess began to sour in the tropical heat, and fumes soon permeated every square inch of the truck. By the time I reached our unit on Bataan late that afternoon, I had developed a life-long aversion to the stuff.

After the second run, the Old Man decided we could probably make another trip before the final withdrawal and sent us back for more food. "It's New Year's Eve," he said. "You guys deserve a break. Stay over in town, have a good meal, get some rest, and come back tomorrow."

That earned him a smart salute, and back to town we went. With thoughts of a pleasant evening ahead, we worked nonstop, cramming those trucks with everything imaginable, then drove to the Manila Hotel, parked down in the garage, and went inside to get a room.

Most of the military had evacuated Manila by this time, but about two thousand American civilians were still there—some too stubborn to leave while they had a chance, others caught by the surprise attack on the island. Quite a few had flocked to the hotel, waiting to see what would happen in the next few days. Rumors about the Japanese occupation of the city took on a life of their own, and confused people milled around aimlessly, uncertain about the future.

We cleaned up, but I couldn't shave, since my razor was the first thing I ditched—a casualty of living in the field. As a result, I went up to the roof garden for dinner a bit scruffy, dressed in coveralls and combat boots.

In contrast, some of the men wore tuxes and others wore the sheer white Filipino shirts that passed for formal wear. Many of the women were elegantly attired in evening gowns or in the lovely native butterfly-sleeved dresses. They sat at beautifully appointed tables with silver and crystal gleaming on starched white linens in the soft lamplight.

Glancing at the guys with me, who looked as shabby as I did, I had to laugh. But even though we looked like hell, everyone there, determined to have a good time despite the worsening situation, welcomed us with open arms. That night, we dined on thick steaks cooked to perfection and served on fine china. The champagne and wine flowed all night long, and we danced until dawn.

We didn't need fireworks that night! As we watched from the roof, the sky was lit with a bright red glow from the port, where storage tanks and warehouses had been set ablaze to keep oil and supplies out of the enemy's hands.

On New Year's Day, as we started back to Bataan with the supplies, a Filipino guard stopped us and said, "Joe, you cannot get back this way. All the bridges were blown last night by the American troops pulling out."

With a sinking feeling I asked, "The Calumpit is destroyed?"

"Yes," he said. In addition, he told us the Japs had been sighted twenty miles south of the city the day before and were rapidly advancing from the north, supported by tanks and heavy artillery.

The twin-span Calumpit Bridge, twenty miles north of the city, was the only way across the deep, swift Pampanga River with its surrounding marshes. Even if we somehow crossed the river, the vast swampland and estuaries that lay between it and our position on Bataan were impassable on foot—and to follow the road was, quite possibly, to meet up with the enemy. Now we had no way back to our unit—at least not overland. There we were: four men with four trucks and without the foggiest idea of what to do! Turning around, we headed back downtown to consider our options.

Under continuous attack from the enemy that day, the city was slowly dying. By now the dive-bombers had destroyed many historic churches, hospitals, and residential areas. Hundreds of people had been killed or wounded. The Filipinos were running around, more confused and hysterical with each successive attack.

Still sleepy and slightly hungover, we kicked it around for a while. I finally said, "It's no use. We've been over it every way from Sunday. Our only way back is blown, and I don't feel like swimming that far."

Reluctantly, we made the decision to give the supplies to the Filipinos in town. "We'll destroy the trucks," I said. "No point in equipping the enemy when they come to town." Everyone agreed. The future looked bleak.

Down at the YMCA, we distributed the food and supplies to the natives and, parking the trucks near the Pasig River, shot them up and set them on fire. We buried our rifles, kept our .45s, then walked back to the Y to wait for the Japs. Sitting near the sandbagged entrance, we watched the Filipino people looting the port area. I think it was one of the most depressing things I ever witnessed. To see those poor bastards scrounging through and taking stuff they had no use for whatsoever was sad.

"Look at that joker," I said. "He's carrying a coffee urn as big as he is."

"Damn, they're going through the warehouses while they're still burning," one guy observed in amazement. "People are even taking army equipment. Now what the hell could they possibly want with all that?"

"Doesn't seem to matter what it is," I said. "They're hauling off everything they can get their hands on."

Suddenly, from our front-row seats, we watched a Jap dive bomber set his sights on the scene below and deliberately dive into the heavily populated area. "Hit the deck!" I yelled moments before his bomb leveled a tree across the street.

After the explosion, we ran over to try to help the victims. But no one had survived. Looking at the terrible, bloody scene and all the body parts of those who had taken shelter under the branches, I began to get an inkling of what lay ahead for us, cut off from our forces. For the rest of the day, I tried hard to shake off the funny feeling growing in my gut. I kidded myself. *Maybe my stomach's just empty*, I thought.

It sounds strange, but after the predictable, even punctual, Japanese bombing raids, life in Manila would resume with some normalcy by late afternoon. When things grew quiet, we decided we'd better get a good meal while we still had the chance, and went into the Y to order a steak. I forced myself to eat it, but the peculiar feeling in my stomach wouldn't go away. It was definitely fear—fear of the unknown more than anything else—a new and unpleasant experience for me.

We must have been the four luckiest bastards alive when a Filipino fisherman happened to come along. Seeing us sitting there, he asked, "Hey Joe, you want to go to Corregidor?"

"You bet!" we said.

He said, "I have boat. I can take you there, but not before nightfall. You wait under Jones Street Bridge."

When we hesitated, he added: "The one closest to the bay. You come there before dark."

We talked for a while and learned that he had fished the waters in and around Manila Bay all his life. He assured us he knew the way. Figuring his plan sounded a whole lot better than ours, we shook hands with the Filipino and agreed to go with him. With a big grin on his face, he took off, promising to meet us later that night.

The small and sluggish Pasig River, running through the middle of town, acted as an artery for the small fishing boats and other commercial vessels going in and out of the city from Manila Bay. A number of bridges crossed it at various places along its twelve-mile length.

At dusk we set out for the bridge a few blocks away; we found three other people underneath it, waiting for the Filipino—a civilian couple and a woman named Ruth Ryder. Talking in whispers, Mrs. Ryder told us that she was married to a chief petty officer stationed on a minesweeper in the bay. "I went back to the States on a ship with the other wives and dependents of the servicemen on Luzon before the war, but I didn't stay very long," she said. "The first chance I got, I came back to be near my husband. I guess it was a foolish thing to do. I don't know where he is, and now I'm trapped."

By now the light was fading, so we were very relieved when the fisherman, true to his word, docked under the bridge. His wooden boat was about twenty feet long. It had a small wheelhouse and was equipped with a single-lunger diesel engine. Climbing aboard, we spread out, trying to hide behind the supplies and equipment, waiting for nightfall.

As luck would have it, the Japs came into the city soon after and set up a guard post right over our heads. The clattering of the sentries' heavy hobnailed boots as they patrolled up and down the bridge above us was like hundreds of steel pellets hitting the pavement. It is a sound like no other, meant to intimidate, and it worked. We froze, afraid to move or make a sound. To add to the unbearable tension we all felt, the moon rose full and bright in a starry sky, illuminating everything around us. Since we could clearly make out objects along the banks, it was obvious we'd be just as visible to anyone looking our way.

We waited there for several hours, until the tide was right, before we cut loose and eased out into the river. The bridge was two miles from Manila Bay. Traveling at a speed of about two knots, it would take us an hour just to reach the mouth of the river.

The boat creaked and groaned, rocking with every move we made. The waves slapped against the hull as we drifted slowly downstream, at the mercy of the current. In the stillness of the night, every sound—every little rustle or bump carried across the water—seemed to be magnified a hundredfold. Any minute, the guard on the bridge would see us and sound the alarm.

Armed and braced for the first sign of trouble, we watched as enemy patrols began to move into the dock areas along the shore. Up ahead, a bombed and burning freighter nearly blocked the entrance to the bay. It was impossible to avoid the large circle of light cast by the blaze. Forced to go through it, we would be sitting ducks for anyone guarding the docks and the port entry.

Everyone crouched down in the bottom of the boat, praying we wouldn't be noticed. As we neared the ship, the heat from the raging fire made us sweat even more. Every minute we spent outlined against the flames was filled with the possibility of being detected and shot.

Finally, after an agonizingly long time, the tide pulled us past the lighted area, and we passed into the relative darkness of the bay. We started the engine and headed for Corregidor, about twenty-seven miles away. What a relief to be in open water at last! Our spirits soared as we chugged along.

Suddenly two men in a sailboat appeared out of nowhere. We drew our weapons, prepared to fight. But when they came within hailing distance and no shots were fired, we identified ourselves and our destination. They yelled back, "We're air corpsmen with a ten-cent compass and a bottle of whiskey, and we're also headed for Corregidor." Trapped in the city under similar circumstances, they had simply helped themselves to a sailboat tied up at a dock and made their escape. The mood was lighthearted, even giddy, as we cruised along together, just glad to be alive.

After traveling for some time, I was lulled by the rhythm of the engine and almost asleep when the skipper suddenly shouted, "Mines up ahead!" I looked in the direction he pointed and saw the "horns" plainly visible in the moonlight. We had entered the minefield near Middleside. The Filipino immediately cut the engine down to a crawl as we began cautiously making our way through what must have been a network of hundreds of mines.

To wake up and find yourself in the middle of a minefield is sobering. Even today, when I picture the scene in my mind I break out in gooseflesh. Spread out before us in every direction, the deadly spheres danced about in lazy circles, tethered by cables to their anchors in the water. I can still feel the motion of our boat, hear the waves slapping up against the metal, and recall in vivid detail how we anxiously scanned the water, straining to see the floating bombs. A couple of times, we got close enough to reach out and touch one.

Tiptoeing through the field was a dangerous and nerve-wracking business. It took a few hours, but it seemed like forever to me. When we finally cleared the last mine without blowing ourselves to kingdom come, I could have kissed the skillful little navigator.

Sometime before dawn, wrung out and exhausted, we approached the dock at Bottomside on "the Rock," as the Filipinos called Corregidor. Suddenly, without warning, blinding searchlights were switched on, pinpointing us in the darkness. At that moment every gun on the east side of the island was aimed at our heads; the cowboys manning them, more than willing to shoot. The questions could come later, they said.

It was understandable that the boys on Corregidor were on alert, ready for possible Japanese landings on the island, the enemy having taken over Manila just hours before. But fully occupied with trying to escape, it never occurred to us that the real danger that night would come not from the Japs but from our own men.

4 "Please Bomb Us, We're Hungry"

Corregidor, an island fortress since Spanish days and only three and a half miles long, lies three miles south of the Bataan Peninsula, guarding the entrance to Manila Bay. The western half of the island, facing the South China Sea, is wider, with higher ground than the eastern half, which tapers down to beaches on the bay. Names like Topside, Middleside, and Bottomside correspond to the various elevations on the island.

Army headquarters, barracks, and housing were located on Topside, while the post hospital, the theater, and more barracks occupied Middleside. Pinching the island in half at its lowest point is Bottomside, with docks and warehouses accessible to the sea. A 13,000-man garrison inhabited Corregidor, as well as 2,000 civilians.

Military guards took us to headquarters for questioning. "Who are you, what are you doing here and how did you get here?" they asked. It took quite a bit of explaining to convince them that we weren't spies for the Japanese. When they discovered that six of us were in the air corps, they greeted us a little more warmly.

Eight or nine of the little Filipino training planes had been hidden in tall grass and weeds next to Kindley Field, a small airstrip on the tail end of the island. Half of them had been destroyed during periods of intense bombing, and headquarters planned to salvage what they could from the wreckage.

Our mechanic and a radioman from some other outfit on Corregidor had charge of the assignment. The rest of us, plus about six other men stationed on the Rock, helped with the less technical aspects. We took the propellers off one plane, the wings off another, and, by the time we finished, got two of the biplanes off the ground.

For the next few weeks we set up camp in an old Spanish graveyard below the airstrip. The open cement tombs made excellent bomb shelters when the Japs came calling. From our vantage point on the Rock, we could see Fort Hughes and Fort Drum a short distance away. Both of these fortified islands were crucial to the defense of Manila Bay. Fort Drum had been rebuilt by army engineers many years before and equipped with a total of eleven big guns. It resembled a lone battleship anchored in the bay.

Taking time out for a smoke one day, one of the guys pointed to the island in the distance and said, "Look at that crazy thing; it looks just like a ship."

"Yeah," I said with a laugh. "I hear it's nicknamed the USS *Never-go.*"

To conserve our rations, the quartermaster had everyone down to two meals a day by the second week of January. Our meals usually consisted of canned salmon and rice, with an occasional vegetable thrown in. One day, swimming and diving in shallow water along the lower end of the island, we discovered a sunken barge about ten feet down, bombed by the Japanese before we arrived. "Looks like it's loaded with army rations," someone shouted when we came up for air.

"Can you believe it? And me so hungry!" I yelled back. Excited over our good fortune, we began bringing up the rations a little at a time. We found crates of raisins, prunes, and other dried fruit and hung them in the trees to dry and to keep the ants away. Once we scraped a half inch off the ten-pound chocolate bars we salvaged, they were fine.

The labels on the gallon cans were gone, so it was a surprise each time we opened one. Sometimes we got potted meat or Vienna sausage, sometimes cheese or jam. In spite of our good luck, I discovered that a gallon of jam without bread is not all that great, even when your stomach growls!

Most days, you could set your watch by the Japanese raids on Corregidor. Our diets vastly improved when the bombs occasionally landed in the water, killing a lot of fish. On the days they skipped us or ran a little late, and all we had to eat was a gallon of jam or some dried prunes (something, by the way, we really didn't need, particularly after some of the more intense bombardments), we'd cuss 'em out, saying, "Come on, you sons of bitches, please bomb us, we're hungry!"

The Japs mainly targeted the huge coastal batteries at Topside and Middleside. The eighteen 10- and 12-inch rifles had ranges of up to seventeen miles; the twenty-four 12-inch mortars had a range of eight miles. Anti-aircraft guns and machine-gun nests, protected by the natural nooks and crannies of the terrain, also dotted the island.

Malinta Hill, east of Bottomside, housed the operational center and a U.S. Navy command unit in a system of tunnels carved out of the rock back in 1922. General MacArthur's headquarters occupied one of the many lateral tunnels off the main tunnel. A kitchen, a mess hall, a hospital, and storage areas—all connected by a narrow-gauge railroad—filled the other laterals. As the fighting went on, the laterals, emptied of supplies, were converted to wards for the wounded.

A couple of storage areas contained freezers of beef that had been processed by the army back in 1918 (the year I was born) and taken there shortly after the tunnel was built. "Man, a gourmet would pay any price for a steak that well aged," said a man in our group who had been a maitre d' in a large New York hotel. We made stew with our share; it went further and was more filling.

Everyone considered the Hill the best place to be when the bombings started. During repeated trips to Malinta for supplies, parts to rebuild the planes, or shelter from the more brutal attacks, I often saw General MacArthur, who had moved his family to the Rock on Christmas Eve. At first they didn't stay in the safety of Malinta Tunnel but chose instead to live in one of the wooden cottages on Topside. After the house was demolished by the Japanese in a raid, the general moved his family to a small bungalow at Bottomside.

Going up to the Hill one day, we suddenly came under attack and began to run for cover. But the general, his wife, his little son Arthur, their Chinese *amah* (nursemaid), and another woman headed for the tunnel at a walk. While everyone else yelled and urged MacArthur to run, he wouldn't; he and his group continued to walk until they entered the opening, a half-second before the bombs hit the ground. The

Lateral in Malinta Hill Tunnel, Corregidor.
National Archives

general was too proud to show fear, and this went a long way with the people on Corregidor.

I jumped into one of the tombs, currently being used as a machine-gun nest, during another raid, banging my foot against an ammunition case and badly twisting my ankle. It immediately swelled to the point where I could hardly walk. When things quieted down, I went to the tunnel to get it X-rayed. Luckily, it turned out to be bruised, not broken. The medics were wrapping it when the Japs started in on us again.

Thousands of personnel and civilians flocked to Malinta for shelter and medical attention that day. But, even with about four hundred feet of rock over me, I found it more unpleasant there than on the outside. Analyzing the situation later, I realized that the bombs didn't bother me as much as the fear I sensed in the people around me. Not only did I feel their panic, I could smell it, too. It resembled the "mass hysteria" I had read about. But at the time I just knew these people were very frightened, and so was I, even in the safest place on the island.

During our stay, several submarines brought provisions and ammunition to Corregidor. When it became obvious that reinforcements were not going to arrive soon, servicemen and personnel critical to the war effort went by sub to Australia.

Washington also ordered General MacArthur to leave the Philippines and proceed to Australia to take command of the Allied troops there. Headquarters talked of shipping me out because my training as a bombardier using the new bombsight might prove useful to the Japs, and they didn't want me to be caught. (They had my vote!) However, space was a factor in the decision, and a major in the top-secret code section took precedence over me. After I left the Rock to rejoin my unit on Bataan, the major escaped by PT boat in March with General MacArthur, the general's family, his staff, and others with critical and secret information.

Before the Japanese invasion, a portion of gold and silver belonging to the U.S. and the Philippines was moved to the Rock from Manila banks for safekeeping. In December, all of the gold and some of the silver were smuggled out as ballast aboard the submarine *Trout*. Late one night, headquarters gave me a singular assignment, to say the least.

"Sergeant, I want you and your men to dump about fifty million dollars' worth of silver dollars and pesos into the bay," the lieutenant said to me.

"Yes sir," I replied, snapping to. Privately, I almost cried. *What sacrilege*, I thought.

Shortly after the Japanese took Corregidor in May, Filipino collaborationists told them about the operation and the exact location of the sunken treasure. American prisoners, sent down to bring it up, found it almost immediately but sat on the boxes as long as possible. Coming up for air, they lied, saying they couldn't see anything.

They continued to lie with each successive dive. Finally, after the third day of this, the Japs told them, "Look, you are going down for the last time. If you don't find anything, don't bother to come back up." That was it. The Americans couldn't do anything else except haul it up.

I understand that the Japanese had a continuous salvage operation there for almost two years. But hardly any of that money went back to Japan; most of it stayed on the Rock. After the Japanese brought up the treasure, for some bizarre reason, they waited too long to ship it out.

By then, the Americans had landed, and the Japs were throwing the stuff overboard again. I think we recovered some of it after the war, but not anywhere near the full amount.

We finished our work by the third week in January. It was time to rejoin our units on Bataan. The night before we left Corregidor, we sat on the side of the airfield facing the peninsula and listened to the big guns go off in the distance. The rumbling sounds and brilliant flashes of light made us think of rolling thunder and heat lightning in a summer storm. Nobody spoke for a long time. Then with chilling accuracy, a despondent voice said, "It looks like some mighty bad weather is headed our way!"

5   To Hell, via Bataan

Bataan was a rough piece of real estate. Twenty miles wide by twenty-nine miles long, the finger of land should have been adequately defended by the 80,000 soldiers under MacArthur's command. But the very things that made it virtually impregnable by the enemy made it tough going for those of us in the Filipino-American army entrenched there.

In the western half, boulders and outcroppings of rock littered the landscape; the mountainous terrain, composed of steep ravines and sheer cliffs, was impossible to scale. Swamps and marshes carpeting the northeast, tall mountains and extinct volcanoes that split the peninsula down the middle, along with numerous rivers and streams, helped to slow the enemy's advances.

Huge trees and dense screens of bamboo shutting out the sunlight in places, together with vines and grasses so tall and thick they could hide an airplane, worked to our advantage in the beginning by giving us cover from Japanese air attacks. Three months later they worked to our disadvantage when, weak and sick from starvation and disease (our real enemies), we had to fight and retreat back through the difficult terrain, almost to the sea. Forced to drink polluted and contaminated water that bred mosquitoes to rival those in the swamps of Louisiana, many of us soon had diseases I'd only read about in books.

After a short boat ride from Corregidor, we landed at Mariveles on the southern tip of the peninsula and hitched a ride to our outfit. Our squad was set up in the reserve line at the base of the mountains and the edge of the jungle, just south of the town of Pilar on the east coast.

A twenty-mile stretch of dirt road, appropriately called the Pilar-Bagac road, connected the villages of Bagac and Pilar. MacArthur's first line of defense lay north of the Pilar-Bagac line, between the towns of Mabatang and Mauban, leaving one third of Bataan undefended. I Corps in the western half of Bataan and II Corps in the eastern half, divided by the mountain ranges in the middle, made their stands against the Japanese.

By the third week in January, after several intense battles resulting in major casualties on both sides, the Japs broke through the line, penetrating gaps left undefended, and threatened to surround II Corps's western sector. The 31st Infantry, along with some Philippine divisions held in reserve at Abucay, rushed in to bolster the troops, buying MacArthur time to strengthen his last line of defense at Pilar-Bagac.

When our forces pulled back into Bataan in December, command told us they would never put the air corps in the front lines. And it's true, they never did; the line simply moved back to us. One night soon after we rejoined our squad, we got word not to fire on the troops coming back through the line; they were our men. Although the 31st did an outstanding job of holding the Japs and beating them up pretty badly in the process, renewed enemy efforts (using fresh reinforcements in all-out attacks) took their toll.

Consulting his generals, MacArthur decided to withdraw, consolidate our forces, and dig in at the Pilar-Bagac line. He vowed he'd fight there to the last man. All night long the 31st Infantry and an engineer battalion filtered through, and the next morning, we were on the front line!

We had converted all the guns in our planes to ground mounts, pretty well beefing up the 220 men in our squadron, giving us thirty-two 50-caliber and sixteen 30-caliber machine guns and enough ammunition to last for some time—certainly until our reinforcements, planes, and supplies arrived. The latest word had them coming in "any day now."

To our right, in our sector, two other squadrons fortified themselves

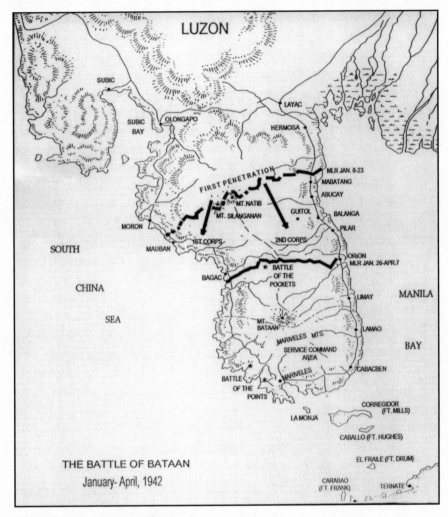

Map of Bataan, January–April 1942.

with even more machine guns, and to our left the 32nd Philippine Scouts were dug in with supporting artillery.

Without planes, we had to devise some means of reaching behind enemy lines. We pulled the 155-mm guns right into our positions on the front lines and began shelling the Japs about two thousand yards away. At about dusk, every one of our guns fired one shot. An hour later, we fired another shot, then a half hour later, one more, then one every fifteen minutes. By midnight, there was continuous firing.

The Filipino gunners were top-notch, the best troops in the world. They really put it to the Japs every night, all night long, for the next two months. When they fired those thirty or forty guns—of which a battery of four was in our position—the ground shook, the concussion jarred your teeth, and the sky lit up like the Fourth of July. We learned to sleep between rounds, lifting our faces off the ground just before the guns went off to prevent brushburns on our cheeks.

Subconsciously, I'd hear the sounds of the breech opening, the shell being seated in the chamber, and the breech slamming shut. Then the battery commander would say, "Ready?"

The gunnery sergeant would reply, "Ready! One ready, two ready, three ready, four ready." Then he'd say, "Tojo, count your men!"

The officer would give the command, "Fire!"

Then the gunnery sergeant would say, "Tojo, *now* count your men!"

All four guns fired at the same instant—one flash, one blast. It's hard to believe the enemy couldn't spot our guns from the flash and the sound, but they never did. It seemed strange, too, that it took so little camouflage to hide them.

The Japs operated a little differently; they fired their batteries one after the other. By firing our guns simultaneously, we never let them know how many we had or their exact positions, but we could easily count and pinpoint theirs. They didn't use the best tactics, but by doing it their way they let us know they had plenty of guns.

The Pilar-Bagac road ran through a little mountain pass and along the face of the mountain in front of us. Even though the road was firmly under the control of the Japs, the Filipino gunners, who knew every foot of the land, had the enemy's positions located to within a few yards. They always waited until the Japanese got a supply depot or some equipment set up during the day, and then they'd work it over at night.

The Nips moved their convoys of trucks with men and supplies along this road, usually after dark, and the sounds carried over the rice paddies that lay between us. The Scouts would fire a few shots at the head of the line and one or two at the rear, ultimately working them over from both ends and tearing them up real good. We could never

Philippine defense artillery 155. These guns dated to World War I. Each was given a girl's name: Betty, Susie, etc.

U.S. Army Signal Corps

figure out why they continued to use the road after the second or third time this happened, much less after the fourth or fifth time. They evidently thought they knew what they were doing, but it cost them.

Barbed wire was strung out in front of us, with just a few openings, to further slow the enemy's advance. Tin cans full of rocks tied to the wire served as warning devices in case of a sneak attack. This was standard military procedure, but any time I went near barbed wire, I got hung up in it.

To get to us, the Japs had to cross about a half mile of open rice paddies. The artillery, the 125 or so machine guns in the three squadrons in our area, plus the barbed wire, slowed them down a good bit. But when they charged across the field in large numbers, we'd have to mow them down like wheat. Getting used to killing the enemy—and I knew I had to do it—took a while. I think every American GI on the line had the same problem, because to us life wasn't cheap.

The Japanese, on the other hand, seemed to have little regard for their men. To intimidate the enemy, they charged across the open rice paddies, following their officers and sergeants, who waved their gleaming swords in the air screaming, "Banzai!" This only showed me who to kill first. They would spend about a hundred soldiers to get one machine-gun nest, instead of trying to infiltrate around it or take advantage of cover. They were trained to fight this way, but it was a terrible situation. After a while, we thinned their ranks so drastically they had to give up those wild charges straight at us. I learned later they didn't care for dying in droves like that; we just proved to be a much tougher adversary than they expected.

After decades of being at war with China for economic reasons, the Japanese finally conquered Manchuria in 1931, renaming it Manchukuo. They invaded northern China in 1937, and by 1938 the cities of Shanghai, Nanking, Hankow, and Canton had fallen, with hundreds of thousands of Chinese slaughtered in the process. In Nanking alone, the Japanese army killed 300,000 civilians and raped 80,000 women and girls—ages seven to seventy.

By June 1940, Holland, Belgium, and France had fallen to Hitler's invasion of Europe, leaving their colonies in Asia defenseless. When Japan signed the Tripartite Pact with Germany and Italy in September, aligning the country with America's "real" enemy, Hitler, Franklin Delano Roosevelt declared an embargo on scrap iron and steel against Japan. He warned Japan against invading Indochina. But the Japanese walked into Indochina in July 1941, with no resistance from the French Vichy government in place there. Two days later, FDR froze all Japanese assets, which meant no more oil from America. Britain soon followed suit.

The surprise attack on Pearl Harbor by the Japanese on December 7, which sank four of our eight battleships and crippled two others, set in motion the successive sea invasions of Pacific territories belonging to America, Britain, and Holland. After striking Pearl Harbor and most of the Philippines, five thousand Japanese troops came ashore on the U.S. territory of Guam on December 8.

Separate, simultaneous attacks and landings were made on the British base, Hong Kong, and the Malay Peninsula—a rich source of rubber and tin. Thailand, which was strategic to their plans to launch attacks on Burma and the road used by the Allies to send supplies and equipment into China, was easy prey.

On December 11, the Japanese invaded Wake Island, another U.S. possession, only to be repulsed by a small garrison of U.S. Marines. But, beefed up by reinforcements, the Japs captured the island twelve days later.

Hong Kong surrendered on Christmas Day, 1941, and less than a month later Japanese forces landed in Borneo and the Celebes. In February the Japs began their relentless drive toward the British island of Singapore, forcing its surrender on February 15. Now the Japanese controlled practically all of the China Coast.

On March 8, the Dutch colonies of Java and Sumatra, an important source of oil, capitulated. Weeks later, Japanese forces landed in northern New Guinea.

By the spring of 1942, the Japanese dominated nearly all of the Pacific. But here, this one little spot of native and Western resistance on the island of Luzon, cost them plenty every day. Losing face was not something the Japanese tolerated easily.

Apparently, they didn't have an accurate count of our troop numbers, because another thirty to forty thousand Japanese soldiers would have done the trick. We couldn't have gotten out; there was no place to go. Within a few weeks, we ran out of gasoline, so the tanks were driven down along the eastern and western shores, buried in the sand, and used for beach fortifications. Live bombs, useless without planes, were also strung out along the beaches.

Food was getting scarce. Not only the military, but the civilians falling back with us into Bataan had to be fed. As things got worse, we began scrounging for food in earnest. Those of us on patrol came back with whatever we could find. Peanuts, vegetables from farmers' fields, fruit on the trees—nothing went unnoticed.

By March, things got really desperate. A can of eight or ten sardines had to suffice a ten-man patrol for twenty-four hours. Anything else we ate depended on what we found. We were so hungry we'd do anything to add to the meager supplies we had. We jumped Jap patrols just for their food.

Our outpost, located in front of the main line between the road and the rice paddies, went right through a cane field. In the beginning, the thick cane would completely hide a man standing five feet away. But by the time we left, the cane was all gone—we'd eaten it.

"Don't disturb any of the foliage around you when you dig in," the manual read. The trouble with that was—it didn't say what you were supposed to do when you were starving! We'd raid a nearby peanut field every night, and every day the Jap observation planes could tell our exact position from the condition of the field.

After the farmers harvested the rice in the paddies in front of our lines and stacked it in the fields to dry, we "harvested" our share as we came back from patrols. We used the Philippine method of knocking the hulls off with big sticks, then we'd grind it up and cook it into a mush.

We began to kill wild animals. Pigs, chickens, carabao, snakes, monkeys—you name it, if it lived in the jungle, we found it. When we first went into Bataan, it was as noisy as any jungle, alive with the sounds of animals and birds. By the time we surrendered, though, it was deathly quiet. We had eaten everything that could crawl, run, climb, or fly.

I found out one thing—if it's alive, it's probably edible. You might not like it, but when you're hungry things start to taste a little better.

The Filipinos would bore a small hole in one end of a coconut, fill it with corn and syrup, and tie it to a tree. A monkey would come along, stick his hand in the hole, and grab a fistful of corn. Always greedy, he was caught when he refused to let go. We ate all the corn and coconuts, so we shot the monkeys. If I had to skin a monkey, I couldn't eat it. To me, it looked like a newborn baby. But if someone else skinned it, no problem.

To capture boa constrictors, the natives built cages from bamboo slats just wide enough for the large snakes to get through and tied a small pig inside the cage. When the snake crawled in through the narrow opening and swallowed the pig, it thereby trapped itself. We ate the pigs, so we had to shoot the snakes, too.

We supplemented all this with wild fruit we found, like bananas, papayas, and mangoes. I had never seen, much less tasted, some of the fruit growing in the Philippines. Most of it was good, and by the time we surrendered the trees were bare.

A bunch of bananas happened to be hanging right over our machine-gun nest, and we watched those bananas every day, waiting for them to ripen. A Filipino came along one day and asked, "Joe, don't you like bananas?"

"You bet!" I said. "But we can't eat green bananas."

Laughing, he said, "Bananas turn yellow after you cut them down. If you wait much longer, they will rot." Feeling kind of stupid, we cut them down to see if he knew what he was talking about. Sure enough, after a day or two, those bananas turned yellow and very ripe.

Cashew trees grew in the area. Most of the fellows had never seen a cashew grow either. We discovered that under the fruit, which resembled an apple, there was a bean. We knew the beans had to be roasted before eating, but we didn't know that the oily hull had to be removed first.

We built a fire from dried bamboo, which gave us a smokeless fire, and put the nuts, hulls and all, into an old Spanish frying pan we'd found. Everything was fine until the cashews got hot. Smoke boiled out of the pan in a big column. We grabbed the pan off the fire, but it was too late! The one Jap pilot flying overhead spotted us and started shooting up the place, scattering us as we ran for cover.

Instead of slit trenches or foxholes, we learned to dig "spider holes"—four to five feet deep and two feet around. For defensive purposes, they were safer than foxholes, with less chance of being hit during an air attack.

I happened to be wearing my "coolie" hat as protection from the sun that day. As I jumped into the hole, the hat proved to be slightly larger than the opening. Since it was tied under my chin, I nearly hung myself. With my feet dangling about six inches from the bottom, I came pretty close to choking before I finally got it off my head.

Well, this is par for the course, I said to myself. Although I had studied aeronautical engineering at LSU, I had never designed any part of an airplane. On maneuvers with the National Guard one weekend, I decided to enlist in the air corps while watching a plane fly overhead. (There's nothing like sitting in a ditch during a downpour, hungry and tired, with only a candy bar for supper, to get a man thinking.) The pilot, high and dry, was going home to a good meal and a clean bed. I made up my mind that that was the life for me. But, although I later trained as a bombardier, I had never dropped a single bomb in combat, and now here I was, back to square one, sitting in a muddy hole, getting my ass shot off.

A little black dog wandered into the area and stayed with us for a while. He had a fine ear. Recognizing the sound of Jap planes long before we did, and associating the planes with the bombings, he'd abruptly take off to find a hole. That was our signal to do likewise. I'm sure he saved a few lives while he lived with us.

Every day the Japs sent at least one plane over our area to check us out. It flew up and down our line from Manila Bay to the China Sea and back. This aggravated the hell out of us, because we couldn't shoot at the plane for fear of giving away our position. We put up with that for about a week before we got permission to do something about it.

A short distance to the rear of our position, and away from the 155-mm cannon, we set up three 50-caliber machine guns in spider holes big enough for two men and dug deeper than the ones on the line. Spread out in a wide triangle, they presented the pilot with three targets. When he dove at number one, the crews in number two and three opened up on him. We hit three Japanese planes this way, and they left smoking. One managed to land in the road, about a mile in front of our lines, where the 155s finished him off.

Soon after, the Japs got wise to our strategy, sending three ships instead of one. They dove on us simultaneously from three directions, but at slightly different angles. Our only option was to fire up their gut. With their rapid-fire cannon winking at us, we were no match for them. We had to abandon the try.

Many of the Filipina women and their kids followed the men into battle in order to survive. Despite our warnings to get back to the rear of the fighting, they constantly hung around, pestering us by offering to do our laundry in exchange for food or cigarettes. Since grub and smokes won out over clean duds, they didn't get our business.

Food was now our number-one priority. Our platoon always kept a fire going in case we found something to cook. One day, during a lull in the action, a friend and I left our area to scout for food. We wandered around looking for cashews, but without any luck. Then the Jap artillery opened up and dropped a few live ones in our direction. We jumped into the nearest hole, ending up in a little dugout belonging to one of our officers. The continuous bombardment forced us to stay there for a while.

When our eyes grew accustomed to the dark, Bill and I discovered that we were sitting on some crates. Straining to check out the contents of mine, I whistled.

"Would you look at this?" I said. "I'm sittin' on a friggin' case of sardines!"

"No kiddin'! Lessee what's in this one," Bill said, squatting down to read the stenciled letters in the gloom. "Holy smoke! It's condensed milk! I haven't seen that since the war started!"

"Dammit, all personal foodstuffs should have been turned in to the general mess," I said. "This guy thinks he's exempt from the rules. We're starving, and he's hoarding food. But he's not gonna get away with this."

We knew we had to get out of there in case the officer came back, so filling our coveralls with about half the milk and as many cans of sardines as we could carry, we stayed until the shelling grew light. We took off then, finding another hole not far away to wait out the attack.

That evening, when they saw the rations, the men greeted us with open arms. "Man alive! Who did you rob—MacArthur?" they asked.

"Ask me no questions, and I'll tell you no lies," I joked, dropping my load of cans in a heap.

"No kiddin', you guys. Where've you been? And will you need an alibi for the dead bodies you left behind?"

"Who cares?" Bill said, tearing into a can of sardines. "I may get shot, but the condemned man ate a hearty meal!"

Our platoon did all right for a little while on the sardines and milk. We never got any flak over the incident. We didn't expect to. Bill and I vowed that if we got a chance to visit the dugout again, we'd carry off the rest of the supplies. We felt no guilt over what we had done. The son of a gun had no right to all that food!

Wild herds of carabao, as well as domesticated herds, roamed Bataan. When war broke out, the constant shelling really stirred them up. Once they took off, nothing could stop them. Occasionally, they became entangled and trapped in barbed wire, screaming and hollering when hit. It sounds gruesome, but as supplies ran out they turned out to be a good source of food.

Although the water buffalo generally avoided us, we would hide behind the trees on little points of land, waiting until they got close enough to shoot. One day, all conditions were perfect to bag one. The wind was right; they grazed close by, headed in our direction. Suddenly, something spooked them and they took off in all directions. I aimed and shot one right behind the horn. As he dropped, all five of us in the hunting party jumped up, ran out, and dragged him back into the little clump of woods as fast as we could.

We were quick—but not quick enough. A Jap plane spotted us taking refuge in that sparse, isolated stand of trees. Trapped, with no place to run, we knew he could drop a lot of firepower on us, possibly forcing us into the open. He made one pass, coming in low, strafing the trees, while we opened up with everything we had. One of us got lucky and hit his fuel line.

A cheer went up when his engine started coughing and he had to land in one of the abandoned airstrips not far from our front lines. He was out of the range of our rifles but not of the 155s. As he landed in plain view of the Filipino artillery, they dropped about three volleys on him and blew the plane and the pilot out of existence.

In addition to reconnaissance planes, the Japanese also used observation balloons to keep track of us. One morning we woke up and there, up in the sky looking right down our throats, was a rubber "cow." With few exceptions, the 155s went into action only at night, but this was too tempting to pass up. Shooting at the base of the balloon, the Filipinos eventually cut its mooring cable with a few well-placed shots, and we watched it float out to sea.

The next day, the Japs put up another balloon, this time just out of range of our 155s. They had us pinned down for a few days, but we still had a trick or two up our sleeves—namely two P-40s, well hidden in the jungle, sandbagged and saved for just such an occasion. One morning right after dawn, one of our pilots in the squadron went up, made a quick pass over the small runway, shot the balloon down, came back, and landed, zipping back into the jungle again.

The Japs went after that airfield, bombing and strafing it with everything they had, but by then the little plane was safely tucked away. This cheered us up no end. We weren't bothered by balloons after that.

As the days and nights went by and we gave no sign of quitting, the Japanese began to use psychological warfare on us. It backfired. In fact, we actually looked forward to each new installment.

Tokyo Rose was broadcast every night from Manila. She knew the names and ranks of many of our men, including their outfits and hometowns. In some cases, she even seemed to know the names of their wives and girlfriends. She'd say something like, "Your wife is running around on you, Joe. You'd better surrender so you can go home to straighten out matters." This kind of talk continued every night. Then she'd spin records of good old American music. When not on patrol, we listened to songs like "Green Eyes," "Marie Elena," and "Frenesi," the top three tunes on the current Hit Parade.

In the background, we could hear people talking and the clink of china as they ate and drank. Then Tokyo Rose would say, "Fellows, I know how much you miss all this. We wish you were here with us. Why don't you surrender so the war can end? Then you can go back home, and we'll all have a good time again." She would end the evening with the song "I'm Waiting for Ships That Never Come In."

Every day we looked forward to the cigarettes a Japanese plane dropped for us. Each "pack" contained a single smoke and had a message on the back: "We know you are out of cigarettes, and we feel sorry for you. Here's a sample. If you want more, all you have to do is join us, and you will get all the cigarettes, girls, and beer you want." Tobacco was the one thing the heavy smokers really missed, and we broke our necks to get out there and get them.

Along with the cigarettes, the plane dropped cards with photographs of movie stars and a nice note on the back: "Isn't this a pretty girl? She'll be waiting for you if you surrender now, and then we can all go home in peace." How ridiculous can you get? The idea that Betty Grable or Dorothy Lamour was waiting for one of us jokers made us laugh like hell! But the pictures made such great decorations for the walls of our machine-gun nests that we began collecting and trading them so we'd all have one of each.

In order to avoid disclosing our positions, we had orders not to fire

One of the more appealing types of propaganda dropped on the front lines by the Japanese in February 1942.

U.S. Army Signal Corps

on "Maytag Charlie," as we called the pilot of the plane that dropped these items. Although we liked his cigarettes and pictures, it was hard to sit there with our fingers on the triggers of those 50-caliber machine guns and let him fly by without blasting him out of the sky.

I really don't believe the Japanese propaganda had any effect on us, except to make us laugh at their clumsy attempts to demoralize us. On the contrary, I think it helped to boost morale. Badly misinformed about Americans in general and about us in particular, they didn't believe that we would fight and die for our country. And for some reason, they didn't think we could shoot our weapons either. Big mistakes. When it finally dawned on them that we weren't buying their line, they stopped flying over with "supplies." We sure were sorry to lose the almost-empty packs of cigarettes.

The Japanese didn't give up, however. Later, they tried selling us and the Filipinos on the idea of "Asia for the Asiatics." The East Asia Co-Prosperity Sphere was a scheme cooked up by Japan to kick the foreigners—namely the British and the Dutch—out of these undeveloped nations and then help these same countries "utilize" their raw materials before taking control of them. But they failed to understand that the people of these nations considered the Japanese foreigners as well. The whole idea was a total flop with the Filipinos; they never did buy it.

Meanwhile, snipers constantly threatened us. They were slipping through our lines, getting in behind us, and making it hard to tell where the next shot was coming from. Sometimes they made it so hot for us we couldn't move at all, seriously curtailing our search for food.

At first, we simply ducked when the shots went whizzing by. After a few close calls, however, my nerves began to fray a bit. I told the men, "I'm getting mighty tired of this. We gotta do something."

"Right," Bill said. "But where are they? We check every bush and tree we come to, but so far, no luck."

We mulled it over for a while, and one day I suddenly realized that we had missed something in plain sight. I told the men, "We've never searched the bamboo groves!"

"No disrespect, Sarge, but are you nuts? Bamboo leaves cut you to pieces and burn like fire. It's the last place I'd wanna be."

"They might be counting on that."

"They're sneaky as hell, that's for sure."

The next morning, I couldn't wait to prove my theory. Sure enough, at first light we found an empty "nest" in a nearby stand of bamboo. By cutting into the middle, close to the ground, the Japs had cleared a small area around the giant reeds, letting them climb up a ways and still be well hidden. The next time one of the snipers took a potshot at us, we hit the little bastard with everything but the kitchen sink. From then on, we made it good and hot for them.

A small, dry riverbed cut across our lines to the left of our position and ran between a cane field and some rice paddies. It was the ideal spot for an outpost. Large trees grew on both sides, forming a canopy over-head and providing a thick screen that shielded us from view. Different squads took turns manning it around the clock to give us ample warning to prepare for enemy incursions.

On our side, the terrain was rugged. By climbing up the side of a steep hill, we could look down over the tops of the trees into Jap territory. Although it was seven to eight hundred yards away, it gave us a clear shot into their backyard. From our vantage point, we could see the Japanese, who thought they were safe enough, wandering around in the open behind the trees on their side of the river. Bill and I ended that notion the day we received the go-ahead to do a bit of long-range sniping.

One day we staked out the opposition from our usual spot high up in a tree. The leaves gave us good camouflage as we picked off the targets on our scopes. Unfortunately, the dry season had set in; the leaves began to fall, leaving us a little more exposed.

I was sitting up there with my shoes off, taking it easy—it had been rather quiet—when without warning they opened up on us with a 20-mm cannon. The shell passed between Bill and me—right through the crotch of the tree. If it had touched even a branch, the shell would have exploded, disintegrating the tree, and what was left of us would have been scattered over a hundred-yard radius. Before the next shot went by, both of us hit the ground. I may have beaten Bill down, but I didn't stop to question him.

We had fun while it lasted (if that kind of business can be called fun), eliminating a few of the emperor's men. After a couple of weeks, the fire we dropped on them and the sharpshooters who joined us from other squads finally persuaded them to draw back into the main woods.

Occasional relief came in the form of a three-day pass to Corregidor. While we might get a few cigarettes and supplies, the trip mostly amounted to trading shelling and sniping for daily bombings. The guys from Corregidor sometimes graced us with their presence, but I could never figure out what comfort they derived from being on the peninsula. Except for the poor exchange of scenery and faces, we had absolutely nothing to offer them on Bataan; we had run out of everything. Anything to break the monotony, I guess. But even this brief diversion was short-lived. After a while, no more passes were issued except for official business.

Although those of us who smoked found it tough to be without tobacco, if I had to make a choice between smoking and eating, eating always won out. People who say, "I'd rather do this or that than eat," don't know what they're talking about. Being hungry for a day or so is nothing. It's the deadening day-after-day hunger, with no relief in sight, that really wears you down. It seems to crowd everything else out of your mind. Even the danger of combat takes a back seat to the complaints your stomach makes. You'll do most anything to satisfy the constant gnawing feeling in your gut, and you'll eat anything, anytime, anywhere. Things that turn my stomach today didn't turn my stomach then.

Most of us were professional soldiers; as the months went by with no reinforcements from the States, we began to realize the grimness of our situation. But when General MacArthur asked us to stay and fight, that's what we did. Actually, we should have surrendered a couple of months sooner. Since most of us were young—all muscle and little fat—it didn't take long for our bodies to burn up the fat and start in on the muscle. Had we given up sooner, we might have better withstood the terrible days and weeks ahead. In our weakened state, thousands of men would die on the forced march and right after we arrived in the camps.

The Japanese began making probing attacks, trying to penetrate our lines. They would shell us—we could hear them fire high and come on in; still, unless a shell found the hole we were in, we felt fairly safe. But we couldn't stay in our holes, patrol, and forage for food, too. The Japs replenished their effort with men and matériel, while the only thing in our favor was strategy and cunning—that and plenty of ammunition for the artillery.

For every shot the Japanese fired, our boys fired back at least ten or fifteen. That was the mainstay of our effort. In the end, the linings had been shot out of the barrels, and the guns were pretty well worn.

Our squadron did okay in combat. I think we lost about five men and had only a few wounded. Even so, with everybody on the front lines and no reserve position since February, the casualties on Bataan mounted steadily. Along with malnutrition, almost everyone suffered from fever by this time—some from battle wounds, nearly all from diarrhea, malaria, dengue, hookworm, and the like. The really serious diseases like dysentery, beriberi, and pellagra also began to show up. But in order to get back to the field hospital, our men had to be either badly wounded or running a temperature of at least 105.

Unless a soldier was shot up, no one could be spared to accompany him to the hospital. If he was only ill or merely wounded in the arm, he had to find a way to get back alone. With the snipers in the woods behind our lines, it was simpler and safer to remain at the front. If anyone did manage to make it back through the jungle to the hospital, all he got was some quinine or aspirin, for by this time we had few medical corpsmen, no medicine, and no food.

When the enemy was unsuccessful in penetrating our lines, they tried a different tack. They planned to come in from the China Sea, attacking our line from the rear and thereby inflicting heavy casualties before we knew what hit us. But unbeknownst to them, there was an R&R area on the southwest coast of the peninsula reserved for men who were unable to fight but still able to perform some assignments. These walking wounded also kept watch from the cliffs above the shoreline for possible amphibious landings by the Japs.

I heard that a special elite guard of the emperor, thinking they had landed on a deserted stretch of beach one night, moved into the valley patrolled by our men. These twelve hundred marines, who were said to be taller than the average Japanese—about six feet—had every expectation of being victorious, winning honors for themselves and their emperor. Instead, they found themselves in a trap, refused to retreat, and all of them were killed. I understand that when it was over, the stinking, decomposing bodies of the enemy lay everywhere. Because they couldn't bury that many men individually, our guys simply dynamited the cliffs to cover the dead.

The Japs were enraged when they found out about the loss of their elite troops. They said we should have cut a finger off each dead soldier and sent it back to Japan. Well, cutting off the fingers of dead Japs wasn't high on our list of priorities. Later, in the camps, we would pay dearly for that little oversight.

By March, we were on constant patrol. Weak and starving, we had orders not to fight unless cornered, but we did jump the smaller Jap patrols for their rations. Many of them carried a sack loaded with rice. Made like a sock without a heel, it would fit anyone. Once the rice was eaten, we had a sock to wear. Not that we needed them, because by then the uniform of the day consisted of coveralls, shoes, no socks, and some kind of hat to protect us from the sun.

We used the lull in the fighting to reinforce our defenses as best we could. We took our artillery pieces, rifles, machine guns, and side arms apart, cleaned and reloaded them. Judging by all the activity taking place north of the road, the Japs were gearing up, too.

Morale was surprisingly high, even though we looked terrible and felt like hell. We lived one day at a time, just trying to hold on for as long as possible. Finding something—anything—to eat took top priority.

6 Surrender

Enemy shelling resumed with a vengeance by the first week in April 1942, and this time the Japs concentrated on the Filipino unit next to us, in the center of our line. They must have had a hundred guns, and they shelled the Scouts day and night.

We tried desperately to reinforce them, but the relentless bombardment made it impossible. The Filipinos didn't pull out of line; they got blasted out. During the next forty-eight hours, the enemy's heavy artillery chopped down the tall liana trees growing in the area as though they were kindling wood.

On the third day, the Japs finally made their drive—right through the middle. We had no reserves to block the hole, so they poured through, fanning out behind us. I assumed the same thing took place on the west side of the peninsula. They didn't even fire a shot as they overran us. They just left us sitting there in our positions.

We got orders to pull back then. Most of our machine guns were 50-caliber, too heavy to haul around. The mounts were cemented down in the ground, so we took the guts out of the weapons, threw them into the jungle, and destroyed them. The few trucks left (sitting on empty) and the other supplies and equipment we couldn't carry, we shot up and burned.

The fine 155s the Filipino Scouts had defended us with for so long were systematically destroyed by the men who manned them so bravely. Lowering the barrels of these big guns, they stuffed them with sandbags, loaded them, and drained the oil from the recoil mechanisms. Attaching long ropes to the lanyards, they sought protection behind trees or in foxholes before firing them. Without oil in the mechanisms, when the shells hit the sandbags, not only did they blow up the barrels, they also destroyed the mechanisms.

We fell back to our second line of defense, but the Japs had beaten us to it and passed that point. The way they cut up the Filipino line and overran us, there was no way we could re-form. Things were truly desperate.

To see an army in full retreat is a shattering experience. Once the Japs had us rolling, they never let up. Sick and dying men, whipped even before the rout, threw down their heavy equipment, fell back, and tried to regroup into some kind of order, but with no success. Dusk found us scattered all through the jungle.

In all the confusion and chaos, I got separated from my squadron. I had been in the rear echelon, and when I finally reached the new position I waited there for some time before Junior came straggling up. I don't remember the kid's given name, but I knew he was only seventeen, the youngest in our group. We stayed there for about an hour, then we began what was to be the pattern for the next few hours—retreat and regroup. As we pulled back, attempting to make a stand, others would join us. We would hold out for as long as we could, engaging in fire fights with the enemy, but in the end we'd be forced to fall back again.

Late that night, nine others from our squadron ended up in a small town with Junior and me. The place was destroyed; every house was on fire. Only a stone building in the public square, probably the courthouse, still stood. The people had not been spared either. Dead soldiers and civilians lay everywhere. The sickly-sweet odor of burning flesh permeated the air. I learned that a burned human body smelled different from that of an animal.

An artesian well flowed in the center of the square, and we stopped to drink all we could hold and fill up our canteens. There was no food to be had, but at least I could quench my thirst and temporarily fill my belly. After everyone had done the same, we decided to bivouac there until first light. We found places on the ground in the square (the only place not on fire), and all of us instantly fell asleep.

When I awoke on the morning of April 8, the soft thing I had used as a pillow turned out to be the body of a Filipino soldier. In the dark, I just assumed it was a barracks bag. *I didn't know this man,* I thought. *But he did more than his share by dying for his country. Even in death he served a fellow soldier.* I wanted to bury him, but there was no time.

We moved out of the village and into a valley before climbing up the side of a mountain to take advantage of the terrain and regroup. We watched the Japanese dive-bombers down below bomb and strafe our retreating troops as they came through the pass, trapping the men like ducks in a shooting gallery.

We spread out and took cover in the grassy recesses of the hill, shielded only by a few rocks and boulders. We spent the next few hours taking potshots at the planes as they came out of their dives, trying to draw the enemy's fire away from our retreating men. As for scoring any hits, we might as well have been using BB guns. Our rifles were no match for the planes' speed and superior firepower, and we failed to knock down even one.

Although we stayed low and tried to blend in with the scenery, the Japanese eventually spotted us. Before long, a dive-bomber came screaming from behind the mountain to take us out. We hugged the ground, bracing ourselves for the coming attack. The pilot dropped his load right in among us. One, two, three, four, five, six—the bombs sounded like giant footsteps as they slammed into the hill. The earth exploded in our faces, the ground shook, and the tall grasses and brush around us burst into flames. Then, as suddenly as it had appeared, the plane was gone. By some miracle, no one had been hit. We counted heads—all okay. We quickly moved off the hill and continued our march to the rear, once more falling back into the jungle. By now it was getting dark.

Most of the eight or ten men in the group had no idea where we were or where to go. After some discussion, we set out in what we thought was the general direction of the peninsula highway to the south of us. It took most of the night to make our way through the jungle. We slogged through a maze of tangled vines and vegetation so thick that, at times, calling out became the only way to stay together. Razor-sharp bamboo tore at our hands and faces. The huge Bataan mosquitoes that we jokingly said were big enough to fly us to Corregidor swarmed over us, sometimes blinding us, taking large bites from any exposed area of skin. In the dark the large exposed tree roots, stumps, and uneven ground continually tripped us up, causing us to stumble and fall repeatedly.

Our squadron got separated again, while men from other units joined us in the darkness. Finally, when I didn't think I could go another step, we came out onto the road—and walked straight into a machine-gun position.

Somebody who could still think quickly identified our group before they could shoot our heads off. The trigger-happy Americans manning the emplacement weren't taking any chances that night. We decided to hold there for the time being. I remember sinking to my knees, my rifle cradled in my arms, and falling into a stupor in the middle of the road.

A sharp jolt followed by a terrible roar woke me. The ground rippled and shuddered beneath me. I tried to get to my feet, but I kept falling down from the severe shocks, each lasting several minutes. All night long the island shook from explosions as our retreating men systematically destroyed one ammunition dump after another. Groggy and confused, I thought a rather large dump had gone up, but then realized this felt more like an earthquake—which in fact it was.

When the ground stopped rolling, I took stock of the situation. Apparently, everyone else had pulled out during the night, leaving Junior and me behind. We were no longer an army. There was no order, no one in charge, only complete chaos. Starving men, sick, exhausted, and demoralized, ran for their lives from the overwhelming hordes of Japanese soldiers.

At dawn on April 9, we started down the road, heading toward the field hospital near Mariveles, with Junior on my left. Trees lined both sides of the highway, so we kept a sharp eye out for enemy soldiers. We hadn't gone very far when I heard the crack of a rifle shot and felt a stinging, burning lick on the inside of my right leg. Junior, beside me, took two steps and fell. Out of the corner of my eye, I saw a slight movement in a tree, and my ears pinpointed the sound. It looked like an easy shot, and I took it. At first, I thought I had missed the sniper; he didn't fall. Then I saw him dangling by a rope. He had tied himself to a tree limb.

I checked Junior, but I think he was dead before he hit the ground. The bullet that killed him entered his body high on the left side, passing through and exiting low on his right side, striking my thigh. It was too risky to stop and bury him, so I moved on to try to find our men. My leg hurt like hell.

Before long I reached the empty hospital, which was now an aid station. The sick and wounded had been evacuated a few hours earlier to Corregidor. Along with a number of other men assembled there, I learned that Major General Edward P. King, commander of the Luzon Force, intended to surrender to the Japanese that day at 1100 hours. General King had made the decision the day before, but, being a student of history, he held off for twenty-four hours so the date would coincide with Lee's surrender at Appomattox on April 9, 1865.

Like most of the others, when I heard the news of the surrender, I was relieved in a way; but like them I broke down and cried, too. We had done our best for our country and the Philippine people. We had fought and many of us had died, holding off the Japanese for as long as we could with everything we had. But without food and replacements, it was impossible to go on.

Thousands of fresh Japanese reinforcements, supplied to Lieutenant General Masaharu Homma in the spring, just overran and overpowered us. Some say that before it was all over, it took 200,000 Japs to finally defeat 80,000 Filipino and American soldiers. It's also said that we killed more Japs than we had soldiers—something else we would pay for in the camps. Was it worth the lives and the time it cost them to clear out this thorn in their side? Maybe not, but by then it had become a matter of saving face for the Japanese.

At 1100 hours, as the American flag in front of the hospital was lowered, we stood at attention and saluted, broken-hearted, tears filling our eyes and coursing down our dirty, unshaven cheeks. Losing is never easy; for the professional soldier, trained to win, surrender is bitter. Historically, the American army had always won the war. But this time, the single act of lowering the flag signified our defeat. At that instant, our status changed from free American soldiers, with inalienable rights, to Japanese prisoners of war, with no freedom and no rights. What happened next was anybody's guess.

A medical officer told us to stack our weapons and get something to eat. Someone gave me a small can of evaporated milk. Those few ounces filled me up real quick and even made me a little nauseated. I collected a few canned goods and put them in a barracks bag I found in the building. Another officer told us to line up and move out to the road. We crossed the narrow strip of jungle that lay between us and the beach. When we got there, I saw one lone Jap standing on a large rock, armed with a rifle. Other Japanese soldiers lined the road at intervals, waiting for us.

The soldiers searched everyone. They made me throw my bag on the ground; I didn't get to carry that food very long. The Japs confiscated eyeglasses, fountain pens, watches, rings—anything of a personal nature. They took my cigarette lighter, my high school graduation ring, and my father's graduation ring from the Tulane School of Pharmacy. They let us keep our canteens and mess kits.

We marched to an airfield at the foot of a hill, near Mariveles, where they organized the prisoners as more of us came straggling out of the jungle. The airstrip was in plain sight of Corregidor, and the Americans there had their field glasses trained on Bataan, watching as the Japs rounded us up. The Japs had moved 105-mm guns in behind the hill, and using us as human shields they commenced firing on Corregidor, thinking that our men on the Rock wouldn't retaliate.

Once more, the Japanese miscalculated the balls of the American soldiers. While the big guns on Corregidor remained silent during this time and were not fired for fear of endangering the prisoners, smaller pieces, in a series of shoot-and-run tactics, began returning their salvos.

The first round into our area was a dud. Whether our guys intentionally used a dead round as a warning to us or not, I don't know, but when that shell hit, the Japs couldn't hold us. We scattered. Filipinos, Americans, and Japanese alike started running off the hill and down the road. Then Corregidor opened up with those 155s and moved some dirt, doing serious damage to the Japs. The last I remember of that hill, a shell landed in the midst of the battery of Jap guns, and I saw Japs and guns go flying.

The Rock's 12-inch mortars at Batteries Way and Geary were instrumental in giving the Japs on Bataan a rough time; they were entrenched in concrete pits and capable of firing eight miles in any direction. Revetments of reinforced concrete six to eight feet thick, together with dirt embankments, surrounded the guns and magazines in these batteries.

When the forces on Corregidor surrendered a month later and the men were transferred to Camp Cabanatuan from Bilibid Prison in Manila, they told us the Japanese had done some pretty fancy shooting of their own across the open water.

One day early in May, from a distance of three or four miles, the Japanese on Bataan lobbed their 240-mm shells against the sides of a magazine at Battery Geary, firing one live round into the cement wall, followed by a dud. Working their way through the concrete, firing a dud to crumble the cement and a live one to blow it away, they finally broke through and got a live round into the magazine. The terrific explosion, felt throughout the island, detonated the shells and powder stored there and blasted the 72-ton mortar out of the pit.

Although the blast killed many people, one man down in the magazine survived. The explosion blew every bit of his clothes off, except for his belt, and it broke all of the blood vessels in his skin. But apparently because he had his mouth open against the concussion, it didn't even burst his eardrums.

Corregidor fought back with everything they had, killing large numbers of Japanese as they attempted to come ashore in droves on landing barges. A Japanese officer told me later, "I commanded one of the barges invading Corregidor. As our craft came around the point from Mariveles, anti-aircraft shells lobbed from Fort Hughes killed forty-eight out of the fifty men on board. When we landed, only one sergeant and I remained alive. The foaming surf turned red from the bloody slaughter that ensued, but we kept right on coming."

Despite the valiant effort of our men on Corregidor, the utter disregard the Japanese had for the lives of their soldiers, plus the support of their air power and the ability to lay down a heavy barrage on Corregidor from the higher elevations on Bataan, spelled defeat for our forces on the Rock, and they capitulated on May 8, 1942.

7 The March of Death

The Japs finally corralled us, and our sad army—defeated, starving, dressed in rags, scared, and unsure of what lay ahead—began the long trek on the road to San Fernando, a town in Pampanga Province, sixty miles north. Five or six hundred men made up the group, guarded by about thirty or forty heavily armed Japs.

At first, the terrain was hilly and hard going. The Japs kept us moving, never allowing us to stop and rest. If I slowed down or stumbled, they hit me in the head or across the shoulders with a rifle butt. Every three or four miles the guards changed while they kept us on the move. If we had to leave the road to allow traffic to go by, we might get a short break, but no one was permitted to sit. Along the way, we connected up with other large parties already captured or men coming out of the jungle to surrender.

The Japs, moving south into Bataan, were gearing up for their assault on Corregidor. They thronged the narrow gravel road with tanks and trucks carrying personnel and supplies. It didn't seem to matter if the prisoners walking toward them got in the way. Unless we moved fast enough, they ran us over. I saw one man, unable to dodge a tank in time, get flattened under the treads. His bloody, mangled body, just left in the road, looked like hamburger.

But what I remember most about that first day was the dust—clouds of thick, choking dust generated by trucks, tanks, and the feet of thousands of men on the move. My tongue felt five times its normal size. I had long ago passed the point of being hungry. I stumbled along in a stupor, like a drunk coming home from a bar.

Before long, I developed a fever from the bullet lodged in my thigh, the same bullet that had killed Junior. Although desperate for water, we had none. The lack of it would be a critical problem for everyone in the days to come.

Although artesian wells dotted the countryside, we couldn't leave the road for water because the Japs shot anyone who broke ranks. If a bridge was out and we were forced to wade across a creek or stream, we'd scoop the water into our mouths as we went, and a little into our canteens. We knew that most of the creeks and streams were polluted and the water unsafe. But in the tropical heat, where temperatures could soar to a hundred degrees and the humidity was close to 100 percent, we became half-crazed with thirst. We no longer cared if the water was safe; we drank it anyway. Under these conditions, it didn't take long for diarrhea or dysentery to spread among the men.

Along the trail of the Bataan Death March.
U.S. Army photo from Corbis-Bettman, New York

The Filipino civilians, who watched us walk by with such pity, were forbidden to give us as much as a boiled egg or even talk to us. The Japanese would have shot them. Neither could we talk to them. But in the days that followed, out of respect for us, they placed jugs of water within reach along the road. Between the water left on the road by the Filipino people and the little we gulped from the creeks we crossed, we at least snatched a drink now and then.

I don't remember the Japanese giving us anything to eat the whole time. Many of the men were near collapse. It became very difficult to stay on our feet, especially when our captors continually struck us with their rifle butts, hitting us out of sheer hatred, forcing us to move even faster. The casualty rate escalated as more and more prisoners, constantly harassed and threatened with extinction, dropped in their tracks, unable to keep up the pace.

In the days to come, when a man fell and couldn't go on, if his friends could help him, the Japs allowed him to be carried. If not, they shot him or stuck him with a bayonet. To save bullets, they beheaded some men with their swords or machetes. Helpless to intervene for fear of suffering the same fate, we watched in horror as they butchered men before our eyes. We quickly learned that if we fell and no one helped us, we were doomed. The Japanese soldiers' treatment of their prisoners was extremely brutal, vicious, even barbaric. We understood the reason for their hatred, since we had killed so many of them in battle; their thinking seemed to be that any live GIs left behind could conceivably return in the middle of the night to cut their throats. They made sure this wouldn't happen.

I have no idea how many soldiers they killed during this forced march, but after a day or so it seemed to me that someone was shot, bayoneted, or clubbed to death every few minutes. To this day, no one can say with any accuracy how many lost their lives during that period. Accounts state that somewhere between seven thousand and seventeen thousand Filipino-American soldiers died of starvation and disease or were killed by the Japanese during the Bataan Death March. Looking back, all I can remember is the wholesale carnage.

With each day much like another, I lost track of time. They kept us moving from sunup until dark. Just putting one foot in front of the

The March of Death from Bataan to POW Camp O'Donnell, April 1942. The men have their hands tied behind their backs.

National Archives

other became my goal. We spent the nights in open fields or in ditches beside the road. With so many men penned up in one place and no latrines, human waste immediately befouled the area. There were flies everywhere.

The wounded and the sick went untended, with diarrhea and dysentery spreading rapidly from the lack of sanitation and potable water. As the men fell out from exhaustion, dehydration, and lack of food, the Japanese stepped up their unspeakable atrocities. Although helping someone else sapped the strength a man needed to keep going, men carried other men whenever possible, at great risk to themselves.

As we left the jungle-clad mountainous areas of south-central Bataan and entered the marshlands, the geography changed. The highway snaked up the eastern coast of the peninsula, with the merciless sun glinting off Manila Bay to our right. To our left, the nearly empty sugarcane fields, which we had stripped during the previous months, stood alongside acres of rice paddies. We had traded the hilly, sometimes steep jungle trail for the flat, sun-scorched bay area. The scenery may have changed, but the temperature remained the same—hot, steamy, and miserable.

We must have spent about five days and nights on the road before we finally arrived at the railhead in San Fernando. The guards divided us into groups and herded us into several small buildings and compounds. They crammed me into a cock-fighting arena with hundreds of other men until it became so crowded we could barely move. We could sit, but there wasn't enough room to lie down.

At last they fed us. That night they gave us a ball of rice the size of a baseball and so salty it was almost inedible. With no water to drink, I barely managed to choke down half of mine. A skinny young fellow standing next to me stared at my rice with eyes big as saucers. He wanted it bad, so I gave him the rest.

Our sanitation consisted of an open-pit latrine dug in one section of the arena. The next morning, as we pulled out, we discovered that a prisoner had fallen into the latrine sometime during the night. Too weak to climb out, he had drowned, which was a hell of a way to go. But I guess if you're dying, you're dying—it really doesn't matter how.

The Filipino trains ready to transport us the rest of the way to the prison camp looked like Toonerville Trolleys. The narrow-gauge steel

Thirty-ton-capacity boxcar, Manila Railroad Company: a "steel trap for 100 men."
National Archives

boxcars, cooking in the sun, felt like ovens as they forced us into them at bayonet point. It was standing room only; they packed a hundred or more men into each car like sardines in a can.

I was more fortunate than most. My boxcar had previously been hit by a shell; the ragged hole in the roof acted like an air scoop as the train moved along. Others were not so lucky. Many men suffocated during the trip. Jammed together in such numbers, when they died they remained upright.

The camp was only thirty miles away, but creeping along at a snail's pace, with frequent stops, it took several hours to get there. The lack of air during these stops made it unbearable. The heat generated by sick men, racked with fever and pressed together, added to our misery. As dehydrated as we were, I couldn't understand how we continued to sweat, but we did. To make matters worse, since we had no sanitation facilities, before long the floor of the boxcar grew slippery from diseased urine and feces. The stench was unbelievable.

We had become like cattle—the sounds of men suffering in that steel trap were like those of wounded animals close to death. At some point my mind turned inward, concentrating only on myself and my own condition. No longer aware of the passage of time or of those around me, I shut out the agony of other men because it was all I could do to cope with my own.

8 "This War Will Last a Hundred Years"

How anyone managed to survive the trip only God knows, but by evening we arrived at a place called Capas. Those of us still alive, though terribly weak, were marched into Camp O'Donnell a few kilometers away. Begun as a Philippine Army camp before the war, with an area of about one square mile, its construction was only a quarter completed. It didn't take a genius to see that the influx of thousands of prisoners into the unfinished camp would be one hell of a nightmare.

Once we arrived, the Japs began to feed us twice a day. The Filipinos called it lugao—rice cooked to a mush, resembling gruel. Like cream of wheat in texture, it was thin, watery, tasteless, and nutritionally worthless. They gave us an average household dipperful of the slop at each meal. A portion barely covered the bottom of our mess kits and did nothing to satisfy the starving men. Hunger was still our constant companion.

The worst problem was lack of water. No lines had been laid. Although there was an artesian well in the compound, it had only one pump and one faucet. To get water, four or five fellows would get together and appoint one man to stand in a mile-long line with their canteens. The others would sit around, resting until the time came to take turns. We'd get up to the faucet about once every other day, resulting in half a canteen of water a day per man. In the tropics, that was not nearly enough for a well man, much less a sick one. As for bathing or washing the crap off our clothes, we could forget that.

Some streets were finished in the camp, and there were a few bamboo barracks under construction, but the hospital was far from complete. It had no beds, no medicines, no instruments, no nothing! It was a place where you went to die.

I still had a Japanese bullet lodged in my thigh. Getting a doctor to help me proved impossible; they were all busy with the seriously ill and dying. Finally, a medical corpsman looked at my leg. The bullet was near the surface, and he removed it without any trouble. Luckily, the wound bled a lot on the march, which kept it from becoming infected.

The wounded and the sick, together with the dead, lay everywhere on the hospital floor, stinking in their own filth, vomit, and blood. Since we had no water to wash them, big greenbottle flies crawled all over the faces of the men and in and out of their mouths or open wounds. Nothing could be done about it. Everything was disorganized; no one had the will or the energy to do anything. We were whipped—worn out both physically and mentally.

I couldn't see any point in hanging around that place, so as soon as they finished wrapping my leg, I went to the area where the rest of the prisoners were mustered. As they arrived in camp, the men began to separate themselves into service groups—air corps, army, navy, and marines.

Within a few days, the rest of the prisoners arrived. About fifty men from my squadron were there, elated at being reunited. Bill was sick and very weak. When I told the men about Junior, they all felt like they had lost a kid brother. I learned that most of the 91st survived the ordeal of the march. It was only later, in the camps and on the work details, that they began to die.

Once we got halfway settled, the camp commander, Captain Tsuniyoshi, gave us a "welcoming" speech. A tall, skinny fellow, he wore a mustache like Hitler's. He stood on a platform with an interpreter, and after he'd say a few words in Japanese, the interpreter would give us the "word" in English. Tsuniyoshi, as I later learned, spoke better English than the interpreter, but officers generally refrained from speaking directly to the prisoners. I guess they thought it was beneath them.

The gist of his speech went something like this: "You are now the guests of the emperor. This war will last a hundred years. Make up your minds that you will die right here. You will also work to earn your keep. If you do not work, you will not be fed."

Some welcoming speech! Not that we believed any of that bull. A little of the American spirit surfaced in our resistance to the Jap's words; men swore under their breath that while we may have lost the battle, this war was far from over! But for the time being, we had to admit they were definitely calling the shots.

No barbed-wire fence encircled the camp, but a cordon of heavily armed soldiers guarded us day and night. Even so, a few men managed to escape and join the Filipino guerrillas fighting in the mountains. Most of us had no chance to escape and no strength to try. But the Japs, in their anger at those who made it out, retaliated by executing scores of men for every one that got away.

Finally, in June, to keep us in line, they ordered the American officers to organize all of the POWs into groups of ten. The rule was: if one of us escaped, the other nine would be summarily executed. This tactic worked for the most part. No man wanted the death of nine others on his conscience.

At night, we slept on the ground. It was the dry season in that part of the Philippines, and sleeping outside was better than being confined in tight quarters in the small, unfinished barracks. During the day, when they provided welcome relief from the sun and the heat, it was a different story.

To save time and trouble, we began to haul water for cooking from a nearby creek. We cut the tops out of 55-gallon drums and mounted them on long bamboo poles. Ten or fifteen men would take them down to the stream to be filled, then carry them back to camp. The Japanese warned us not to drink the river water without boiling it, and most of the Americans didn't. But the Filipinos ignored the warning, and dysentery soon struck them down. They began dying at the rate of two or three hundred a day.

The more able-bodied men formed burial details to deal with the many deaths. About a quarter of a mile from camp, they dug continuous trenches six feet wide and the depth of the short shovels they used. They hauled the dead off in blankets and stacked them three deep in the graves. As I look back on those first weeks, there is no doubt in my mind that quite a few men who were comatose were presumed dead and buried alive. We'll never know, since conditions didn't allow the medics to pronounce them dead with any degree of accuracy.

Americans were dying, too. No latrines had been dug yet, so whenever nature called, the soldiers took off for the fields, away from the sleeping and eating areas. Facilities for bathing or washing didn't exist, since we needed the little available water for drinking and cooking. Mix in the flies that plagued us during the day and the mosquitoes at night, and we had the perfect breeding ground for disease.

Although some men developed beriberi and pellagra, in those first few weeks at O'Donnell it was diarrhea and amoebic dysentery that ran rampant. It was common for a man to go twenty or thirty times a day. But if he began to pass blood, he could figure he'd be dead in a day or two. We had no medicine for either disease, but word spread among the men that if you ate charcoal, it would stop the runs. We tried it. Hell, at that point, we would have tried anything. But all it did was color the watery crap we passed.

9 Girocho Rides Again

The word *blivet*—army slang for the ultimate in constraint and dis-comfort: two pounds of shit in a one-pound bag—aptly described life in O'Donnell. While no one can be 100-percent sure of the numbers, statistics would later show that of the eighty thousand men in the Fil-ipino-American army, approximately fifty thousand made it into the camps. Many men familiar with the terrain escaped during the rout, and more than five thousand may have melted into the jungle while on the death march.

Things were about as miserable as they could get when, on May 9, we heard that Corregidor had fallen. Although we didn't expect any last-minute miracle from the men on the Rock, the news put the cap on things, really sealing our fates.

Shortly after that, the Japanese began releasing the Filipino pris-oners. They also began using the Americans as slaves to repair bridges and roads and to build runways. While it was hard physical labor, it beat staying in camp where there was only sickness and death.

Every morning the Japs announced that they needed a hundred or so men for a particular detail. The men who wanted to work on it lined up at the gate to be counted off. This would be repeated until the jobs for that day were filled.

It's been my experience that given half a chance southerners tend to gravitate together, and I became friends with several in camp. Two of the guys, Freddie Barr and Allen Laurence, hailed from Fort Worth.

Back in Texas, Freddie had been a truck driver and Laurence, as we called him, a successful florist.

One day as we sat around discussing our limited options, we decided we'd better volunteer for the next assignment to come along. Although Bill was still too sick to work, Freddie, Laurence, and I did not have dysentery yet, only diarrhea. Instead of going to the latrine twenty or thirty times a day, we only went ten or fifteen. So far, we had not passed any blood—a good sign. We were in better shape than many of our comrades, but the time had come to get out of there before it was too late.

The next morning, Freddie went down to the gate to check out the work detail for the day. In a few minutes he came running back on the double. Hurrying over to Laurence and me, he said, "Hey, y'all, the Japs want forty men to drive heavy trucks!"

"Man, I've never driven a heavy truck before," I said. "What do they mean, a tractor-trailer rig?"

"What difference does it make?" Freddie said. "I've driven some large rigs in Texas. It's no big deal."

Laurence chimed in. "It seems to me, if we stay in this hell hole another day, we're not long for this world."

"Yeah, but if we wreck a truck, we've had it," I argued. Then I shrugged and said, "Either way, there's not much choice, is there? Let's do it!"

We volunteered, and the Japs put us and the rest of the men in the back of two stake-bed trucks. We took off, holding on for dear life as we bumped along the rough highway. Having to stand all the way back to San Fernando in the jolting, bucking trucks really aggravated our swollen and painful guts.

That afternoon, we arrived in the center of town, where the trucks we were to drive sat parked in a row down one side of the street. I was relieved to see that the so-called "heavy trucks" were the ordinary GI kind we'd used on Bataan. Although we did our best to destroy all of them before we surrendered, obviously we missed a few.

A Nip interpreter told us they had made some repairs to those trucks we abandoned in order to form a transportation outfit. (My guard later told me that this group constituted what remained of the Third

Chrysanthemum Cavalry Unit after we decimated their numbers on Bataan.) In 1942, maybe 50 percent or more of the American population owned a car or truck, but in Japan the average man or woman didn't even know how to drive. They needed our GIs to fill the bill.

They lined us up and, as we walked down the street, each man peeled off to climb behind the wheel of a truck, accompanied by the soldier appointed to ride with him. After we'd each been given a vehicle, they divided us into groups of ten or so and assigned us to the squadrons we would be ferrying into the field. I was billeted with twelve others in the town of Cabanatuan.

As I got into my five-ton Dodge, the interpreter told me it didn't run too good, so take it slow. I started the engine and after rolling a few feet, I realized it was a power wagon with four-wheel drive. Following the instructions on the dash, I disengaged the front wheels with the lever on the floor alongside the gearshift, put her in gear, and she smoothed out, running like a top.

This made me an instant hit with my Japanese companion; I became an expert in his eyes. I guess he'd expected that we'd be bringing up the rear of the convoy, eating everyone's dust.

After we got under way, the *haitai* or *gunjin* (soldier in Japanese) started to talk a little.

"You smoku?"

"Yeah, I smoku," I answered.

"You got cigarette?" he asked.

"No, no cigarette," I said.

He reached into his jacket, brought out a sample pack of three or four Piedmonts (a popular brand of American cigarettes in the 1920s and '30s, now a favorite in the Philippines), and handed it to me. This was my first smoke in many days, and the first whole cigarette I'd had since "Maytag Charlie" dropped his samples in the field. Boy, it tasted great, but it was so strong it nearly knocked me out! I handed the pack back to him, but he said I could keep it.

"You hungry?" he asked a little while later.

"Yeah, I'm hungry."

"You eat?"

"If I had anything to eat, I'd eat," I told him.

He hesitated for a minute, then he reached down into a leather bag on the floorboard, pulled out a boiled duck egg, and gave it to me. I took the egg, cracked it on the steering wheel, and began peeling it, driving with my knee. When he saw that, he almost had a fit. He grabbed the egg and finished peeling it himself, then handed it back to me.

I took two bites out of that big duck egg and it was gone. It hit bottom with plenty of room left over. He observed all this without a word. Before long he asked, "You like egg?"

"Yeah, I liked the egg."

He went through the same procedure as before, and it disappeared as quickly as the first. He laughed as he handed me another and yet another; he must have given me six eggs. I ate them all, and I could probably have eaten six more.

As we drove along, he seemed to admire my skill in handling the big truck. He kept the conversation going, practicing his English on me, while I tried hard to understand what he said. Thanks to our Nip escorts, the soldiers waved us through the numerous roadblocks along the way. But at least once every hour, we'd have to make five-minute pit stops. The diarrhea and dysentery still dogged us. We'd stop the trucks and head for the side of the road.

It was dark by the time we came to a crossroads. The Japs made us park the trucks near a small food stall called a tienda. They told the couple who ran the stand to feed us. Things were looking up!

The woman got busy making what looked like flapjacks. The smell of them cooking on the small charcoal stove made our mouths water. I must have devoured at least a dozen of the tasty little rice cakes as fast as their teenaged daughter could serve them off the griddle. They punched holes in big green coconuts for us to drink. The clear liquid, running down my chin as I sucked on the slightly salty "milk," was refreshing. Hot, freshly roasted peanuts and some of the raw-sugar candy they make in the Philippines rounded out the first real meal we'd had in months. We almost cleaned the place out. Although the Filipino couple wouldn't take any money from us, as soon as they saw that our hosts were paying, they didn't hesitate to rack 'em!

Somewhat revived by the food and drink, we continued on to the town of Cabanatuan. We drove to headquarters—the town's schoolhouse—arriving about midnight. The cook was still on duty, ready to feed this contingent whenever they showed up. Our guards lined up to be fed, motioning us to get in behind them. This time, we got rice and tea, and they said we could have more if we wanted. Things were definitely looking up!

We went back for seconds and even thirds; each time, they filled up both sides of our mess kits. When we finished, they threw us a pack of cigarettes, then showed us where to park the trucks. We drove into the schoolyard, where they turned us over to another unit. They gave us tarps to spread between the trucks, and we bedded down for the night.

The next morning, all the Japs came over to see the POWs. What a crummy-looking sight! Having gone for months without a bath, no doubt we smelled pretty ripe. A couple of the younger men were unable to raise a beard or a mustache, but the rest of us had four-month-old beards, full of cockle burrs, with God knows what living in them. (In the field, we hardly had enough water to drink, much less shave with. I had a pocket comb on Bataan, and when on patrol or at an outpost, I'd sit there and comb my beard, looking for all the world like Karl Marx. Along the way, I lost it, making it impossible to keep my beard even halfway clean.) Our coveralls, stiff with sweat, grime, and in some cases crap, could have stood by themselves. The Nips took one good look at us (probably got one good whiff, too) and broke out the soap, towels, razors, and scissors. They pointed to the water faucet in the middle of the schoolyard and said, "Take a bath!"

Situated on the corner of one of the busiest intersections in Cabanatuan, the school faced an open market directly across the street. The main hospital occupied the opposite corner. A continuous throng of people walked by—men, women, and children—and we had nothing to hide behind.

We stood there, hesitating, not comfortable with the idea of public bathing, when along came a haitai in a G-string with a towel slung over his shoulder. He strode over to the faucet, peeled off the G-string, and proceeded to bathe right out in the open. Since he didn't attract undue attention from the people passing by, we looked at each other and agreed that if he could do it, so could we.

I've had plenty of baths, before and since, but none ever felt as good as that one! We used a whole bar of soap among us, lathering up our bodies and washing our hair. Our skin was so dry that it seemed to soak up the water as we played and splashed in it like a bunch of kids. For once, we drank as much water as we wanted.

Next we washed our coveralls. Without the dirt, they almost fell apart. I had worn the same pair all through combat; they were torn and full of holes from the countless times I had gotten hung up in barbed wire while out on patrol. We did the best we could to clean them, then spread them on the ground to dry.

Busy with organizing this new detail, the Japs didn't press us to do any work for the next few days. We got a chance to take it easy, rest up, and recuperate. We sat around cutting our hair and beards with scissors, then shaving with razors. They made us shave our heads as well, saying it would get rid of the lice. But once our hair was gone, we discovered a layer of gray scum covering our scalps. It came off in sheets, but it took a good bit of scrubbing to get rid of it.

During this interval, we also fixed up a place to sleep. Like most buildings in the Philippines, the school, built on pilings, left a space under it almost tall enough for the average American to stand. We loaded a truck with rice straw and spread it around under the school. We covered the straw with our tarps, and we were in business.

The day finally came when the Japs put us to work. Through the interpreter, they told us what our duties would be: "You take Japanese soldiers to various areas in the field and haul food and supplies from nearby warehouses to different units housed in the town. You take care of trucks, keep them washed, gassed up, and in good running order. A soldier is assigned to each of you. He will see you have food, he will travel with you, and generally be responsible for you."

Next they handed out ribbons with Japanese characters painted on them to the thirteen men in our group. The interpreter went on, "As your Amelican names are foreign to us—very difficurt to pronounce—you are being renamed after characters in Japanese folklore. There is ancient fairy tale about a man like your Amelican cowboy Jesse James and the English thief Robin Hood. He stole, all time, from rich and gave to poor. All little Japanese children know story, bereeve he was champion samurai and hero to the people. His name was Girocho. He had ten captains under his command, and these ten captains had a hundred men under them. Two women in the group assisted the men."

He walked up to me and pinned a ribbon on my collar. "As ranking man," he said, "you will be known as Girocho." To Laurence, who was standing next to me, he said, "You are renamed Omasa, Girocho's Number One captain, since you are tall man with rots of hair on chest."

They gave the rest of the captains' names to the men, matching their descriptions with the characters in the story. But that left two in our group unnamed. The Nips solved this problem easily. Because of their youthful good looks and inability to grow beards, they named the youngsters after the two women who acted as gun molls for the group (or so the story went).

To the Japanese this was a big joke, a game. They laughed and pointed at us as we walked around with those nametags pinned to our collars. We really didn't care what they called us; we had a few choice names for them, too. But to memorize our new identities, we started calling each other by the Japanese nicknames, and we soon dropped our given names almost entirely.

One day, one of the haitai made a proper name tag for me, cut from a piece of copper lantern. Etched into the oval shape were the Japanese characters for "John Poncio." I had to wear it around my neck, but it didn't make much difference because before long, everyone in the area knew me and the others by our new monikers. As we drove by, they would wave and call out, "Girocho!" or "Omasa!"

In the early summer of 1942, General Homma made the rounds of all the installations on the island. His pending visit generated plenty of excitement and activity within the various units stationed in Cabanatuan. Inspections were ordered every day as the rank and file swept and tidied the barracks, offices, and grounds. Our trucks had to be washed and parked in neat rows, just so.

On the day General Homma arrived, the Japanese soldiers lined up, spit-polished and at attention. They made us fall in behind them. By then, our uniforms had disintegrated; most of us were dressed in makeshift shorts and torn shirts without sleeves. Still, we had shaved, and our hair was clipped to *ni cinchi*, the Japanese army's regulation length of two centimeters.

After the general finished his inspection of the Japanese troops, he got around to us. He stopped, looked us over real good, and aimed a few questions at the Jap commander. The CO explained who we were and where we had come from. Standing there dressed in rags, but perhaps with a certain glint in our eyes or pride in our bearing, we must've had "Made in the USA" stamped all over us, for the general remarked that we looked like pretty good soldiers to him. Coming from Homma, whose shock troops had overrun us in the end, the Japanese officers considered this high praise. Most of them didn't have any respect for us. Surrender was not in their vocabulary. But when they took stock of how many of their men had been killed by a relatively small number of Americans, they grudgingly acknowledged that the general might be right. After Homma's pronouncement, our treatment by the Japanese soldiers in the truck detail improved even more.

When we were not delivering food and supplies or hauling Japs around, they made us work around the kitchen and help with the cooking. That suited us just fine. One thing appeared on the menu every day three times a day: rice. We cooked everything in a big iron pot. First, the rice, then after we washed the pot, the soup, meat, or vegetables would go in.

The troops took their *bentos* (lunches) into the field. The covers of the mess kits held enough dry rice that, when cooked, it filled up the bottom part of the kit as well. While this portion satisfied the average Japanese soldier, we Americans could easily put away two of them. The Japanese were amazed at how much we could eat. Larger than the average Jap and half starved at that, a measly cup of rice didn't stick with us very long. Fortunately, they put no limits on how much food we could have in this camp. After a few weeks, most of us finally got rid of the runs and even managed to pick up a little weight. Even so, a few of the men in the group never recovered.

A young fellow in our group, one of the two who had been renamed for one of the Japanese women in Girocho's merry little band, went steadily downhill. Most of the time, he lay under the schoolhouse in a curled-up position. Coaxing him to eat got us nowhere. One morning as I watched him give up, knowing he would die soon, I picked him up in my arms, carried him to the steps of the building, and sat him down none too gently. I stuck my face close to his and said through clenched teeth, "You son of a bitch, you've got two choices: You're either going to sit there until you eat something, if it takes all day, or I'll cram it down your throat right now!"

His pale blue eyes widened. His mouth flew open for a split second before he came to life. Then he drew back, saying in a surprisingly strong voice, "God damn it, if I ever get well, I'm gonna beat the living hell out of you."

"Listen, you bastard," I yelled at him, "if you give up and refuse to eat, you won't live long enough to whip my ass."

Over the next few days, he managed to choke down some soup and began to show signs of regaining a little strength. But before he could make a full recovery, the Japs trucked him and four other men in the same shape to the camp outside of Cabanatuan. Although I heard a few of the guys eventually got better, some didn't make it. Later, after I had been moved to the big camp, I saw the youngster walking across the compound one day. I smiled to myself. He had somehow beaten the odds.

The school building also housed a field aid station where the Jap soldiers came for medical help. The medics dealt harshly with their own, showing them no sympathy. Many times a gunjin would come in, sick as a dog, and have to stand at attention while announcing his complaint to the medical officer in a loud voice. I saw one medic roughly pull the scabs off a man's sores with no regard for the pain he inflicted.

If something ailed us, we could go there for medicine, too. But we really couldn't complain about the way they treated us. It puzzled us for a while until we learned that in Japan a truck driver ranked only second to an airplane pilot in importance.

This jibed with their strict code regarding class and privilege. Because I was ranking man in our group, the Japs made me responsible for everything the prisoners did wrong. But that same system also entitled me to the privileges they thought I should have.

Not long after we fixed up our "barracks" under the school, a couple of the haitai dragged in a broken-down cot and set it up especially for me. "Giro, you head honcho over your men," they said. "You sleep on cot."

It made no difference to them that I really preferred to sleep on the ground rather than on the busted cot. The "code" forbade it. As top banana, I was permitted to grow a mustache, too. This mark of distinction was strictly reserved for officers or ranking noncoms.

Their system of military justice, very different from ours, included corporal punishment. Frequently, when I saw a haitai do something wrong, the corporal would knock the hell out of him; he'd hit him four or five times while cussing him out good and proper.

A GI in the U.S. services usually got put on report for wrongdoing and maybe sent to the guardhouse or the brig, but unless the Japs did something really serious, they received punishment on the spot. Usually, that ended the affair—forgive and forget. The officers didn't seem to hold it against the man once they had "corrected" him. I guess it's all in how you look at it. I wouldn't have liked some guy pounding on me, but then I wouldn't have liked the guardhouse, either.

The Japanese also believed in plenty of exercise on their day off, whereas the American soldier, even today, believes in lying around. The Japs couldn't understand that, so they always included us in their fun and games.

Shortly after we arrived, they came up with the foolish notion that we had to play baseball and hold races. Ignoring our poor physical condition, the Japs, of course, beat us at everything. In baseball, they knocked us out of the park, and we didn't stand a chance in the footraces. The soldiers also liked to arm-wrestle us because their short arms gave them superior leverage. Quite often they won, which thrilled them no end. They naturally began to swagger and brag, "Americans, no good! Not strong like Nippon. Nippon, *kirei na* [pure]. Americans, *kato* [inferior]."

Maybe so. They might have beaten us physically, but we stayed on our toes when it came to the mental games we played with our captors. All the Nips wanted to learn English so they could talk to the Filipinos. They would come up, offer us a cigarette, and try to carry on some sort of conversation, attempting to learn new words. It always cost 'em! We'd find a way to chisel them out of something of value every time. With me, it was nearly always food—candy, eggs, or, if I could get them, canned goods.

Everything the haitai did, we had to imitate. They made us learn the Japanese numbers (*bango*) and report in when they did. Every morning, the soldiers fell in for *tenko* (muster). Then they faced east, bowed low, and recited a prayer, saying that they worshiped the emperor, who was a god, and that they would fight and die for Japan.

After the head count, we too had to bow and face east, but our prayer went something like this: "The emperor is a son of a bitch. We won't die for him and, better yet, we'll try not to die at all!"

We said it in English, of course, in a singsong voice. Had they understood us, heads would have rolled right then and there. Once it registered how much they revered the emperor, we cut that out. Too dangerous.

A few of the battle-hardened Japanese soldiers and officers hated all Americans on general principle. You couldn't expect anything else. But most of them kept their feelings fairly well hidden and didn't give us a hard time, especially when they got to know us individually. We quickly learned which ones to cultivate and which ones to avoid.

Unlike some of his cohorts, my guard Taiota just seemed to be marking time until he could go back to Japan and resume his life. He was married and had three kids; all he wanted was to get back to them after the war. Under the circumstances, we got along okay.

The cook for our detachment, Ota (I called him Otayo), although not exactly a simpleton, wasn't too sharp. Having lost a brother on Bataan, he was hostile toward us at first. But after a while he lowered his guard and became somewhat friendlier. Occasionally, when he went to town, he'd bring back something he knew we liked. He learned that Americans like corn, so whenever he could get it, he'd buy some to roast in the coals under the rice pot. The Japs always laughed at us, saying only horses ate corn. They didn't like sweet potatoes either, but Otayo kept us supplied.

Since most of the soldiers couldn't read English, when they bought canned goods from various markets—some of it American made—they often ended up with food they didn't like. One guy bought what he thought was a can of corned beef. He took one bite, made a face, and spit it out. He ended up giving it to the crazy Americans, who the Japanese said would eat anything. Passing the can around, several of us got to savor the delicate taste of asparagus, a food we had almost forgotten.

The assignment to run supplies to the different army detachments took us to the town of Gapan, the capital of that province, located a few miles south of Cabanatuan. The Japs commandeered houses all over town, putting a single squad in a small house or several squads in a larger one. With no central mess hall, each unit had to cook its own meals.

Every day we picked up the fish, meat, vegetables, and rice the Japs appropriated from the Filipinos, plus staples such as soy sauce and mustard shipped from Japan to a warehouse in town. Then we made our deliveries. If ten men occupied a house, we'd drop off rations for ten, then continue down the line to the rest of the houses. Say what you will, all GIs, whether Japanese, American, or any other nationality, behave the same. They'll steal you blind, and if something's not nailed down, it'll be long gone! Taiota, the man assigned to guard me, was no different.

"Giro," he said to me one day, using a combination of sign language and pidgin English we'd worked out between us in order to communicate. "We fix up truck real good. Have more food and supplies for us." As I was still somewhat weak and very hungry, he had my undivided attention.

"You take out boards here," he said, pointing to the middle section of the wooden floor of the truck bed. After I lifted out a couple, he handed me a rifle-shipping box and motioned to me to lay it between the planks.

"Now put boards back," he said. When I finished, he gave me a big grin, put his finger up to his lips, and climbed into the back of the truck, where he usually rode during our deliveries. I hopped into the driver's seat and we took off for the warehouse.

From then on, whenever we picked up supplies and nobody was looking, Taiota would pull up a plank, fill the box underneath with a variety of whatever food we got that day, and replace the plank. As we made our rounds, he'd distribute what was left, shorting the other detachments. Although we occupied the last house on the route, we never came up short; we drew our full rations for the day, plus the extra rations in the box, making ours the best-fed unit of all. On special holidays, such as the emperor's birthday, we got extra rations. Naturally, since our truck made all the deliveries, we came up with more food, more candy, and more beer than anybody else.

In the event that we drew both meat and fish, the Japs always opted for the fish and gave us the meat. That suited us just fine. Their favorite was fresh tuna, caught at sea and frozen aboard the ship en route to the Philippines. When they brought in one, often weighing fifty pounds or more, it gave them an excuse to hold a big celebration. They either cooked it in soy sauce or shaved it into real thin slices and ate it raw, usually with cucumber.

At first, because I wasn't starving anymore, I turned up my nose at it. But after I learned to fix it with a little lemon juice and chase it with a lot of sake, it began to taste pretty good. After enough sake, I couldn't tell the difference between the raw fish and the cucumber. We gradually developed a taste for Japanese food, but it always helped if you were hungry to begin with.

One day Laurence and I made a run up to the town of Baguio. After we made our deliveries, cooked supper, and served it, a few of our Japanese friends invited us to a party. Soldiers from another unit came too. Things went pleasantly enough until one of the soldiers got drunk. He started shooting off his mouth about how he hated Americans. Then he tried to slap us around to prove it.

He didn't get very far. Much to our surprise and delight, our little cook Otayo sprang into action. Using his judo skills, he gave the haitai a good karate chop on the arm, then swung around and kicked out with his left foot, planting it squarely in Big Mouth's midsection. That ended the evening's festivities. We didn't attend any more private parties, but Otayo, who turned out to be a black belt in judo, would protect us from transient soldiers more than once.

We managed to corrupt the Japanese a little, as time went by. They never used salt in their rice, but after sampling some of ours and liking it, a few of them started adding salt to theirs. They called us nuts because of the way we drank our tea. After making hot tea, we'd cool it, put lemon in it to make it tart, then sugar to make it sweet. By the time we left, though, some of them had switched to using sugar in their tea.

Calling upon my vast culinary talents, one evening I threw a hand-ful of rice into the soup. (Except for a few sad-looking pieces of carrot and daikon—Japanese radish—floating on top, we had nothing else to put in it.) When we served dinner, the Jap corporal in charge of the kitchen got hopping mad.

He called me and Laurence over and asked, "What happened? You boiled rice and didn't wash pot before you made soup?"

"Oh, no!" Laurence answered. "That's the way Americans make soup."

"Right," I said. "My mother always puts rice in hers."

Looking unconvinced, the corporal tasted the soup again, trying to decide whether he liked it. He swallowed it, looked up at me, and grinned. "Dai jobu. Okay," he said. From then on, we had to put a little rice in the soup. All things considered, I guess we learned a few things from each other.

Shortly after we arrived in camp, the Jap brass instructed their men not to take valuables from the prisoners but to offer to buy them in-stead. Unfortunately, the order came too late. Within the first few days of capturing us, the haitai had ripped off everything of value.

While manning a machine gun in the height of battle, I chipped the crystal of a small watch I wore on the inside of my wrist. I stashed the watch in the pocket of my coverall leg for safekeeping and forgot about it. Sitting around one day, I suddenly remembered it. I reached into the little pocket. The watch was still there! I tried to wind it, but no luck. It had rusted from all my tramping through the swamps and creeks on Bataan.

Noticing my attempts to fix it, an officer came over and said, "You have a watch?"

"Yes sir, but it's broken," I replied.

"You want to sell it?" he asked politely.

"Yes, I guess so," I said, figuring if he really wanted it, he'd take it, anyway.

"How much do you want for it?"

"I don't know. Anything you give me will be okay."

"No, no, how much?" he insisted.

"Well, I paid seventy-five dollars for it, so how about fifty pesos?"

Nodding, he said, "Come into the office."

We walked in, and he asked me, "How do you want it, big bills or little bills?"

"If I ever get a chance to buy anything, it probably won't cost much, so give it to me in small bills."

Using the little machine each outfit had to print occupation money, he ran off fifty pesos in small denominations. No serial numbers, or much of anything else except the denomination, appeared on the bills. I could have asked for a thousand pesos for the watch; he would have given it to me. What did he care? All he had to do was run the printer a little longer.

I exchanged the watch for the money and went back to my quarters to tell the other guys about it. "Boys," I said, laughing, "this is hot off the press!"

A Jap working in the kitchen and hearing the laughter and commotion, as well as the cruder comments regarding the worth of the bills, came over and wanted to know where I got the money. Then he asked, "What means, 'No good for shit'?"

I explained that I had sold a watch to the captain, adding, "But we all know this money is no good. There's no gold or silver to back it up."

"Yes," he said, pointing to his bayonet. "But it's backed with steel—just as good."

A year or two later, the Japs began to print better-looking money. No gold or silver backed it either, but at least it had serial numbers on it and looked more official. At first, though, their money was a joke; I saw some of it that was printed on regular tablet paper with the blue lines running right through it. Worthless or not, the Filipino people had no choice; they had to take it in trade from the Nips.

Once the Japs captured the Philippines, it didn't take long for Filipino and American money to disappear from the open market. I went to buy coconut milk from the market across from headquarters one day and noticed that the old woman in charge was grinning from ear to ear as a haitai finished his purchase and moved off.

"You look very happy today," I said. "What's so funny?"

Coming closer, she whispered, "You see that soldier who just left?"

"Yes."

"Well, he bought less than one peso's worth of food and paid me with an American silver dollar." Chuckling, she added, "I gave him only fifty centavos in change. He is so stupid he doesn't realize the silver dollar is worth more than two pesos." As she tucked the money in her pocket, she vowed, "No one will see this until the war is over."

Like most of the Filipinos, the woman had faith that MacArthur would keep his promise to recapture the islands from the Japanese. Anyone who had pesos or dollars hoarded them against the day the Americans would return.

Although some prisoners got paid by the Japanese (according to the Geneva Convention rules they later observed), I never received any pay in the Philippines. When they transferred me to the POW Camp Cabanatuan a few miles from the city of Cabanatuan, the only money I got was smuggled in by the underground that had been formed by civilians to aid the POWs.

In the meantime, we continued to eat well in the transportation unit, and the Filipinos, who often stuck their necks out, slipped us money, cigarettes, candy, or other little luxuries. The risks they took made our blood run cold. At the same time, it did us good just to receive a smile from these naturally friendly people or a surreptitious V sign flashed behind their backs. We tried to discourage their boldness, knowing that if they were caught by some of the more perverse Japanese guards, they would be severely punished. But they didn't seem to care. By their unselfish generosity and words of encouragement, they proved over and over that they were pro-American.

As the months rolled by, learning to live and work as hostages to Japan became a matter of surviving. On day one, the thirteen men in the truck detail got together and decided that we would not try to escape. The ten-man-squad death penalty, which called for executing the other nine men if one escaped, pretty much tied us together. At this point, we felt that we couldn't afford the heroics. We bided our time, did what they told us, and didn't give them any trouble. We concentrated on building up our health and strength, living one day at a time.

One afternoon Laurence and I, busy cooking the evening meal, noticed a couple of trucks driven by American prisoners rumble past the schoolyard. They continued around the block then drove into the yard opposite our quarters. We didn't pay much attention until a voice be-hind us said, "Hey, you guys, do you have a place around here where my men can sleep tonight?"

We turned around, expecting to see an American, but saw only a Japanese soldier standing there. He spoke again. "Can you make room for my men tonight?"

Still not believing our eyes or ears, we continued to look past him for a GI. He said, "It's me. Do you have a place where my prisoners can sleep tonight?"

"Well, yeah, we have plenty of room under the building," I replied. "Spread out wherever you want to."

The fact that he spoke English without any accent really intrigued us. Curious as hell, I waited until after he had gotten his men settled, then I plucked up the courage to ask him where he'd learned English.

With a laugh he said, "Man, I'm as American as you are!" He told us that he was a Hawaiian-born Japanese from a well-to-do family in Hon-olulu, and to please call him Mike.

"Back in 1932, my father arranged for me to go back to Japan to con-tinue my education and renew my cultural ties to the old country," he said. "Unfortunately, while I was pursuing my studies in 1935, they con-scripted me into the army. I protested. I argued that as an American cit-izen I had certain rights. They told me that my place of birth didn't matter; they considered anyone of Japanese descent a citizen of Japan forever."

He was silent for a while, remembering his ordeal, then he went on. "I was sent to China and forced to fight in their bloody war under Gen-eral Homma, in Shanghai and northern Manchuria." With a rueful smile he added, "I arrived in the Philippines in March, just in time for the fireworks."

Mike had another strike against him. "I'm also a Christian, and al-though I have a good education, the authorities distrust me because I am not Shinto. I hope this damn war is over tomorrow, but even if it lasts another hundred years, I could never rise in rank above PFC."

We talked for some time. Frustrated as hell, he told me, "I sure am homesick." He wasn't referring to Japan, either! I really felt sorry for him. Not until I learned more about the traditional Japanese way of thinking did I understand why the Japs considered him a traitor and kept him under close wraps. To them, Mike and his family had been disloyal. His father and mother had left the home of their ancestors to live in a foreign country. Furthermore, they added insult to injury by adopting another religion.

The Japanese put me in the same boat. "Since you are Italian, why you not fight on the side of Italy and Germany?" they would ask. (Trying to explain the difference between Sicily and Italy got me nowhere.) They accused me of turning my back on my "mother country." Mother country, hell! Why should I care about Italy? Just because my grandparents were Sicilian didn't make me a citizen of Sicily, much less of Italy. The fact that I was born in the United States and owed my allegiance to America made no sense to them. They had no concept of what America was all about.

It never occurred to them that our nation was stronger precisely because our people were made up of all races, religions, and nationalities. They couldn't get over the fact that some of us had brown hair, while others had blond, black, or red. The color of our eyes, whether blue, brown, or green, or the way we were built, either tall and thin or short and stocky, usually resulted in some comment from them.

They really had no basis for bragging about their race. I saw quite a collection of Japanese characters as time went by. One in particular stands out in my memory. He was so short his rifle came up to his shoulder. He had buck teeth, and the thick glasses he wore magnified his slanted eyes. His drawers hung down about an inch below his shorts to complete the picture. He looked like the proverbial caricature in the propaganda posters. He was the funniest-looking guy I'd ever seen. But even though I had trouble keeping a straight face in his presence, I knew—and respected the fact—that he'd fight me to the death, if necessary.

At any rate, because of our mixed-up heritage, they regarded all Americans as just a bunch of mongrel dogs, a much lower class than the Japanese. They thought of their race as pure, and the fact that they all looked alike proved it. If it made them feel any better about themselves, that was okay by me. But it always made me laugh when they looked down their noses at us. How can you look down your nose at someone who is twice as tall as you?

At first, we experienced frequent cases of culture shock. An American-style toilet graced the post office in Cabanatuan. Never having seen one before, the Japs working there would mount the thing backwards, stand up on the seat, and never flush after using it. They'd leave the damnedest mess! But what I thought of as ignorance was just a lack of experience with western plumbing. Their toilets in Japan looked nothing like ours; they had no concept of how ours worked.

We found their social customs equally strange. Now and then when Taiota went to a dance, he'd have to drag me along since he didn't drive. He'd tell me to sit on the sidelines where he could keep an eye on me. Then he'd warn, "Don't dance with the girls, either."

On another occasion, I drove an officer in the outfit and his date to a dance. He had the girl by the hand, and before climbing the stairs to the dance hall, he paused af the first step to take a leak, right there in front of her. His behavior appalled and embarrassed me, but he never gave it a thought. This was a perfectly normal and natural thing to do; there was nothing at all unusual about it.

USO-style shows provided entertainment for the Japanese troops, and I drove Taiota to several of these as well. After the performance, the dancers, actors, and actresses would hand out signed pinups of themselves to their fans. I usually sat in a front-row seat, so they always generously gave me some, too.

The Japanese army had a longstanding tradition of prostitution that existed for the soldiers' well-being. The "comfort girls," as they called them, were not Japanese. They were basically culled from among the female population of conquered nations; the ones in the Philippines mostly came from Korea or Formosa. I've heard that one girl might be forced to "handle" as many as twenty-five Japs in a single day. When the detachments they serviced moved, the girls moved with them.

As with most things in the military, rank had its privileges. Every month, the Japanese issued tickets to the gunjin that allowed them to visit the houses set up for these women. A private got one ticket, a corporal got two, and a sergeant got three—the officers, naturally, got the lion's share. Their "generosity" in this department, however, did not extend to me. I never got any "skivvy tickets."

10 "Hey Joe, You Want to Get Even?"

Our coveralls finally disintegrated, and I couldn't salvage enough material for a pair of shorts. The Japanese uniforms simply didn't fit most of us, especially when we began to put on a little weight from eating regularly. Their shoes were impossible for us to wear—too wide and too short. All that summer, I drove the truck dressed in a G-string (our hosts thoughtfully issued a new one every three months or so), a pair of Japanese wooden geta, and a sun helmet. As I traveled up and down the roads in my skimpy attire, I became well known to the Japanese and civilians alike. By the end of the summer, I looked as dark as the Filipino natives, only a little bigger.

I'm not much of a flower fancier, but on these trips I saw flowers and plants that were out of this world. Steep, verdant cliffs, densely populated with huge trees, rose up on both sides of the road. Tangled vines, jumping from limb to limb, formed lush, green canopies overhead, shutting out most of the sun. Driving along in the dim light gave me the feeling of being in a grotto; the air so cool and invigorating after the heat of the plains. Massive ferns, with fronds big enough to hide a truck, grew in outcroppings of rock. Wild orchids in every delicate shade imaginable, even pale green, hung from the trees and vines.

Coming out into the brilliant sunshine moments later, I'd almost be blinded by the splashy flowers decorating the slopes with every color under the sun—reds, yellows, pinks, and purples. They always reminded me of the brightly garbed gals I'd seen crowding the Escolta in Manila during happier times.

Laurence, now known as Omasa, had owned a florist's shop in Fort Worth before he joined the army. It always tickled me to look at those big mitts of his and picture him arranging fragile bouquets. The first time he caught sight of all the rare and exotic plants and flowers up in the mountains, he got real excited. On subsequent trips, he'd give me botany lessons, naming the many species we had seen that day, his eyes shining with wonder and amazement. "Giro," he'd say, "if only I could take these back to Texas, I'd be a rich man in no time!"

Our forays all over the island took us to places we would otherwise never have seen. Beautiful little villages, or barrios, off the beaten path, looked pleasant and peaceful. But to the Japs, who were only interested in chasing guerrillas, they represented places for possible ambush.

As Americans right in the middle of the action, we tried to make sure the Filipinos could tell us apart from the Nips. Most of the drivers didn't wear shirts, and several were big enough to be conspicuously American, but the smaller guys, who were also dark from the sun by now, could easily be mistaken for Japs.

One day I ferried a truckload of troops to check out the increasing guerrilla activity near Baler, the birthplace of Manuel Quezon, the former president of the Philippines. The town was north of Cabanatuan on the eastern coast, in what is still unexplored territory on Luzon. Situated between two mountain ranges, the winding gravel road we took was very primitive, only wide enough for one vehicle in many places. We had made this rugged and dangerous trip once or twice before, hauling supplies to the Jap detachment stationed on that side of the island.

On an earlier run, heavy rains had washed out a portion of the road. Taiota ordered some of the Jap soldiers riding in the back of the truck to find some bamboo. In a short time they came back with several pieces, which they cut and plaited into a thick mat, installing it over the area of the road that had fallen away.

I was driving the lead truck in the convoy, and when they finished the soldiers motioned me forward, calling out, "You first." I looked at the bamboo patch, trying to quickly calculate the weight of the truck plus the approximate weight of the soldiers riding in the back, but I didn't have time; they kept yelling at me, "Sa! Sa!" Come on! Come on!

I pictured myself, the truck, and everybody in back plunging into the deep ravine below, yet I had no choice but to drive across. I put the Dodge in gear, held my breath, and started forward, fully convinced that this was the end. Unbelievable! Not only did the mat hold for my truck, but the entire convoy passed over it. On the subsequent trips we made, it was still in place, and, to my knowledge, was never improved or replaced while the Japs occupied the Philippines.

Another time, we came to a spot where a bridge had been blown. That didn't faze the Japs either. They simply took the planks from the truck beds, nailed cleats on either end, then laid them across the bridge pilings and ordered us to drive across. Once on the other side, they picked up the boards, replaced them in the trucks, climbed back in, and we continued on our way. No sweat!

President Quezon had built a summer camp in the mountains above Baler. The large, rambling bungalow, surrounded by beautiful trees and flowers, overlooked a mountain creek, which had been dammed up to form a swimming pool. We stayed there one night then continued to Baler the next day.

About a mile below Baler, as we circled down the bare face of the mountain, we could see a perfect half-moon-shaped beach of snow-white sand. The deep, aquamarine waters of the bay, sparkling in the morning sun, resembled a picture postcard.

Then a tiny fishing village came into view. Bamboo and coconut huts, jutting out of the water on their spindly legs, lined the little inlets along the shore. We could see men getting ready to put out to sea in their brightly painted boats, each more colorful than the last. The people seemed untouched by the war, their life peaceful and serene. In this setting, the horror of being a prisoner of war seemed to fall away, as though I had discarded a dirty shirt. I felt almost normal again.

In addition to fishing, the natives of the village harvested peppercorns to sell in Manila and ran a small cottage industry, manufacturing sisal. During our stay, they showed us how they beat the large, succulent leaves of the agave plants to expose the fibers then placed them in a swiftly flowing stream. They weighted them with rocks and left them there until the water had scrubbed them clean.

After the fibers dried, the villagers wove them into various articles such as hats, purses, belts, and cigarette pouches. They earned a mere seven and a half cents for a hat that would later sell for fifteen or twenty dollars in the States. The little Philippine horses carried the goods over the mountains into Cabanatuan. From there, they were shipped to Manila, where finishing touches were added before they were sold.

One of the men in the village made a hat for me and put my initials into it. The workmanship was excellent, and I had fun wearing the stylish fedora as I made my runs up and down Luzon.

Every day the Japs sent out patrols from Baler to scour the jungle for guerrillas. But due to the nature of guerrilla warfare these expeditions hardly ever succeeded. It's hard to sneak up on someone who's sneaking up on you. The Japs could be seen from miles away, and by the time they arrived on the scene the jungle fighters were long gone.

Under Japanese occupation, everybody worked. They didn't go for the Geneva Convention rules that stated that prisoners had certain rights and should not be mistreated or made to work. As we had been warned by the commandant at Camp O'Donnell, "You don't work, you don't eat!"

We heard that conditions at O'Donnell had gotten so bad that in late May just about all of the American prisoners were moved to a larger camp near the town of Cabanatuan. As we hauled supplies and troops all over Luzon, we saw many POW work details from the camp. Literally used as slaves, they rebuilt the roads and bridges destroyed by the American army engineers as they pulled back into Bataan.

At one location, we saw Americans making a new span out of wood over a major river. Everything had to be done by hand, from cutting down the trees and hauling the heavy timbers to driving the pilings. Using a series of ropes and pulleys, about one hundred men, straining with all their might, pulled the massive weights up to the top of a makeshift pile driver before letting them drop. This process had to be repeated over and over to drive the piles into the soil.

Such grueling labor, forced from sick and malnourished men in the tropical heat, without adequate sanitation or medicine, took its toll;

they died like flies, only to be replaced by more men from the camps, who were in even worse shape.

Other POWs told me similar tales of their less than humane working conditions. A friend said, "I used a wheelbarrow to haul dirt, cement, and gravel all morning. Then at noon I had to cook lunch in the same wheelbarrow. After dumping the dirt or cement, I'd simply rinse it out a little bit, set it up on some rocks, build a fire under it, and use it as a boiling pot for rice or soup. After lunch, I'd go back to hauling dirt, sand, and cement in it."

This was typical of the treatment of our men imprisoned in the Philippines. No wonder so many died of dysentery.

The convoy split up after a month or so, and Laurence and I moved to the village of San Carlos. Guerrilla activity had cooled down a bit, so for a while we didn't have much to do. We cooked for ourselves without much success, since neither of us excelled in that department. Mostly, we just hung around and observed the local customs.

The center of activity was the river that ran alongside the village. The women washed their clothes there, beating them on the rocks bordering the stream. The kids splashed and played in the water while their mothers, keeping a sharp eye on them, gossiped about everyday things.

The river was also used for communal bathing. If others were present when we bathed or washed our trucks there, we kept our G-strings on. Sometimes it was hard for us to ignore the women; no doubt it was just as hard for the Filipino men.

Their method of fishing was interesting. They spread bamboo fences upstream and downstream across the twenty-foot-wide river. Two or three men walking between the fences and each carrying what looked like a bottomless birdcage with a hole in the top would suddenly stop and throw them into the water. Reaching into the trap, they occasionally came up with a small fish. As they did this, the others gradually moved the barriers closer together, forcing the fish to concentrate in a smaller area, which made catching them easier.

Our house in San Carlos, commandeered from a local Filipino family, was built on stilts. It had a split-bamboo floor, and any food crumbs that fell from the table were swept through the cracks to the chickens penned up below.

The day we moved in, I noticed a little shack in the backyard and assumed it was the outhouse. It, too, stood on pilings about three feet off the ground, with walls about four feet high and covered with a *nipa* (thatch) roof. A little picket fence wrapped around three sides of the house.

There was a hole in the floor of the shack, but no latrine had been dug in the ground under it. In spite of this, I could see no deposits on the ground. This was mighty strange! "What happens to the crap?" I wondered aloud.

Looking around some more, I noticed a very large pig snoozing under a tree. I told Laurence, "I hope he's not somebody's pet. He looks about the right size for a luau."

"You're right," Laurence agreed. "I don't remember the last time I ate ham."

Later that day, I abandoned my plans for a feast. I climbed the steps to the john, walked into the hut, and looking down through the hole in the floor, I saw the pig underneath, waiting for the fallout. He was the clean-up man! We could roam around the backyard, go in and out of the house, and he'd just lie in the shade of the tree, never stirring. But the minute one of us made a move toward the shack, he was "Johnny on the spot," so to speak.

The pig amazed everybody. We all got a kick out of watching him watch us. We spent a lot of time trying to outwit that hog by attempting to sneak into the hut without being seen, but he never missed a trick.

The Filipinos told us that once a pig had been fattened up this way, they would tie it up and feed it nothing but rice for a few weeks before butchering it. They swore that after it was roasted, it tasted delicious. They didn't convince me. It would be a long time before I could eat pork. Once I was back in the prison camps, though, the day would come when extreme hunger blotted out the memory of that pig and his "diet," and I was glad to get even a small taste of the meat.

Laurence and I didn't have a Japanese interpreter in San Carlos. By this time we spoke a little Japanese, and a soldier or two might speak some English. But if we wanted to communicate anything more complicated than hello or goodbye, we had to rely on two small boys in the village, one Japanese and one Filipino.

Whatever I had to say to a Japanese soldier, I would say to the Filipino boy in English. He would tell it to the Japanese boy in Tagalog, and the Japanese boy would repeat it to the soldier in Japanese. It was a time-consuming business, and I felt embarrassed by these two little kids, five or six years old at the most, who spoke several languages while I spoke only one, and not so well at that.

One of the first Japanese words we picked up was *ohaio,* or "morning." Whenever a Nip greeted us in the morning with a slight bow and said, "Ohaio," Laurence or I usually responded by saying "Texas" or "Louisiana." Learning that the word *taii* meant "captain" in Japanese but "shit" in Tagalog, we took great delight in bowing low and addressing every private we saw as "taii." It always got a great response, but after a while, when the Japanese became more conversant with English and Tagalog, we kicked the habit before we got our heads knocked off!

One day, Omasa and I decided to wash our trucks in the middle of the street. Squatting down, intent on getting the wheels clean, we hardly noticed the foot traffic going by. Suddenly, I noticed a pair of good-looking legs standing next to me. When I heard what sounded like an American voice, I followed those legs up past a slender waist and looked into the pretty face of a young Filipina, who was with several of her friends. They laughed when they saw our expressions, explaining that they were GI brides. We enjoyed basking in the company of these gals until a Jap guard, suspicious that we might be breaking the rules by talking to the natives, came over to investigate.

The girls immediately began to charm him with looks and giggles, all the while calling him every dirty name they could think of in Tagalog. He must have thought they were flirting with him, because he wore a grin from ear to ear. As he moved off, they told us what they had said to him. It wasn't nice. Walking away, they gave us the V sign behind their backs and whispered, "Keep your chin up, boys!"

After a few weeks of doing very little, we got a break when the Japs sent us down to Manila to pick up a truck. We left by train early one morning, accompanied by our guards. What a day! It was late afternoon by the time we reached the city, but the trip was well worth the money.

Traveling on the small Philippine trains reminded me of a three-ring circus. Every so often, we'd stop so the crew could gather more fuel to throw on the wood-burning engines. The slow-moving bunch never seemed to be in a hurry, so sometimes the passengers got out to help. I guess they figured if they didn't, they'd never get where they were going.

Six cars with old-fashioned wooden seats made up the train. Top speed: twenty miles per hour. The engineer didn't seem to adhere to a schedule. We stopped in all the small villages and towns along the way, and we also stopped in the middle of nowhere. People came out of the bushes and rice fields to board the train, carrying their children, belongings, and even livestock. They climbed in through the windows, bag and baggage, and often got off the same way. I didn't see how the conductor kept them all straight. They must have been used to it, but I just sat there totally amazed, taking it all in.

The noise was deafening. Babies cried, pigs squealed, chickens were all excited, and the people talked loud enough to be heard over the din and racket.

Whenever we slowed down or stopped, the ever-present vendors ran alongside the cars selling water, eggs, candy, rice, and all sorts of other stuff. The Filipino vendors picked up the Japanese and American lingo quickly. If they saw a haitai, they hollered at him in Japanese to buy this or that. If they spotted a Caucasian, they switched to English just as easily.

The average person had two ways to get around the island at that time, by rail or by bus. The buses did not resemble any I'd ever seen. The Filipinos had mounted specially built wide wooden truck beds onto regular cabs. Seats with storage compartments above and below ran across the bodies of the trucks, which operated much as the trains did—no scheduled stops, just people jumping on and off—always with a big hurrah.

We had been in San Carlos a few weeks when a Filipino approached me one night as I gathered bamboo to build a fire for the evening meal.

"Joe," he asked me softly, "you like Japs?"

"Not much," I answered.

"You want to get even with them?"

"You bet!"

"Would you like to join our group in the hills?"

I explained that while I would like nothing better, it was not that simple. "If I take off, the Japs will kill nine of my friends."

He said escaping was not necessary. I would be more useful to the cause if I stayed in town and reported on enemy truck and troop movements.

"I'll do anything to help the cause," I said. "Just tell me what you want me to do."

"Act normal. Do whatever the Japs order you to do, only we'll be watching you all the time. You will be contacted soon," he said. And with that he was gone.

I had no idea how this would work. What sort of information could I give them that they wouldn't already know? I began to worry about whether I had done the right thing. Maybe the Japs were trying to trick me. Fifth columnists spied on everyone, ready to turn in those who opposed the enemy. In any case, I couldn't back out now!

I heard nothing from the underground for about a week. Then one day, as I washed my truck down by the river, a couple of small boys swam by. As he passed me, one of them ducked under the water and grabbed my leg. Thinking he was just playing around, I reached down to give him a gentle swat, and he put something in my hand. Stooping down in the water, I slipped it into my waistband. The boy came up for air a few yards away and, joined by his friend, swam on downstream, laughing and yelling like kids do while playing.

I waited until I was alone that evening to read the note. In it, the guerrillas told me what my role would be. They wanted the earliest possible advance notice of convoys, their destinations, troop numbers, and a list of the supplies hauled. I would convey this information daily when I bathed or washed my clothes. If I had any news for them, I was to hang my wash on a bush or a tree. This would be their cue to watch where I hid my note containing the details. To signify any change in plans, I must place my clothes on a large rock before bathing in the river. The plan was simple, but it worked.

The guerrillas began stepping up their attacks. The Japs increased their patrols and began to deal harshly with any Filipinos suspected of working with the guerrillas. One day they arrested a fellow they accused of being a spy. The Nips showed everyone what they meant by maintaining "law and order."

During his lengthy interrogation and torture, the man never did confess, but as the local Filipinos looked on, the Japs forced him to dig his own grave, stood him on the edge of it, and shot him. After he fell in, they made the people standing around cover him up.

On another occasion, I saw the Japs execute two suspected guerrillas. They had been betrayed by a Filipino collaborationist who was married to a Japanese woman. Like the others, after being alternately beaten and questioned without success, the men had to dig their own graves. But this time they weren't shot. The Jap officer in charge beheaded them. Kneeling, with their hands tied behind their backs, the condemned men were directed to extend their necks forward. I watched the officer raise his sword with both hands then bring it down in one swift and powerful stroke.

My stomach turned over as the first man's head separated from his shoulders. Blood spurted out of the severed arteries, spattering me and everyone standing nearby with a warm, sticky spray. His head fell on the ground with a sickening thud and rolled a few feet from his body. Then the officer repeated the terrible procedure on the second man.

When it was all over, they motioned to me to drag the bodies into the graves, pick up the heads, and throw them in with the corpses. I had learned by this time that to show emotion in front of the Japs only made things worse. Screaming or crying, protesting or pleading, only served to reinforce their feeling of superiority over us. Reacting much like dogs in a pack, any display of weakness drove most of them into a frenzy.

Horrified and revolted by the mutilations, I kept swallowing the vomit rising in my throat. I had to keep my face impassive while I shoveled dirt into the hole. But the whole time I worked, I fought an overwhelming urge to hit the officer in the head with the shovel then kill the son of a bitch with his own sword.

News of the executions traveled like lightning via the underground grapevine. The next night, swift and violent justice came rolling down from the hills. When the fifth columnist's body was found, it had been hacked to pieces, execution style, by the silent, vengeful men in the bush.

Every time the Japs returned from raiding suspected guerrilla outposts, they brought back fountain pens, watches, or cigarette lighters. One night the captain of the outfit came back from one of these forays carrying an American-style suit over his arm. He motioned me to accompany him to his quarters and wait outside. After a few minutes he opened the door, dressed in the suit, and waved me inside. He closed the door and said in excellent English (since we were alone), "Giro, how do the Americans wear their suits? Are the sleeves too long? And what about the length of the trousers?"

As he twisted around in front of the mirror, looking at himself dressed in the pale-gray Palm Beach fabric, the surrealism of it all struck me, and I just stood there, staring. Looking past his reflection, his eyes met mine in the mirror. He repeated the question. "What do you think? Are the sleeves and trousers a little bit too long?"

Coming back to "reality," I quickly replied, "Yeah, maybe about an inch in the sleeves and the pants."

Pointing to some pins in a dish on his desk, he said, "You will please mark the places for alteration." When I finished, he smiled and told me to wait outside.

A few minutes later he opened the door, handed me the suit and told me to take it to the tailor in town. It occurred to me that walking down the street in San Carlos with a new suit over my arm might get me arrested by one of the soldiers. Before I could explain where I got the suit, I might suffer a severe beating from said soldier. When I expressed my concerns to the captain, he told me not to worry. He would pass the word to everyone down the line.

The tailor shop was across the street from the Catholic church. After delivering the suit with instructions to fix it as soon as possible, I reported back to the captain that it would be ready in the morning. I added, "If it's all right with you, I would like to attend church before I pick up the suit."

"Ah," he said. "You are Christo."

"Yes, and it's been a long time since I've been to Mass."

He said, "It is no problem. I will arrange it so that no one will question you when you enter the church."

Surprised and pleased to be allowed to attend church, I spent a few moments the next morning on my knees in prayer in the quiet coolness of the little chapel. The typically Spanish architecture of thick whitewashed plaster walls and massive wooden beams was beautiful in its simplicity. I felt comforted by the familiar surroundings of my faith and experienced the peace that only comes from God. The padre seemed a little startled by my presence, but he gave me his blessing before I left.

An elderly Filipino man walked out with me. We paused on the steps of the church to chat, and I commented on his intricately carved walking stick. He looked around carefully to see who might be watching before he asked, "Have you ever seen one like this?" He pressed a button near the handle, and a six-inch stiletto slid soundlessly from the tip of the cane. He smiled at my surprised expression, and I got the distinct feeling that, despite his age, he was actively engaged in the fight for his country.

After church, I took the captain's suit back to him, and he insisted I check it out to be sure it fit properly. Looking at his image in the mirror, he seemed very pleased. I gave him a thumbs up, thinking to myself, *Who cares? Once he gets home and puts on weight it won't fit anymore anyway!*

As the guerrillas made their presence felt all over the island and their efforts to make life miserable for the Japs began to pay off, I was issued a set of Philippine Army dungarees and a pair of Japanese tennis shoes and transferred to a province farther north to ferry troops and supplies for a Signal Corps outfit. My friend Laurence didn't move with me.

In the meantime, the Hukbalahap movement, a Communist organization, started its own little war in the rural areas. Picking up weapons and ammunition that had been abandoned by us on Bataan, they joined the guerrillas for a time to fight the Japs. We frequently saw evidence of the hit-and-run tactics of this group when we took Japanese soldiers on patrols to check out trouble in the western provinces.

One day, driving down the remote Baguio Trail, we nearly hit a body lying in the road. A few feet away, a Model-A Ford had skidded off the track and plowed into a tree. We stopped, and the soldiers in the truck quickly deployed on both sides of the road. All five people in the car were dead. The man in the road had apparently been shot while riding on the fender of the car. He probably never knew what hit him. The top of his head was gone. Pieces of his brain littered the highway, and his blood splattered the road. These men appeared to be merchants hauling supplies from the town of Baguio.

Robbery didn't seem to be the motive—their goods were still in the car. The Japanese said this looked like the work of the Huks, who sometimes attacked civilians at random, but they never found out for sure. While the Japanese occupied the Philippines, they kept the Huks in check. After the war, the Huks became a real problem, attacking in strength and trying to take over the country. By the mid-1950s, the Philippine government finally brought them under control.

Baguio, located about fifty miles northeast of San Carlos, was the capital of the subprovince of Benguet and considered to be the summer capital of the Philippines. The city, often with its "head in the clouds" at an elevation of 4,500 feet, could be reached only by a steep road zigzagging up the side of the mountain. Surrounded by pine forests and beautiful scenery, the ideal climate made it a popular summer resort before the war. It is also one of the few places on the island where fireplaces or stoves are needed for heating.

There were several way stations or construction camps along the Baguio Trail that had been used in building the highway to the city. Sometimes the guerrillas attacked the area, killing off a few Nips in their attempt to cut the supply lines, so the Japs took over the sites and stationed troops there to keep the road open. They called them Camps 1, 2, and 3.

I was stationed at Camp 1 at the foot of the mountain with two other truck drivers. I was the only American in the group. The other drivers for the Signal Corps were Japanese.

Every other day I took supplies to both of the other camps up the trail. The scenery was breathtaking, each level more beautiful than the last. To find yourself in the middle of a forest of tall, blue-green Christmas trees after the heat and harshness of the plains was to be transported to a different world. The pure, crisp air, laced with the pungent scents of pine, spruce, and cedar, seemed like heaven. Magnificent waterfalls cascaded hundreds of feet into deep emerald gorges, only to be dissolved into veils of mist by the wind and tinted in delicate rainbow colors by the sun. It was balm to my soul.

As I climbed higher and higher, my old truck fought to make the grade. I'd put her in double low and keep her there, gears grinding and straining all the way, until I reached the top. At times I drove through thick clouds that suddenly blotted out the road, making it a bit tricky to negotiate the sharp curves. Then, just as suddenly, I'd break out into bright sunshine, able to trace the pencil outline of the Agno River below. From this elevation the trees down in the valley resembled grass, and again, surrounded by incredible beauty and peace high up in the mountains, I would almost forget the war.

There was nothing like a good dose of reality to bring me back to earth. Coming down the mountain could get a bit dicey. Due to a chronic shortage of parts, my brakes were not always up to snuff. I had a few close calls, forcing me to do some creative driving—downshifting, using the emergency brake, and once deliberately scraping the side of the mountain to slow the truck's forward speed.

I continued to pass information on enemy troop movements to the underground, using the same method of communication I had used in San Carlos—making contact with a go-between and hiding my notes in prearranged spots. I still considered myself at war and was willing to take the necessary risks. I wasn't alone. One night during my second week at Camp 1, shots rang out in the hills farther up the trail. A Jap patrol quickly moved into the area, firing rifles and machine guns into the bushes and trees lining the road. After a while, when their fire was not returned, they came back to camp.

The next morning, the phone line that connected the three camps went dead. The Japs sent the telephone-repair crew up the trail to fix the problem. Several hours later, the phone rang at Camp 1, bringing news that caused general excitement and alarm among the soldiers. They yelled at me to get the truck. "Speedo, speedo," they commanded. I turned the Dodge around and they piled into the back, armed with their semiautomatic rifles. We flew up the road, with the Japs firing into the heavy brush at every turn.

The cliffs overhanging the narrow, twisted highway running between Camps 2 and 3 made it an ideal place for an ambush. To make matters worse, I had to slow down and crawl up the mountain in the old truck. Staccato bursts of machine-gun rounds echoed back from the canyon walls as the nervous soldier manning the cab-mounted gun in the back of our truck "sprayed" for guerrillas.

Coming down from a crest in the road, we saw the phone crew's truck in a small clearing up ahead. The attack probably took only a few minutes. There were six men in the group. Five of them were now dead. One lay in the road, his face shot away. Another partially hung out of the back of the truck, hit by a grenade. Two had been killed halfway up the steep slope, their bodies riddled with bullets, and the fifth soldier got it in the chest as he stood guard a few yards away. The sixth man, barely alive, dangled from the telephone pole, held only by his safety line.

The Japanese soldiers climbed up the embankments on either side of the road, shooting up the area, employing *ni* (two) mortars to fire at the cliffs above. But the Filipinos had long since melted into the hills. When the Japs saw that they were wasting ammunition, they put the bodies of the dead men into the truck, gathered up the equipment lying around, and hauled the wounded man down from the telephone pole.

He was in bad shape. He looked like he'd been used for target practice; the blood just poured out of the terrible wounds in his body. He had been shot while repairing the line but somehow managed to call in the alarm. It didn't make any sense that he was still alive.

When we reached Camp 1, everyone came out to see the bodies and to look over the wounded man in the back of the truck. He lay there in his blood-soaked uniform, barely conscious, obviously in a great deal of pain. The Japanese didn't attempt to do anything for him, not even offer him a smoke or a drink of water, probably thinking he would die anyway.

I didn't hold out much hope for him either, yet I found their manner strange and unfeeling as they just left him lying in the truck. In fact, a couple of soldiers standing nearby were laughing about something moments before the man died. Maybe they were just nervous; maybe they didn't like the guy. But their lack of human compassion toward a dying comrade made my blood run cold.

One man in the camp, though, won a certain amount of respect from me. He was the sergeant in charge of Camp 1. Much taller than the average Japanese (he was about my height, six feet) and a fine-looking soldier, he wore his uniform exceptionally well. Deploying his men to hunt down the guerrillas who ambushed the phone crew, he directed his men to take cover while he himself refused to do so. He proudly stood in the middle of the road commanding the operation, seemingly without any regard for his personal safety.

I thought his tactics were foolhardy, but he did remind me of the way MacArthur refused to run to the tunnel during bombing raids on Corregidor. Like the general, the Japanese sergeant showed his men he wasn't afraid of anything or anyone. Knowing I wouldn't have done what he did, I had to admire his style.

I, on the other hand, had a different reason for distancing myself from the soldiers. Just in case the guerrillas were still around and planning to attack, I didn't want to be confused with one of the haitai. When the sergeant noticed that I stood in the open, apart from the group, he appeared impressed by my "bravery" and motioned me to hide under the truck. It was the last place I wanted to be, so I remained rooted to the spot, no doubt further impressing him.

The guerrillas didn't always act on information received from their informants. They picked the times and places for their raids, keeping the Japs off balance and frustrated. Not knowing when or where my truck might be the target for their next attack made things a bit hairy for me, too.

Driving around a sharp curve one day, I ducked as bullets suddenly pierced the cab of the truck, whizzing past my head and missing me by just a few inches. I slammed on the brakes and skidded to a stop. The soldiers riding in the back jumped out, firing their rifles into the brush on either side of the road. By then it was too late. The phantom band of men was gone. But once again they accomplished their mission. Before the truck came to a halt, they had shot the machine gunner standing behind the cab, along with four others in the group.

The next day, while I was washing the truck down at the river, my Filipino contact got near enough to ask me if I'd heard about the daring raid made by his fellow countrymen the day before on a Japanese supply truck. Pointing to the bullet holes in the cab of my truck, I said, "Your compatriots damn near killed me yesterday. Who do you guys think are driving most of the Jap trucks?"

"Oh, I'm so sorry, Joe," he said, "I didn't know you would be driving! Next time, we will be more careful."

But my near miss was not the only time I came close to getting killed. During the months I drove for the Japanese, I came under fire at least ten or twelve times, in many cases because of information I generated about enemy movements—standard operating procedure for any of the GIs working on details where they had access to useful knowledge.

I heard of another case up in the mountains where the guerrillas, acting on a tip from the POW truck driver stationed up at Camp 3, lobbed a grenade into the back of his truck, killing the nine Japs riding with him. The prisoner, one of the original thirteen POWs in our group nicknamed Otsuna, escaped injury. Like me, he received word through the underground grapevine apologizing for the attack, saying the guerrillas hadn't known an American was driving the truck.

Somehow, I didn't quite buy their line. While it was somewhat reassuring to know they weren't intentionally trying to kill us, I think they were so intent on killing the Japs they would have viewed an American casualty or two philosophically. I realized there was no use worrying about the bullet with my name on it; the one marked "to whom it may concern" was the problem.

It was on the Baguio Trail that I saw a Japanese soldier riding down the road on a bicycle, and tied to the fender was a bundle with a familiar red, white, and blue design. I recognized Old Glory right off with a stab of pride, but then it made me mad to think the soldier had probably wrapped his dirty laundry in it. Seeing the flag desecrated ruined my whole day, and I felt even worse knowing I could do nothing about it.

Not long after, a large pile of rags was delivered to the camp for cleaning the Japs' rifles. I could see cut-up pieces of the American flag, as well as pieces of the flag of the Philippines, mixed in with the rest. As soon as I got the chance, I removed the strips and burned them. I just couldn't let the Japanese clean their guns with the Stars and Stripes. And after fighting side by side with the Filipino army Scouts on Bataan, witnessing the unselfish and courageous acts of the civilians during the march, the flag of the Filipino people had come to mean almost as much to me.

One of the Japs caught me burning the scraps. He asked what I was doing. There was no point in lying to him. "I have always been taught to respect my flag," I said. "I just can't stand to see it being used as a cleaning rag."

Surprisingly, he said, "Yes, Giro, I understand. It is all right to do what you are doing."

As I learned more about the Japanese people and how they stood on ceremony, I could see why he understood my love for my country's flag and the symbolism it represented. I learned, too, that while the Japanese might not have that kind of fidelity to their own Rising Sun, they revered the emperor's insignia of the chrysanthemum.

Occasionally, when our paths crossed, Otsuna and I exchanged books we scrounged from different places in our travels. Even the Japanese soldiers who went on leave obligingly brought back whatever reading material they could find whenever I asked them. The books provided welcome breaks from the monotonous routine and, at times, from my own thoughts.

Two buses that traveled to Baguio every day were forced to stop at Camp 1. The passengers had to step out while the Japs searched the bus, looked over their papers, and questioned them about their destinations. Although the Filipinos still couldn't talk to prisoners, their friendly smiles and signs of encouragement gave me hope. The arrival of the buses with their lively passengers was the high point of most days.

The national pastime for the Japanese soldier stationed in the Philippines, I believe, was a hot bath at the end of the day. Every afternoon I had to gather the wood to heat the water for the haitais' baths at Camp 1, which they took in a 55-gallon drum set up on rocks. As with everything else in the Japanese army, this was done according to rank.

When steam rose off the water in the barrel and the temperature was hot enough, the captain got in. He would sit and soak awhile. The only thing visible was his bald head and his slanty little eyes peering over the rim. He looked just like a turtle, surveying the world from inside his shell.

The sergeant came next. Eventually, the rest of the rank and file, the corporals and privates—twenty or thirty men in all—took their turns in what was by now gray lukewarm water.

"Hey, Girocho, you bathe now," someone would say.

"Iie kekko desu. Oh, nooo thank you. Americans don't like hot baths!" I'd lie. "We prefer cold water."

Every day, this went on, the soldiers trying to persuade me and me just as determined not to be persuaded. Actually, I'd have given my eyeteeth for a good hot bath, but no way was I going to climb into the dirty water used by all those little bastards.

The alternative method of washing was pretty rough. The good-sized Agno River near the camp, which resembled a pencil line from high up in the mountains, was fed by streams so cold the water could turn a man blue in thirty seconds. But to give credence to the lie and to demonstrate my point, I'd jump in, soap up, rinse off, and jump out in record time, pretending to enjoy it while my teeth chattered like a Spanish dancer's castanets.

The soldiers called me crazy for bathing in the frigid river. I thought they were just as nuts for bathing in one barrel of water. We had reached an impasse on the subject.

A Japanese soldier at Camp 1 fell in love with my truck. Something of a simpleton, he hung around and helped me wash the truck or repair it. One day, after one of our brushes with the guerrillas, he ran up to me, eyes shining, all out of breath. "Girocho," he said, "I have good idea."

"What's that?" I asked in my pidgin Japanese.

"Well, you know, maybe Taiota will get killed, and I can take his place. Then maybe you get shot, then I can drive the truck! Wouldn't that be good?"

"Yeah," I answered, thinking, *You simple son of a bitch, you don't know what you're saying.* I'm sure Taiota wouldn't have cared for his idea either, but you had to feel sorry for the poor devil because in his mind he meant well. It was just that driving a truck was his ultimate goal in life.

Due to the constant shortage of gasoline, the Japanese began to switch to alcohol made from sugarcane for fuel. In a pinch, it wasn't half-bad drinking material either. Beer was available and rationed to the troops at the rate of four bottles a week. Many of the soldiers didn't drink much, some not at all. A couple of beers or some sake was about all they could handle. Thanks to the ones who didn't drink at all, I always had a nice cache of beer on "ice" down at the river. Like their sake, the Japanese drank their beer warm; but after noticing that I preferred mine cold, a few of the men tried it and decided that it tasted better that way.

My time as a truck driver for the Japanese was drawing to a close. The day before I left Camp 1, the sergeant gave me a memento. Most of the Japanese officers and soldiers usually brought some small talisman from home. Nearly all of them carried a fan, as well. He handed me his fan and then gave me a small samurai doll he called Girocho.

He said, "Giro, you good soldier. You take samurai doll. Also fan. All Japanese soldiers carry fan. I give them both to you." Then he bowed low—always a sign of respect between two parties. The gesture surprised me, and frankly it touched me. I returned his bow.

I had driven trucks for the Japanese army from May 1942 to October 1942. I had gained weight and was now in fairly good shape. The decision that Laurence, Freddie Barr, and I made to get out of Camp O'Donnell and drive "heavy trucks" proved to be one of our better moves. Without that six-month interval, during which we ate fairly well and did light physical labor that kept us fit, we would have never made it through the next few years. The ordeal to come would test us to the limit. Not all of us would make the grade.

11 Inside the Wire

In October 1942, I left the Baguio detail and went back to the town of Cabanatuan to operate out of a truck pool. Baguio had been a lonely assignment, what with my being the only American up there for miles around; and although I had learned enough Japanese to hold a conversation, my captors and I weren't exactly on what you'd call social terms. Still, it hadn't been a bad little interlude, all things considered. I would miss the beautiful scenery, the cooler weather, and the relative freedom I enjoyed as Girocho.

For the last two months, as the Japanese geared up for the push south to Australia, horses and new recruits arrived daily at the port of Manila to replenish the former Third Chrysanthemum Cavalry. By the time I arrived in the fall, arrangements were complete, and we ferried the now-defunct truck company back to Manila to rejoin their cavalry unit and ship out.

I met up again with Laurence and most of the other drivers from the "pool," but Freddie Barr was not among them. Quartered at the University of Manila, we hoped to go to Australia with the Third Chrysanthemum and maybe get close enough to the front to escape and rejoin the American forces at some point. But that was only a pipe dream. Later, in Japan, I would ask about the Third Chrysanthemum and learn that most of the men had been killed in the fighting on New Guinea. Taiota probably didn't make it. A simple man, he just wanted to go home and live his life in peace.

Rather than shipping us back to camp, the Japanese we had worked for apparently respected us enough to try to get us assigned to the university. But the school didn't need any more POWs, so we ended up at Bilibid Prison in Manila.

Bilibid was a civilian prison. A gloomy place behind massive walls, it had been built by the Spaniards more than a hundred years earlier. A mixed bag of Chinese, Dutch, and American civilians, along with other nationalities picked up by the Japanese for various reasons, made up the prison population. The Americans and Filipinos captured on Corregidor were imprisoned there briefly on their way to Camp O'Donnell and Camp Cabanatuan. Bilibid also served as a way station for POWs going to and from the camps and to various work details. The prison also housed a large makeshift hospital for the gravely sick POWs.

In a macabre twist of fate, our group, plus ten other American POWs, had to stay in the execution chamber of Bilibid for the short time we were there. A new electric chair sat in the middle of the room. I heard that sometime before the war capital punishment had been abolished in the Philippines, so the chair had never been used. We took turns sitting in the only chair in the room and cracked a lot of grisly jokes about it.

As I took my turn in the chair one day Laurence pretended to turn on the juice, asking, "How do you want it, John, rare, medium or well done?" Hell, we had no illusions about the future. I wouldn't say we'd lost hope. As long as we were breathing, we had hope. But we were realistic about our chances of survival in the camps.

It's difficult to recall exact dates or stretches of time in the tropics. Only the dry and monsoon seasons helped us mark time. Special holidays, like Christmas or the emperor's birthday, gave us some idea of whether it was winter or spring. But with no clocks or calendars to aid us, each day was pretty much like another. We got up on command, went to work on command, ate on command, and slept on command. With our lives so ordered and our "schedules" prearranged, it was hard to be more specific about the exact passage of time.

We stayed in Bilibid for about ten days to two weeks before we boarded the train for the "big camp" outside Cabanatuan. It took two days to reach it. No one seemed to be in a hurry. I could've beaten the train to camp by walking. We must have averaged all of five miles per hour, stopping at every little crossing for pedestrians or to let the Filipinos lead their water buffalo across the tracks to safety.

No one complained, though. This train trip was much better than the first. About twenty of us rode in the boxcar, with the sliding door rolled back. I sat in the opening, dangling my feet just above the rails. Armed guards accompanied us, but they didn't mistreat us or confiscate the food and medicine we had accumulated. And thanks to the open door, sanitation wasn't a problem.

That summer, the Japs transferred Allied POWs out of Camp O'Donnell and divided them into three camps known as Cabanatuan 1, 2, and 3. By the time I arrived, Camps 1 and 2 had been closed due to various problems such as lack of water, and Camp 3 had become Camp 1, or Camp Cabanatuan—the "big camp." Located about six miles from the town of Cabanatuan, it was roughly the same size as O'Donnell. But unlike O'Donnell, which had about fifty thousand Filipino and American POWs, Cabanatuan held only about seven to ten thousand American prisoners.

Plopped down at the foot of the Sierra Madres, on the edge of unexplored territory, the camp had been built on flat, virtually treeless terrain. It was begun as a training facility for the Philippine Army but, in contrast to O'Donnell, was nearly completed.

The camp was divided into three sections: the eastern section assigned to the healthier POWs; the middle section occupied by the Japanese; and the hospital zone and "Zero Ward" in the western sector. A barbed-wire fence enclosed the entire compound, and four guard towers stood sentry outside the wire. Heavily armed soldiers constantly patrolled the perimeter inside as well as outside the camp.

We marched into camp, lined up, and first off, the American medic confiscated our pitiful supply of medicines. "We'll have to take your quinine, Sergeant," he told me. "And the sulfa tablets are badly needed for the worst cases. Sorry."

They let us keep the few items of food we had, but they didn't last long. Things were getting tough in camp. Food was downright scarce. About all we could get was a little rice and some sweet-potato vines.

They tell me there are vitamins in sweet-potato vines. Maybe so, but bitter didn't quite describe it. It tasted worse than quinine.

It made me think of the time when I was about twelve and living with my grandparents. For as long as I can remember, my grandfather ate only one thing for lunch—Campbell's vegetable soup. One day he put his spoon down after the first bite and announced to my grandmother in his Sicilian accent, "Hot dammi, thisa no good!"

"Well, I put a can of water, some salt, pepper, anda hot sauce in the soup, just likea always," she declared.

"I don'ta care," he said. "It tasta real bad!"

"Well, something musta be wrong with you. Just shuta up and eata your soup!"

"Okay, okay," he replied. "I eata, but I no likea."

They ate the rest of the meal in silence. But that evening, while emptying the kitchen trash, Grandma laughed like a fool when she discovered that in her rush to fix lunch and serve customers in the store, she had seasoned and heated a can of fruit cocktail instead of the Campbell's soup.

Poor guy! I knew just how he felt when I had to eat sweet-potato vines. We forced ourselves to eat the damn stuff because it was a source of vitamins. I atea, but I no likea!

We also ate whistle weeds, which grew in the marshy places at the edge of camp, but I'll bet you couldn't find a vitamin or calorie in a ton of the stuff. We boiled it, added it to the rice—trying to spike up the meal—but our stomachs weren't fooled. It was just godawful!

In August 1942, the Japanese allowed the prisoners at Cabanatuan to plant a garden to feed the men. What started out as a project to supplement the diet of the starving prisoners soon got out of hand, requiring more than a thousand men to cultivate it. By the time I left for Japan in 1943, the garden had become a plantation of more than seven hundred acres that encroached upon the base of the mountains.

Nothing much had been harvested when we arrived in the fall of 1942. A tremendous corn crop, planted months before, was ready to eat, but the Japs refused to let us bring it in. They insisted that we leave it in the field to "mature."

The Japanese only grew corn for fodder, so we couldn't convince them of its goodness if harvested while still tender. By the time we got it, we could only make hominy, which we did by putting it in a barrel with wood ashes. The lye leached from the ashes dissolved the tough skin off the corn, making it edible. I never liked hominy, yet I loved fresh corn; everyone did. The vitamins and calories in it would have made a big difference in our conditions. It was another case of plain stupidity and unnecessary stubbornness on the part of the Japs.

At first everyone looked forward to all the fresh vegetables we could eat. When the crops began to come in our diets did improve. We could make a fine flour from the cassava roots. There was taro, grown for its starchy, edible root; several vegetables native to the Philippines; eggplants; okra; and sweet potatoes. At that point, anything extra was an improvement in our diet. But the price we paid for a few sweet potatoes far outweighed the benefits.

Like almost everyone else, I put in some time on the farm. We worked in the broiling sun during the dry season or in the pouring rain during monsoons, under backbreaking conditions and cruel, sadistic overseers who did not spare the rod. They forced us to farm without shoes, tools, or protection from the elements. We had to devise implements from scrap metal, wire, and bamboo. These conditions caused even more POWs to sicken and die. Most days, we couldn't find enough well men to work in the fields.

Before long, everyone hated the whole idea of farming and would do almost anything to avoid the detail, especially when it became evident that the Japs were taking the lion's share of the crops. What they didn't want, they sold to the Filipinos for rice to feed the prisoners— or so they said. The vegetables they stole would have been much better for us than rice. It was another no-win situation.

To my great relief, the Japs took me off the farm after several weeks of working in the fields and reunited me with some of the ex–truck drivers. Because we looked somewhat fit and strong after our six months on the road, they put us in charge of the newly formed loading detail.

Our job consisted of loading and unloading everything going in and out of camp. About the only thing going out was an occasional load of buffalo hides. Meat was a rarity. But when they killed a carabao, we dried the hide and saved it until we collected enough to fill a wagon, then took them to town to sell. Every other day, we brought in several hundred sacks of rice from the rice mill to feed the prisoners. Laurence and I often ended up working together.

Water buffalo powered the little two-wheeled carts we used for the job. Since the buffalo have no sweat glands, they overheat quickly. We had to stop and dunk the animals in a creek or a stream every thirty minutes. The hotter the sun got, the more stops we made. Although we'd leave early in the morning, it would be dusk before we returned to camp.

If you're in a hurry, I don't recommend water buffalo for transportation. They might be able to move a house, but at a snail's pace. "Hey, Omasa," I'd kid Laurence during one of our frequent stops, "driving trucks beats driving cows, don'tcha think?"

"Don't bother me," he'd grumble. "You don't exist, neither does this cow, and right now, I'm halfway up the mountain in my truck, cool as you please, just drinking in all the beautiful scenery. Remember the orchids in the trees?"

"Yeah. Man, compared to this, we had it made!"

"You said it. We also had enough food."

"You had to remind me. God, my stomach's been complaining all morning."

"Yeah, mine, too. Musta been something we didn't eat."

As the plantation grew to an enormous size, the Japs gave us another pleasant assignment—hauling fertilizer from a slaughterhouse outside of town. The ancient structure stood near a bluff overlooking the valley; as animals were butchered, their internal organs and manure were simply thrown over the cliff to collect at the base. Over the years, a huge pile of crap had accumulated there, well seasoned and ripe—just the thing for our "garden." As we loaded it into the carts, memories of our time in the mountains began to fade.

Besides the farm, the Japanese came up with another scheme to "beef up" our diets. The word went out that they needed twenty Texans for a special work detail. Most of the Japs believed that if you came from Texas that automatically made you a cowboy. As far as the boys in camp were concerned, if they thought there might be something in it for them, well then, everybody in camp became a cowboy, "sure 'nuff."

The Japs chose twenty of the stronger-looking prisoners from the hundreds of so-called cowpokes and gave them the job of herding a bunch of Brahman cattle, commandeered from an experimental ranch near the town of Cabanatuan, into camp. Already high-strung and nervous, the cattle strongly objected to being jammed into a stake-bed truck for the journey. Some of them jumped ship a few times before the Japs finally got them corralled.

Really wild after their ride, unloading them was as dangerous as loading them. Kicking and bellowing, they nearly tore the truck apart as they gored and trampled each other to get out. The flimsy five-foot-high fence around the corral couldn't hold them; they flattened it as they stampeded across the camp to open ground.

Laurence signed up for the rodeo. While most of the men took off after the cattle on foot, a few rode the little Filipino horses, their feet nearly dragging the ground as they sat astride ponies slightly larger than jackasses. I laughed like hell watching the big tall "cowboys" give chase, yahooing in the best western tradition as they tried to lasso those "little dogies."

It was late afternoon before they finally rounded up most of the cattle; some they never caught. Those Brahmans, easily outdistancing the horses, simply took off for the hills. To keep the rest of the ill-tempered beasts from breaking out again, we had to reinforce the fence and increase its height to seven feet.

On the surface, their idea of raising beef cattle to feed us seemed like a good idea. But this scheme came off like the rest of the long-range plans the Japs made—it didn't. We got no benefit from the enterprise whatsoever. Convinced the war would last a long time, they tried making provisions for it. But since the war ended before the five or six years it would have taken the herd to breed and mature, we would have been better off if we'd simply had a big barbecue.

For the first few months I was there, until things got better organized, life in the big camp consisted of little more than work and sleep. There were drainage projects, buildings to be completed, cleanup details, hauling, sanitation projects—you name it, we did it. It seemed to me that the Japs kept us busy from morning 'til night. Whatever time we had off we spent just lying around in a stupor. Sheer drudgery on almost empty stomachs was bad enough, but the lack of amusement in our pitifully dreary existence began to affect us, too. We were bored as hell. But it was basically up to the individual to combat the colorless existence any way he could and to find purpose in living.

To break up the monotony, I tried working different details. A few times, I helped gather firewood for cooking. Only the strongest and healthiest men could manage this necessary job. But it allowed us to leave camp—an important element, I felt, in the game of survival. Contacts outside the prison could be made, we might get more food, plus a degree of normalcy lay outside the wire. Every chance I got to leave, I took it.

Most of our wood came from the foothills of the Sierra Madres. We'd fell the trees, cut the logs into cordwood, and haul it back to camp. Occasionally, we ran into huge anthills, some as tall as five feet. But these were not your average household ants. Much worse than the fire ants of Louisiana or Texas, the large cannibal ants in the Philippines can strip a calf lying on the ground clear down to the bone before it can get up and run.

Busy chopping down a tree one day, I didn't notice the line of ants running all the way up the trunk. Dressed in my usual attire of G-string and no shirt, I must have looked like prime meat to them; they fell out of the tree onto my back. I started yelling for help, and everybody came running, but before they could brush them off the bastards had chewed several good-sized chunks out of me. The holes they left later turned into nasty sores that lasted a long time.

It seemed to us that the Japs constantly changed their minds about the layout of the camp. On a whim, they would decide to move a building here one day or there the next. Most of the lightweight structures, built from bamboo, had woven walls and nipa roofs. Once we removed the floor, even a large building that housed a hundred men could easily be moved by the three hundred men scattered around the inside. It was common to see a building take off across the compound like a centipede walking on its three hundred pairs of legs—just one more odd job we had to do, usually during our noon break.

Despite the promise of a better diet from the farm, serious ailments and diseases began percolating in our bodies, and we began to look like animated skeletons with potbellies that hung over our shorts or G-strings. It helped to have a sense of humor, especially when you caught sight of a stranger reflected in a pond or stream, and he turned out to be you!

A few of the guys in camp couldn't see anything funny about our situation, but most of us could find the humor in it. Some of the things that went on were so ridiculous, you couldn't help but smile, even if you felt like dying. Besides, we had to laugh to get through the rough times without going crazy.

I met a young man at Bilibid Prison who had lost both legs below the knee. One day a Red Cross shipment of clothing came in and was distributed among the prisoners. Some of us got shirts, while others received pants or shorts as needed. When they got around to the fellow with no legs, he rolled over onto his bed and, kicking his stumps in the air, declared, "All I need or want is a pair of socks!"

He got his socks, all right. He also won a lot of admiration and respect from the rest of us. In spite of his loss, he had somehow managed to adjust without giving in to depression and even retained a good sense of humor in the bargain. It was a fine thing to see in someone so young.

The nearly finished barracks in Cabanatuan, built on pilings four feet off the ground, measured fifteen feet wide by fifty feet long. They were open on either end, with no doors. Ten bays divided the interiors, with sleeping accommodations consisting of upper and lower platforms built of bamboo slats an inch apart. It was originally intended to house two men per bay, but ten or twelve men often found themselves jammed together in one bay. This meant that a hundred or more men inhabited a space designed for twenty. Food rations were issued according to the current population of each barracks.

During the worst days, when so many men were dying from a combination of disease and malnutrition, they often expired in their sleep. If the man was lying on the top deck, when his bowels relaxed in death the fellow below got a rude awakening. He'd get up mad, fussing and raising Cain, even though he knew the poor dead bastard above him couldn't help it. No one thought that was funny, but we weren't above using it to our advantage.

That man represented a ration of food, so it became common practice to hold up the dead in line for tenko. Before dawn, another POW and I might support a corpse between us, calling out his number at the appropriate time so that his ration would not be subtracted from the barracks's total for the day. Then we kept the body in the barracks, not reporting the death until it began to smell so bad we couldn't keep it any longer. Divided among one hundred men, the dead man's portion didn't amount to much, but we were so starved that every grain of rice seemed critical. In retrospect, this might seem like a cruel thing to do. However, we knew the soldier was beyond caring, and we felt justified in doing this if it helped others stay alive a little longer.

Nearly everyone in camp had diarrhea. The shallow, open latrines made excellent breeding grounds for the big greenbottle flies. Although we moved the latrine locations often, we couldn't keep the pests off the food and out of the mess quarters. The flies transmitted the dysentery and intestinal diseases that killed so many. Sometime in 1943 we finally got permission to build a new, permanent installation in camp. This time, we dug the latrines fifteen feet deep. We built new platforms over the trenches and cut twelve seats into each one.

If you saw someone take off across the compound at a trot and about halfway to the latrine slow down to a walk, you knew what had happened. Those of us in the air force, who wore coveralls in the beginning, soon discarded them for shorts or G-strings. Simply put, we didn't always make it to the latrine and get the suits down in time before we crapped on our collars.

By the fall of 1942, diseases such as beriberi, tuberculosis, malaria, dengue, and the ever-present dysentery took hold, and the Americans began to die. We buried as many as fifty to a hundred men in a single day. In that setting even a cold was serious. A tiny scratch, turned infectious, could end up killing a man.

Pellagra caused the tongue to split. The corners of the mouth and all the tender parts of the body putrefied. All of us suffered from various stages of these diseases at one time or another. A few nicotinic-acid pills from the corner drugstore, for instance, would have cured pellagra.

A man could get one of two types of beriberi, wet or dry. The dry kind was characterized by general muscle weakness in the limbs, followed by inflammation of the nerves in the feet, causing great pain in that area. If a man had the wet kind, he could swell to three hundred pounds or more. Besides causing edema, wet beriberi enlarged the heart, causing cardiac arrest. Like dry beriberi, it could also affect the nerves in the lower limbs, making the legs and feet ultrasensitive. The slightest pressure felt like electric shock waves. We called it "electric feet." If it hurt to put on your socks, you knew you probably had it. In severe cases, simply blowing on a man's feet made him scream in pain.

Beriberi was brought on by the lack of vitamin B1 in our diet, which consisted almost exclusively of rice. Something as simple as a slice of bread from the grocery store would have contained all the vitamins and minerals we needed to prevent this potentially fatal disease. But we had almost no food, and the only medical supplies we had to fight the serious ailments were aspirin and a few sulfanilamide tablets. The scarcity of the latter gave the more cunning "entrepreneurs" in camp another opportunity to con the Japs.

In the Japanese army, the men had to pledge to leave whiskey and the local women alone. The "comfort girls" were given medical checkups to make sure they were free of venereal diseases. Although the men received weekly rations of sake and beer, their superiors inflicted all kinds of punishment upon any man who got drunk or contracted a venereal disease. That didn't stop the Nips from screwing the local talent, though, and they frequently turned up with a good case of clap.

They knew that sulfa tablets cleared up the problem, but they were afraid to report the disease to their superiors. Instead, they tried to get the tablets from our medics. We didn't have enough of the drug for our own men, and the idea of sharing the little bit we had with the Japs was downright un-American.

One day, coming back from a trip to the latrine, several of us passed a Japanese guard who was talking to one of our medics behind the hospital ward. Someone made the comment, "Betcha two bits he's tryin' to worm some sulfa outta the Doc."

"Yeah, he probably went to town Saturday night and came back with one of those 'sociable' things," said another.

"Lucky stiff."

Ignoring the faraway looks and wistful sighs of our little group, I suddenly had an idea that began to take shape as we walked. Boy oh boy! It was almost too simple—diabolically so. I started to laugh. Laurence, who could read me like a book, demanded, "What's that dangerous Sicilian brain cooking up now?"

"I was just thinking, we're out of money, and the only difference between the APCs [all-purpose capsules] and the sulfa tablets is that groove down the middle."

"So far, you don't make a whole lot of sense."

"Well, it occurs to me we could kill two birds with one stone."

"Go on, I'm listening," Laurence said. "I like the part about the money best."

"Let's open a drugstore. The sign above the door could read 'Poncio's Potions.' After all, my father was a pharmacist."

"And just what are we selling?"

"We've still got plenty of aspirin, right?"

"That we do, ol' buddy, and maybe you could use some."

"No, just think. What would happen if we carved a line in the APCs to match the ones on the sulfa tablets?"

"And sold them to the Japs!" they all finished in unison.

"You guys catch on fast!"

"Girocho," said Laurence, bowing low, "you do honor to the family name."

The word went out, and a few days later, we had more trade than we could handle. The Nips never noticed the difference, readily accepting the tablets as bona fide.

Although we made them pay through the nose for the "cure," no one was interested in money; instead, we made a killing in cigarettes, food, and candy. We got a kick out of the scam, more than anything else.

"Hey John, can you die from the clap?" someone asked me a few days later.

"Hell, I sincerely hope so. If they depend on this stuff, they'll be dying like flies."

We all laughed, as we went about "manufacturing" more tablets. We did a brisk business, until we finally ran out of aspirin.

12   The Zero Ward

Unfortunately, for the first few months after I arrived in camp, the burial business was just as brisk as our phony sulfa enterprise. Burying the dead had to be the worst detail of all. We took the bodies to a building located at the end of the hospital area, called the Zero Ward, to await burial. During those first terrible months, the corpses quickly piled up in the little house by noon, with the overflow left lying outside.

Because we had little or no medicine or supplies, the hospital amounted to just a place where they kept the really ill. But the only difference I could see between the sick and the general prison population was that the sick people didn't have to work.

Since we had no anesthetic, if a fellow needed an operation, he either chose to have it without or not at all. This was life in the raw, and men accepted the fact that if they were dying, nothing much could be done about it. Forget about a bedside manner. The few doctors we had called a spade a spade. They bluntly told a man, "Look, if we don't do this operation or that procedure, you're going to die. Do you want it or not?" Thanks to the bravery of both patients and surgeons, radical techniques tried in "meatball surgery" saved many lives in the prison camps of the Philippines.

Every morning men lined up at the gate to the Zero Ward to bury their comrades who had died the day before. The bodies were counted and compared with the tenko from that morning. We'd better come up with the right number of men, either dead or alive. The Japs didn't care which.

In O'Donnell, we had buried the dead in their uniforms or fatigues. In Cabanatuan, necessity forced us to strip the bodies so their clothes could be washed and reissued to the living.

If one hundred men died the day or night before, the first two hundred men at the gate in the morning formed this grim detail. Once they buried the dead in the graveyard, a mile or two away, nothing more was expected of them that day, and they could return to camp. Sad to say, since the Japs always made us work unless we were flat on our backs or the medics pronounced us unfit for labor, burial became the detail of choice for those who felt unwell or had a minor injury.

The primary causes of death were beriberi and dysentery. If you were already in a weak or sickened condition, it made a lot of difference whether you and your partner carried a body that weighed three hundred pounds or seventy-five pounds. It's a terrible thing to admit, but when that gate opened, the men on the burial detail—including me—would rush in and fight over those poor dead souls, yanking and tossing them around, trying to find the body that weighed the least. It had become a matter of life or death; the man carrying the litter today might be the one carried out the next day.

I worked the detail more than once, but it never got any easier. The first time, always the hardest, usually stopped a man in his tracks. But if you or your partner hesitated, you'd wind up with a heavy body. Even with two men on either end of the litter, hauling a swollen corpse for two miles sapped what little strength we had, especially if rain made the path slick and slippery.

With so many men dying every day, we had no choice but to bury them in mass graves. We dug continuous trenches, like the ones in O'Donnell, and laid the bodies three deep in the ground. During the monsoon season, water quickly filled the shallow holes. To keep the first body from floating to the surface, we had to hold the fellow down with a shovel before placing the second and third men on top.

Packs of wild dogs roamed the countryside at night and frequently dug up the bodies, forcing us to rebury the dead time and again. It was gruesome. We never got used to things like that, but we learned to live with them. It was either that or give up and die.

We tried to keep track of the dead. When we buried a man with identification tags, we called out his name and wrote it down for the record. But if friends or acquaintances did not identify someone when he died, he was buried as an unknown soldier. Many men who had lost their dog tags in battle, or had had them confiscated by the Japs, were laid to rest as unknowns.

One day I helped bury a man I didn't know—that is, until they called out his name as they lowered him into the ground. It was my friend Bill Williams. Memories came flooding back of our times together in the National Guard and on the rifle team, the months fighting side by side in the jungles of Bataan and the days spent sharpshooting high up in a tree. I had lost track of Bill when I left O'Donnell for my months with the trucking outfit. Now he was so swollen and bloated from beriberi that I didn't even recognize him.

Mercifully, the deaths began to taper off by November 1942. The weaker prisoners had died, and those who had made it to this point were helped by the produce from the farm and the first shipment of Red Cross boxes. Now instead of one hundred deaths a day we had only twenty or thirty.

We were making progress in fighting disease, but in the tropical heat the burial details rushed to get the bodies into the ground to prevent worse epidemics of dysentery and other contagious diseases. But sometimes the dead lay in the Zero Ward for more than twenty-four hours before we buried them. You'd think, in all that time, that if a man wasn't dead but only unconscious he'd have sufficient time to come around.

I remember one miserable morning when the rain came down in sheets as we gathered at the gate to the Zero Ward. After tallying up the living and the dead, we headed out down the long, gloomy road to the graveyard. Slipping and sliding in mud up to our butts, my partner and I tried hard to balance our load and keep from falling.

A couple of men walking ahead of us carried the body of an American Indian. When we reached the trenches, we waited in line as each body was counted for the second time by an American prisoner and the number verified by a Jap guard. This was a very serious business. If the count was short, nine men would be executed for each one who had presumably escaped.

After they checked off the Indian, they lowered him into the hole; his was the first of three bodies that would be laid in that section. As the men held him down with their shovels and the water closed in over his body, he suddenly moved. Total immersion in the chilly water had revived him, and he began to thrash about as he struggled for air.

The fellows standing over him with their shovels were taken aback, to say the least, by this apparent miracle. One of his litter-bearers peered into the grave and exclaimed in amazement, "Look at that son of a bitch! He's alive!"

Reaching up, the newly restored Indian grabbed the edges of the trench and tried to climb out, but he couldn't make it without help. Leaning over the grave, several of us grasped his arms and pulled him out.

The second litter-bearer, suddenly realizing that he and his partner would now have to carry the sick and just barely breathing man two miles back, said, "Hit him in the head with the shovel and throw him back in the hole. I'm not hauling his ass back to camp."

"Aw, come on, we can't do that," a third man objected. "I mean, look at him. Poor devil, we nearly buried him alive! Besides, the Japs'll raise holy hell if we kill him."

"Well, don't look at me," someone else snapped. "Let the guys who brought him here bring him back!"

The Chief's two litter-bearers really balked at the prospect and kept threatening to toss him back in the hole. At that point, I wasn't sure whether they were joking or deadly serious. This was the first time any-one had come out of the trenches alive. It would take some doing to get him back to camp. The men argued about it for a bit, but with the final consensus against killing the guy, they grudgingly and without much compassion rolled him onto the stretcher, and carrying him in shifts, we took him home.

Back at camp, "Chief" was the main topic of conversation. Since they had stripped him of his clothes and given them away, he spent the rest of the day in the buff before more clothing could be reissued in his size. Even so, he counted himself lucky. If he'd been the last man in the

"Hit him in th' head with th' shovel ——— I'm not carrying him back to camp!"

Burial detail, POW Camp Cabanatuan, Philippines.
Illustration by Lauren Y. Pursley

grave, instead of the first in the water, he might not have come to before we covered him over.

From then on, everyone on the burial detail did his best to be certain a man was dead before we planted him. The word also went out that while you slept you'd better do one of two things: snore or move around a lot. If you were too still or too quiet, you could end up like Chief!

By the way, Chief came through the rest of the war okay. We ended up in Japan together, and the last time I saw him he was sitting on top of a red fire engine on liberation day, waving a bottle of sake in the air and letting out war whoops.

I had another friend in camp, a fast-talking manipulator from Chicago nicknamed "Greek," who acquired some mongo beans, a type of soybean that took forever to cook. This guy always had some angle or other, and one day he said to me, "John, let's get on the burial detail tomorrow, and when we get back, we'll have the rest of the day to cook these things."

"Greek, you don't really want to do that," I said. "The last time I went out, I swore I'd never go again. You've never done it before and, man, it ain't pleasant."

"Yeah, I know. But look, we'll go and get back real quick and be through for the day," he argued.

We knew we couldn't put the soybeans on the fire and leave them; someone would steal them, surer than hell—and not only the beans, but the can they were cooking in and the fire as well. So Greek finally talked me into it.

The next morning, as we waited at the entrance to the Zero Ward, the sight of the dead lying around, with flies walking in and out of their open mouths and noses, stunned the Greek. When the Japs opened the gate, he hung back, letting everyone else rush by. I yelled at him, urging him on, but it was too late. We got stuck with a body that must have weighed at least 350 pounds. That made me mad, and I cussed him a few times. But Greek was unusually quiet as we put the guy on the litter.

I took the foot of the stretcher; as we lifted it up, the dead man's arm fell down, dangling in front of Greek's face. All the way out to the graveyard, the guy's hand bounced up and down, his fingers occasionally brushing Greek's cheek. By the time we arrived, ol' Greek was green!

It had been raining—par for the course when I worked that detail. Staggering under our heavy load, we walked along, one of us on either side of the grave, looking for a slot for the body. Suddenly the edge of the trench caved in under Greek's foot and down he went, into the hole, landing right next to a corpse.

When he lost his balance, he dropped his end of the litter, and our man fell in on top of him. For a split second, all I saw was a tangle of arms and legs down in the water. "Aaarrgh!" Greek screamed at the top of his lungs. Then he came flying out of the hole, and I swear his feet never touched the ground until he was well clear of the grave!

After he calmed down, we finally finished the job. Always glib, he usually had an answer for everything. Today, we walked all the way back to camp in silence. We started cooking the mongo beans, but when they were done, I ate by myself. Greek wasn't hungry.

I kidded him a little, trying to get a laugh out of him, but I had little heart for it. Burying our dead always shook me up. In the back of my mind, I figured I might be next. The Greek—well, he never volunteered for burial duty again. For that matter, neither did I.

Those days are still engraved in my memory and the pictures don't get any prettier as time goes by. For the lack of basic food, care, and a small amount of medicine, some 28,000 Filipinos and more than 4,000 Americans died in the camps—and died painfully.

13 Miss U's Boys

Thanks to an intrepid soul named Margaret Utinsky, we had a very good underground system in Camp Cabanatuan. She was an American nurse who was married to an engineering consultant for the government on Bataan. Prior to the war, they had lived and worked in Manila. When war with Japan became a certainty, Margaret refused to leave on the last ship taking American army wives and dependents back to the States. Knowing full well that she was risking her life, she stubbornly remained in Manila to be near her husband. Before the invasion, she bought up all the food, medicine, and supplies that she could get her hands on and hid out in an apartment in a quiet section of town.

After Bataan fell, Margaret Utinsky, pretending to be Lithuanian, changed her name to Rosena and, with the help of a Catholic priest and a few well-connected acquaintances, acquired the necessary forged documents to wangle her way into a Filipino Red Cross expedition going to Bataan. They were going there to set up emergency hospitals and clinics for civilian relief work under the direction of the Japanese. Once on Bataan, she hoped to find her husband, Jack.

Leaving Manila in a station wagon with four Filipino doctors and five Filipino nurses, the Red Cross group traveled the same road leading into Bataan that the defeated soldiers had taken on their way to Camp O'Donnell. They arrived so soon after the forced march that the dead still lay where they had fallen, strewn along the Bataan Trail.

The horror of what she saw filled Margaret with shock and anger.

As she forced herself to search for Jack among the dead, each foot of the road revealed scenes of torture and assassination by the Japanese, wild dogs tearing at the limbs and faces of the dead bodies—scenes that she was never able to blot out of her mind.

Every day, little by little, she learned the details of the Death March from civilians who had witnessed the massacre from the towns and villages along the way. They told her of the cruelty and suffering these men had to endure and how they, the villagers, had been helpless to stop it.

What Margaret Utinsky saw along that trail made her vow to move heaven and earth to help the men who survived. She was outraged! And she had the guts and brains to carry out a bold plan of action. Nothing was too hard or too dangerous for her to try. Every weapon and trick that could be used on behalf of the soldiers who had endured so much was not only justified but mandatory. If Jack was being held prisoner, she would be helping him as well.

In her nursing capacity, she offered assistance to any American prisoners she came across in the field. Truckloads of men, on their way to work and suffering from different diseases, were given all the drugs they could carry by Mrs. Utinsky, in many instances over the objections of the Japanese. She never let that stop her, and she convinced the Japs that if they did not treat disease in the camps, it would soon spread to the Japanese themselves.

After the fall of Corregidor, she witnessed the March of Shame in Manila, when the captives from the Rock were paraded through the streets on their way to Bilibid Prison. Once she was beaten in the street by some Japs for no reason. Even that did not stop her from hiding and nursing sick American officers, who managed to elude the Japanese, in her apartment. She was almost caught several times. Her bravery, spunkiness, and quick-wittedness were the only things in her favor.

In order to be near the prisoners—and hopefully her husband—Margaret applied for the position of field nurse on Bataan. In her travels up and down the peninsula, she was able to make contact with American officers who were allowed by the Japs to forage for food during the day. With information gleaned from these men, she started a list of the dead and the sick. The day was to come when she would have the most complete list of prisoners in the Philippines. After the war, she would help the War Department trace many men whose whereabouts were unknown.

When Margaret almost died from dysentery, she was taken back to Manila to be hospitalized. After she recovered, a Filipino doctor asked her to join him at a clinic in Capas, and together they treated the sick Filipinos as they were released from Camp O'Donnell. Thinking she had finally found a way to help the American POWs in camp, she loaded up the food and provisions she had hoarded in her apartment in Manila and transported them by train to Capas. With the help of the doctor and the officers she met on Bataan, she smuggled in desperately needed supplies to the prisoners.

This was just the beginning of the work this brave and tireless woman accomplished. She enlisted the aid of many people in Manila, some of whom were wealthy and influential, to smuggle food, money, medicine, supplies, and clothing to the men in O'Donnell and later to Camps Cabanatuan 1 and 2.

Before long, it was said that one could order almost anything and it would somehow be delivered. Mail from the POWs reached Manila within twenty-four hours. Another twenty-four hours brought an answer. Eyeglasses, artist's paints, musical instruments, even birthday cakes came through the underground established by Mrs. Utinsky and her band of volunteers.

The money filtering into the camps made a difference in the health of the enlisted men. Now, as they left the prison to work on some detail or other, they could stop and buy food from the carts outside the gates. Many of the vendors were Miss U's conscripts; along with their purchases, the prisoners were given even more money.

Several times, the Japs sent me to buy food from these vendors because, they said, I could get more for their money than they could. And it was true. If I bought bananas for ten pesos, I got all the bananas I could carry plus fifteen pesos in change to boot! The Japs couldn't get over the fact that after two years in the camps, we had more money than when we were captured—and occupation money, at that!

Shortly after I went to work as a loader, Lieutenant Thompson from our old squadron quietly approached me with a proposition, saying, "Sergeant, you're in a perfect position to help us smuggle things into camp." Then he handed me a letter.

I opened the envelope. It was from "Miss U." She wrote that she knew of my work with the guerrillas on the Baguio Trail and asked me to continue the work in camp. I looked at the lieutenant and said, "No problem."

We kept the system very simple. Each of us who participated in the underground had only one contact. If we were caught and tortured, the damage was limited to two men.

We brought in two types of rice: polished and unpolished. The unpolished rice was for the POWs and the polished for the Japs. With the cooperation of the civilians who worked in the rice mill, supplies, mail, and money were put into the sacks of unpolished rice, so there was never any mix-up.

Another surefire way to get stuff in was through the burial detail. During the night, mail and packages would be left in the tall grass near the graveyard. At least two men in the underground volunteered nearly every day to help bury the dead.

While the Japanese guard and an American POW verified that the number of dead carried out of camp tallied with the number of buried, the men on the burial detail had to stand around and wait. Several of them would take this opportunity to casually check around for mail, slipping it into their clothes or pockets when no one was looking. No one ever searched them when they returned to camp, because they had supposedly been under guard the whole time. On the way back to camp, an empty bamboo litter, folded in half, provided the perfect hiding place for packages or anything too big to fit in their pockets.

We used every means of communication in the fight against the Japanese. The aborigines in the hills, many of whom were in the underground, acted as go-betweens, helping to get word to the guerrillas. Night after night, the constant throbbing of tribal drums could be heard in camp as their messages went out, with the answers echoing back from the unexplored territories a few miles away. Although they outnumbered us and had all the advantages, the Japs never let down their guard. We made them nervous; they hated to turn their backs on us. But the drums had an even more visible effect on them and played an important part in the psychological warfare against our common enemy.

One dark night, when an oppressive heat lay over everything like a thick wool blanket and the Negrito campfires winked down on us from above the camp, the language of the tom-toms seemed to promise swift retribution for the unprovoked, savage acts the Japanese were committing against the Filipinos. Once the eerie sound of the beating drums began, extremely tense and jumpy guards forgot about us and stood with their backs to the barbed-wire fence, their eyes focused on the darkness beyond. The steady rhythm, reverberating through the hot, sultry night air, accentuated the danger they felt all around them. I felt it, too; as I tossed and turned in my bunk, my heart kept pace with the beat.

These same natives helped deliver mail to the prisoners by shooting it over the fence into camp at night, using bows and arrows. It may sound primitive, but it worked. Because of the sheer volume of goods and supplies, no doubt they used other methods, but these were the only ways I knew about and in which I personally took part.

While smuggling was a risky business, even punishable by death, it wasn't that hard to escape detection. Our captors were cruel, but in a way they also seemed childlike, naive, and simplistic. Although they occasionally hauled in those suspected of being in the underground for interrogation, slapped them around, and even tortured them, they couldn't prove anything; I never heard of anyone being executed for bringing in contraband during the year I spent in Cabanatuan.

Over time, Miss U sent me several letters, money, and once, on my birthday, she even sent me a cake. Only a quarter of the cake reached me. I guess I was lucky to get that.

Not long after the war, I had the pleasure of meeting Miss U in person. One day in 1947, while stationed in El Paso, I read in the paper that Margaret Utinsky had come to Fort Sam Houston in San Antonio to have surgery. Since our annual leave started the next day, my wife and I decided to stop at Brooke Army Hospital to see her on our way home. As I stepped up to the reception desk and asked for her room number, the nurse looked up and said, "Oh God, not another one!"

Miss U—Margaret Utinsky—the "angel of the underground."
National Archives

"Another what?"

"Another of Mrs. Utinsky's boys. Ever since she's been admitted, there's been a steady stream of military through here. Everything from privates to generals."

Remembering those terrible days in camp, I looked at her and said, "I wouldn't be at all surprised."

We walked the length of the empty ward and found Mrs. Utinsky sitting up in bed holding court with several lady visitors. She was a tiny thing, thin and brown like a sparrow, with eyes that sparkled with vitality and love of life. As we approached, she stared at me and said, "I know you!"

When I told her my name, she got all excited. "I knew it, I knew it!

The Japanese called you Girocho. You drove a truck for them up and down Luzon, but you worked for us. I used to see you sometimes when I rode the bus to Capas and Cabanatuan. Then later, in the big camp, you were a loader, helping to get mail and money to the men."

We talked for a long time while her friends hung on every word. I thanked her again for the cake she had sent me in the camp. "I got your note, and you're very welcome," she said.

"By the way," I said, "something has puzzled me for a long time. Did you send a whole cake, or only part of one?"

"Why, I sent you a whole cake, of course!"

We had a good laugh when I told her that apparently, at each juncture in the route, some of my "trusted" associates in the underground had helped themselves to a piece.

Tragically, Miss U said that she had received word through an American officer in December 1942 that her husband Jack had died of starvation on August 6, 1942, in Cabanatuan and was buried in a mass grave with his fellow soldiers.

Before MacArthur returned to the Philippines, the Japanese had arrested her for suspected underground activities. They tortured her and almost killed her before releasing her, but she wouldn't talk. She eventually escaped to the hills with the help of the guerrillas.

She told me that, during her surgery two weeks earlier in San Antonio, she had been declared clinically dead on the operating table, but the medical team had revived her. "I'm hard to kill," she joked.

The United States government has acknowledged her bravery, her unselfish devotion to her country, and her willingness to risk everything for the cause of freedom. All of us who were in the camps owe a debt of gratitude to Mrs. Margaret Utinsky. In many instances, we owe her our lives.

14 R&R

Unlike Camp O'Donnell, Camp Cabanatuan had two wells in its compound. Due to the thinning of our ranks by the large number of deaths and the transfer of prisoners to work details outside the camp, we had sufficient drinking water. By 1943, improvements made to the camp even allowed us to take baths on a regular basis. We'd fill five-gallon cans, set them out in the sun for a few hours, and have water just as hot as if it had come from a water heater. After days of driving the carabao along dusty roads and then letting them wallow in mudholes, or loading and unloading heavy sacks of rice and buffalo hides, not to mention shoveling manure all day, I looked forward to a good hot bath at the end of the week.

Once we had cleaned up—usually on Saturday night—and eaten our evening meal, we began to look around for something to relieve the boredom and get our minds off being sick and wondering how long we could last. Some of the fellows broke out harmonicas that they had somehow managed to hold onto when they were captured. More musical instruments began to appear one by one, sneaked into camp through the underground, while others were brought in (with permission from the Japanese) by a Catholic priest from Manila. At one point, we even got a piano. From such small beginnings, our entertainment business was born.

The Japanese allowed us to build a stage and agreed to keep the lights on until nine o'clock for our shows. The musicians in camp formed a sort of dance band. They serenaded us with old-time favorites as well as the songs that had been popular when we left the States. Amateur contests, using costumes and props courtesy of the underground, featured singing by either solo acts or groups, the reciting of poetry written by the more gifted prisoners, and jokes.

Some had talent. Some didn't. A lot of the material was repetitious. We listened to the same tunes week after week, like "San Antonio Rose" (a favorite with the Texans) and "At the Close of a Long, Long Day," a popular encore with the men. But the repetition made no difference to us. We enjoyed it all. For a while, at least, we could forget our misery.

The men in charge of the programs came up with some very clever skits, mostly panning our conditions in camp. We had become a bunch of pack rats, collecting all kinds of junk or *quan*, as we dubbed it (using the Filipino word for personal possessions), that we figured might come in handy down the road. Once you emptied a tin can of food, for example, you hung on to it for dear life. It became a cup that you drank from, a pot you cooked in, or a scoop to use when you bathed. One skit featured this joker, liberated and going home to his father with a dozen or so of his prized quan tied around his neck. When he ran up to his "dad" and jumped into his arms, the clattering racket sounded like the tin cans tied to the bumper of a just-married couple's car. We laughed so hard, we cried.

In another skit, the "Cabanatuan Theater Players" treated that last terrible day before the surrender in the same irreverent way. Back at the Filipino command post, the phone rang and an officer answered it. On the other end of the line, a young soldier in the field reported on the desperate situation. "Sir," he said. "The Japs are behind us. What shall we do?"

The reply came back loud and clear, "Turn around, you damn fool!"

The Japs failed to see the humor in all this. They couldn't understand how we could poke fun at ourselves and our terrible circumstances. In the Japanese culture, surrender was a disgrace, not only for the soldier who had been captured but for his entire family. Although we later took some prisoners, the hard-core Japanese fought to the death or committed hara-kiri rather than surrender. They considered us cowards, but we felt no shame. We had given our all in battle and had done a lot of damage to the Japs. They were the first to admit it.

On Sunday, our so-called "day off," those of us who were able had to participate in the footraces and baseball games the Japs insisted on playing. We also held religious services in camp, conducted by chaplains from the various branches of the service. Just about all denominations were represented, and Communion was celebrated on a regular basis. Attendance was good at all of the services. Many GIs found God in camp.

One of the chaplains gave me a little Bible. In fact, every man in the service got one to carry into battle. It was very compact and printed on extra-thin paper. During my off hours I carefully read each page of Scripture, committing much of it to memory, before tearing it out of the Book and using it to roll a cigarette from the butts I'd saved. I hope I don't sound sacrilegious when I say that I truly "inhaled the Word."

In spite of our efforts to build the latrines deeper and to keep our living areas washed down, the greenbottle flies posed a constant nuisance. Twice a day, a bugle blast signaled those of us who were sick or between work assignments to stop all activity, pull out the flyswatters the Japs had issued us, and commence killing flies. To encourage the men to really get into the spirit of the thing, the Japs awarded prizes. For every milk can full of flies, they gave us an egg or a few cigarettes. Such incentives brought out the inventiveness of some and the genius in others.

It took about a thousand flies to fill a milk can, so several of the guys would pool their catch to collect the cigarettes—eggs usually being in short supply. But a few men who had "the fly concession" down at the latrine always walked off with the biggest haul. Someone in their group came up with the brilliant idea of draping mosquito bar over the wooden toilet seats. When everything was in place, they lifted the covers, trapping the flies that swarmed into the nets by the jillions. Jealous as hell, everyone else wanted a piece of the action, but nothin' doin'! The financiers of the outfit guarded this successful monopoly closely, effectively shutting out the rest of us.

In a camp as large as Cabanatuan, all kinds of people, thrown together under terrible conditions, made up the very diverse population.

Besides the average Joes, there were crooks, the usual con men—always working some angle or other—the toughs, and a few intellectuals.

The happiest of all, though, were the homosexuals. It didn't take long for the hundred or so of like persuasion to gravitate under one roof. They made no bones about their preferences and were probably the only ones there who had a good time. For the most part, we adopted a live-and-let-live attitude toward them; they bothered no one, and no one bothered them. Up until then, I had never known that this type of lifestyle existed. My education was becoming very broad.

One of the fellows in the group, a medical corpsman from San Francisco, treated me as gently as any woman the day he took a splinter out of my hand. Frankly, I didn't care about his personal life, as long as he did his job. The homosexuals did seem to be more sensitive and solicitous than the average man when someone got hurt.

The rumor mill generated most of the excitement in our drab little world. Working outside of camp, we sometimes had the opportunity to talk to the Filipinos, picking up tidbits here or there about the war's progress. Since we didn't have much to eat, rumors were like food and drink to us.

In the early days of our imprisonment, we waited hopefully for the day when General MacArthur would return to liberate the Philippines—and us. As months passed and nothing changed, we became starved for news; in our off hours, we would dissect every piece of information, real or imagined.

Some of the guys in the navy, who were familiar with almost every inch of that part of the world, drew maps of the Pacific on the backs of labels from canned goods. When the Japs bragged about their conquests, telling us that they had won a battle here or had beaten the socks off us there, we would consult the maps in secret.

For a while, the news looked hopeless. The U.S. and our allies suffered huge casualties. But early in 1943, when the Japs talked about their victories at Midway, Guadalcanal, or New Britain, we began to take note that they seemed to be marching in the wrong direction. When the Japs boasted of winning in the Central Pacific in the fall of 1943 and early 1944, the American sailors, putting two and two together, became convinced that at last the tide was turning and we were on the offensive. What a boost to our morale! Knowing that this war would have a happy ending, we felt that we could take whatever they dished out.

In the meantime, food remained high on our list of priorities in Cabanatuan. We spent a lot of time plotting how to get it, keep it, or cook it. Staying alive meant indulging in some bizarre practices. Woe to any dog or cat that ventured under the wire and into the compound; it didn't stand a chance. Rats, iguanas, lizards, earthworms—anything that moved—we utilized in some sort of stew or soup.

Everyone in camp attended the midnight mass held on Christmas Eve, 1942. Christmas Day was celebrated in an extra-special way when we learned that no one had died in the last twenty-four hours. The Japanese also issued the first Red Cross packages that day. Thanks to a wise choice of items, our conditions improved almost overnight. (Because the Japs usually handed them out at Christmas, they became known as "Christmas packages," although they really weren't.)

In the three and a half years I was held prisoner, I only received four Red Cross packages. Had they been issued on a regular basis, we would have been in better shape. If one box a year cleared up a few ailments for a time, think what three or four a year would have meant. One box a month would have been sufficient to keep most of the guys alive. Sadly, not until the last months of the war did the Japs distribute them more frequently. By then, it was too late for many of the men.

Each box, labeled "American Red Cross Standard Package No. 8— For Prisoner of War," weighed twelve pounds and contained:

Evaporated milk, irradiated (vitamin D)	1 14½-oz. can
Lunch biscuit (hardtack)	1 8-oz. package
Cheese	1 8-oz. package
Instant cocoa	1 8-oz. tin
Sardines	1 15-oz. tin
Oleomargarine (vitamin A)	1 1-lb. tin
Corned beef	1 12-oz. tin
Sweet chocolate	2 5½-oz. bars
Sugar, granulated	1 2-oz. package
Powdered orange concentrate (vitamin C)	2 3½-oz. packages
Soup (dehydrated)	2 2½-oz. packages

Prunes	1 16-oz. package
Instant coffee	1 4-oz. tin
Cigarettes	2 20s (20-cigarette pack)
Smoking tobacco	1 2¼-oz. package

By scrimping and saving, we could stretch the supplies out for a month or more, bolstering our meager and monotonous fare of rice, rice, and more rice.

Every now and then, someone would try his hand at baking a cake for a special occasion or just to lift our spirits. We could make flour from rice by grinding it with a bottle or a rock—hard work! Later, we found that dried cassava root made a better grade of flour. Without much in the way of ingredients, though, it was quite a challenge to come up with something tasty. We had no coloring or flavoring, and we usually had to scrounge up the sugar to sweeten the cake. But one day, some inspired thinking led a fellow to put a little tooth powder in the batter, and it gave the cake a peppermint flavor. Looking back and remembering how much we enjoyed the taste of that cake makes me realize how truly hard up we were.

What we lacked in the way of food, our fertile imaginations more than compensated for. In no time, we could be transported back home with our feet planted under Mom's kitchen table. We spent a lot of time dreaming up menus, things like shrimp cocktails or a dozen oysters on the half shell with hot sauce, followed by a thick steak, french fries, and Creole tomatoes with onions, sliced real thin. Of course, there was all the beer you could drink, topped off with apple pie and vanilla ice cream, chocolate layer cake, or whatever your heart desired.

On Thanksgiving and Christmas we traded traditional down-home recipes and recalled the customs we all observed. Dreaming of the homecoming dinners we would eat when the war was over was a favorite pastime.

We could not write ordinary letters to the folks back home. Instead the Japs issued preprinted postcards with statements for us to check off. Unfortunately, when they distributed these cards to the men in camp, I was driving a truck up and down Luzon for the Japanese. Not until sometime in December 1942 or January 1943 did I get to send the first

From: *John H. Poncio*
Name

JOHN H. PONCIO

Nationality   AMERICAN

Rank   STAFF SERGEANT.

Camp   PHILIPPINE MILITARY
PRISON CAMP NO. 1.

To: MRS. LOUISE LOMBARDO,

203 CAFFERY ST.,

FRANKLIN, LA., U.S.A.

IMPERIAL JAPANESE ARMY

1. I am interned at THE PHILIPPINE MILITARY PRISON CAMP #1

2. My health is — excellent; good; fair; poor.

3. I am — uninjured; sick in hospital; under treatment; not under treatment.

4. I am — improving; not improving; better; well.

5. Please see that   ALL THE KIDS ARE TAKEN CARE OF

   _____ is taken care of.

6. (Re: Family);   BEST WISHES TO ALL.

   _____

7. Please give my best regards to   ALL MY FRIENDS.

John Henry Poncio's first postcard to his mother from "camp," received in August 1943.

of two cards to Mom, letting her and the family know I was alive. A few months later I sent another. But because of the strict censorship and the haphazard—often whimsical and cruel—handling of the mail by the Japanese, she did not receive them until August and September of 1943. And so for more than a year the officials had me listed as missing in action. While other men received mail now and then, I got nothing from home while I was in the Philippines, for by the time my mother answered my cards, I was on my way to Japan.

Mom was not idle during those months while she waited for word of me. As early as April 1942, she contacted the Louisiana State Service Commissioner, who in turn wrote to the War Department in Washington asking for news of my status. The War Department officials said they couldn't reveal that information but had searched the records for known dead; since I wasn't listed, they concluded that I must be okay.

In July 1942, Mom received an official letter from the War Department stating that, with the surrender of Corregidor, all persons serving in the Philippines were now considered missing in action. Finally, in May 1943, she received a telegram confirming my status as a prisoner of war of the Japanese government. Letters from the provost marshal's office followed, telling her how she could communicate with me.

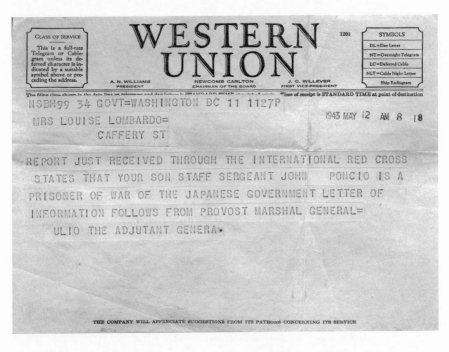

Telegram from the U.S. War Department, May 12, 1943. Thirteen months after our surrender on Bataan, my status as a POW was finally official.

In June 1943 she sent a package and cabled me through the Red Cross, but I didn't get either the package or the message. In the meantime, she clipped newspaper articles about other prisoners of war and tried to glean as much information as she could.

She continued corresponding with the War Department officials in Washington and also wrote to a congressman from Louisiana for help in contacting me. She also tried through church channels; I believe she would have gone to the Vatican itself if she thought it would have helped.

In September 1943, U.S. government censors returned two of her letters because they exceeded the twenty-five-word limit imposed by the Japanese. In the letters, she told me of other friends and relatives who had written to me. By November, the provost marshal's office informed Mother that I had been sent to a prison camp in Japan and gave her an address where she could send mail. She sent another package.

Finally, in January 1945, she received the first of several one-page letters from me telling her that I was getting mail from home and I had at last gotten one of the packages she sent back in June of 1943. I wrote the letter on my twenty-sixth birthday, July 21, 1944, but it took almost six months to reach her.

Mother said that when she got my first card from the Philippines in August 1943, she thought anyone could have typed the information in the blanks or checked off the state of my health. But overjoyed at seeing my signature on the return address, she knew for certain I was alive. "No one but John Henry," she said, "writes that bad!"

The mail from the States was heavily censored. Instead of blacking out words or phrases that they found objectionable, the Japanese censors simply cut them out. Later, in Japan, I got a letter from an aunt that read, "Dear John . . . Love, Annabel." The whole body of the letter had been cut away, leaving a large square hole in the middle of the page. I don't know what Aunt Annabel wrote, but it must have been hot!

Even though the Japanese did their best to keep us in the dark about world events, they weren't always successful. It's one thing to speak English; it's another to understand it, especially the way Americans speak it. The folks back home used slang or hidden messages to get their news across, and it was never lost on us.

In the fall of 1943, one of the fellows in my barracks in Camp Ca-banatuan got a letter telling him that, "The Benitos, next door, moved away." Puzzled, he said, "I never heard of any Benitos living in the neighborhood."

After kicking it around in one of our endless bull sessions, we all agreed the only Benito we knew was Mussolini, and we correctly construed he must be in trouble. Much to our delight, the underground confirmed the news of Italy's surrender a few days later.

15 Going Asiatic

Escape from the camps was next to impossible. Even so, some managed to make it out. A few officers and enlisted men, stationed in the Philippines before the war and familiar with the territory, took off for the hills during the rout. Men on the death march melted into the jungle whenever they could. In O'Donnell, a cordon of heavily armed soldiers guarded us because no fences had yet been erected. Some of the prisoners, seeing their chance, simply walked out in the first few days.

But the majority of us were so weak and exhausted, escape seemed fruitless. Where would we go? How would we survive? Four months of scrounging for food in the jungles hadn't netted us much. The island was crawling with the enemy, and our chances of surviving on our own seemed remote. The Japanese did not subscribe to the Geneva Convention, and our military code encouraging a soldier to escape meant nothing to them. If you got caught—and the Japanese apprehended nearly all those who tried to escape—you could hang it up. The soldiers in O'Donnell beheaded the first fellow they captured and put his head on a pike at the gate as a warning to the rest of us. That sort of discouraged the notion of taking off.

Before they established the regulation regarding ten-man squads, the Japs executed scores of POWs for every one who tried to escape. Later, in Camp Cabanatuan, a few men, despite the risks, were still hellbent on making a run for it—a perfect example of why it paid to choose the other nine men in your squad with care.

Two officers decided to break out one night, lie low in the drainage ditch at the edge of the compound, and go out under the fence as soon as it got quiet.

A sleepy prisoner, suffering from dysentery, which usually resulted in frequent urination, wandered out to the trench to take a leak. Unfortunately, he chose the very place the men were hiding. The minute the poor guy began to pee, he was startled out of his wits by the yelling, cursing officers who came boiling up out of the ditch, mad as hell. The commotion attracted the attention of the guards, and they came running and hauled the two officers off to the guardhouse.

The next morning, the camp was all abuzz with the news. But something strange happened. Turns out no one had much sympathy for the officers, even though I never heard anything more about them, and very probably they were beaten, maybe even killed. In the first place, they had risked not only their lives, but the lives of eighteen others. (Officers didn't hang together in a particular ten-man squad, but the rule—nine men executed for every one who escaped—still applied to them as well.) In the second place, most of the men in camp felt the stupid SOBs should have had enough sense to keep their mouths shut, no matter what.

"Going Asiatic," a term coined by the POWs for fixating one's mind on a single object and putting the reflexes on hold, gave us a way to endure and withstand interrogation, punishment, or torture. We learned it from the Filipinos. When harshly questioned, beaten, kicked, and even killed for information regarding guerrilla activities, they put this blank expression on their faces, their eyes glazed over, and no amount of mistreatment by the Japanese could break them.

Near the town of San Carlos, the guerrillas attacked a Jap convoy one day, wiping it out and leaving no one alive to give the alarm. The Nips tore up the area trying to find the men responsible. They chased all through the jungle, searching the towns and villages nearby, but no one would tell.

The Japanese usually got most of their information about resistance movements from the fifth columnists. This time, they rounded up some civilians for questioning and took them to headquarters in San Carlos, right down the street from our house. I watched them pick up men, women (some with small babies in their arms), and even children. They locked them up in a small back room for several days without food. Although the Japs beat the adults and knocked them around, they got nothing from the people.

The Filipino is partly Asiatic. Like the Japanese, if a Filipino decided he wasn't talking, he just retreated into his shell. They could beat his brains out, and he wouldn't crack; he'd just give them a blank stare. I knew from experience that if a Filipino chose to remain silent, even though he understood the language, he wouldn't talk.

Eventually, the Japs gave up on the adults. Turning to two small boys in the group, they tried scaring them into revealing what they knew. They slapped them and yelled at them, but the kids gave their tormentors the same blank stare. The more the children held out, the more it infuriated the Japs. Their voices grew high-pitched, their actions became frenetic; I thought the soldiers would lose their minds. They beat the boys, picked them up and threw them at each other, and still they said nothing. The Japs finally had to give up on the children as well.

Occasionally, they hauled in a few prisoners they suspected of working in the underground. Usually they slapped them around, kicked, beat, and (in one case I heard about) mutilated them during interrogation. But the benefits of an active underground often meant the difference between life and death for many of the men, and we felt they far outweighed the risks.

Some of the prisoners in camp were less than noble. Not everyone was brave. They may have wanted to be, but the ability to endure torture is an individual thing; one man might have a higher threshold for pain than another. Yet I believe the majority of the men would have died rather than betray their fellow prisoners or their country, and most of them who were caught breaking the rules were able to hold up under the cruel treatment meted out by the Japs. Through it all, the man who controlled his thoughts stood a better chance of surviving the ordeal. If you didn't talk, they might not kill you.

A few months after I made contact with the guerrillas in San Carlos, the captain suddenly called Laurence and me in for questioning one morning. Through an interpreter, he accused us of encouraging the local people in their resistance to the occupation. This was the same captain who, in private and in perfect English, had asked my advice on how Americans wore their suits and allowed me to attend church in the village for a few minutes.

Several guards stood on either side of his desk, and a couple of big bruisers blocked the door leading outside. Although the captain had always been fairly jovial to me, calling me Girocho, today his baleful look nailed me to the wall. He said, "We have heard you are perpetrating the myth that General MacArthur will soon return to the Philippines to liberate the Filipinos. It is also said that you have told them they must continue their guerrilla activities in the hills and be ready to join the fight against the Japanese when the time comes. This is a most grave offense!"

He continued, "How can you say this? Look at the maps." Pulling out a map of the Pacific, he angrily whacked his swagger stick across the Solomon Islands and Guadalcanal. "We control everything a thousand miles from here. MacArthur can never regain the Philippines."

Laurence and I exchanged the briefest of glances. In that split second we both knew that whatever we said or did from then on had better be good. Fighting the temptation to vehemently deny the accusation, I shrugged and said in a mild way, "Sorry, Captain, I don't know what you're talking about." Turning to Laurence, I asked, "Have you been talking to the Filipinos about MacArthur?"

The picture of innocence, Laurence replied in a similar low-keyed manner, "Who, me? No sir."

The captain looked from me to Laurence and back again. Shaking his finger at us, his voice straying into a higher key, he said, "We have it on good authority that you have done this thing. Do not deny it!"

A trickle of sweat ran down my back. *Oh Lord,* I thought, *who ratted on us? A lousy collaborationist, no doubt. But who?* Unfortunately, you couldn't always tell the good guys from the bad. Some Filipinos would sell their mothers, if the price was right. But whoever it was, it was his word against ours.

I continued to bluff my way through the endless questions that followed, with Laurence backing me to the hilt. We looked the captain straight in the eye and refused to budge an inch in our answers. I also reminded him, "Taii, we are under supervision by our Japanese guards twenty-four hours a day. There is no opportunity for us to meet with the Filipinos singly, much less in groups."

Not waiting for the interpreter, he jumped up from his desk and, slamming his hand down on the top, screamed, "You lie!"

Here we go, I thought. This was the usual method of intimidation. The Japs hoped to get the accused so rattled with their scare tactics that he couldn't think. We'd seen it all before. There was only one way to deal with this. Stay calm, stonewall, and let him wear himself out.

The captain was working himself into some kind of a state, pacing up and down; the interpreter could hardly keep up with his torrent of words. Now and then, he'd stop and look at us coldly. Even with our sketchy understanding of Japanese, his threats came through loud and clear.

More questions, more stonewalling. The captain's face turned dark with rage. The veins in his neck stood out against his sweat-stained collar, and his eyes were about to bulge out of his head. I noticed a tiny bit of spittle at the corners of his mouth. Almost idly, I wondered how long he could keep this up before he had a stroke.

As the light began to fade and the shadows lengthened in the room, I began to doubt that we would ever leave this place alive. *Don't even think it,* I mentally shook myself. Bracing myself for the blows that surely would come if the Japs followed their usual routine, I hardly dared to look at Laurence. I didn't want to see the fear on his face. I hoped the captain couldn't see the fear on mine.

The interrogation continued for hours without interruption. Over and over the captain asked, "Who are the local leaders in the movement? How many in the group? What methods do you use to communicate with them? How often do you meet? Where?" We remained mute, staring at nothing.

Whether from fatigue or hunger, my thoughts began to drift, and soon I was back home with all the folks. Mother, Grandpa, Grandma, and I all sat around the dining-room table talking and laughing about old times. They were so real to me, I felt like I could reach out and touch them.

I don't know how long I was "away," but when I woke from my reverie it was dusk and the lights were on in the room. The captain sat at his desk, silent. He looked extremely frustrated and unsure of how to proceed. Clearly, he had run out of steam. After some minutes, he pushed his chair back abruptly, barked an order, and strode from the room. The interpreter turned to us and said, "You are free to go, for the time being." Giddy and lightheaded with relief, we left on shaky legs; we had been standing the whole time.

For the next few weeks, we lived with the threat of being hauled in at any moment, tortured, and maybe shot. Under the circumstances, we played it safe, passing no information to the guerrillas on troop or supply movements. We managed to get word into the right ears that someone had talked, and that now the Japs suspected us. But oddly enough, they didn't pursue the matter any further. That was the last we heard of it. We couldn't explain it. They hadn't been play-acting in there; they were deadly serious. Someone had definitely tipped them off.

At around the same time, the guerrillas executed the Filipino traitor with the Japanese wife for turning in two of his countrymen to the Japs. When we had no more trouble after that, we concluded that he may have betrayed us as well, and when he died, any evidence he had against us died with him.

Patriotism and loyalty were strong in camp. They were all we had left. That and the acts of defiance toward our jailers helped keep us going. Wherever we were, whatever we did, we constantly looked for ways to get even. We watched, waited, and observed the various chinks in our hosts' armor, seizing any opportunity to avenge ourselves. We had fun targeting the more sadistic guards; by playing one against the other, we returned the favor by getting them in hot water.

Since fraternizing with the locals was strictly forbidden, we slipped love letters, supposedly from Filipina women, into their unattended equipment where they might be discovered by their superiors. More than once, a couple of the guards were accused and soundly beaten in front of everyone as an example.

Plotting ways to get more food, even if it meant taking terrible risks, filled most of our waking thoughts. Stealing from the farm was a serious crime, in some instances punishable by death. Starving men were severely beaten, put in the guardhouse, or even killed for taking a turnip or an onion out of the field. But that didn't stop us. The work was so hard we needed more food than the normal day's ration.

Although we harvested very little in those few weeks I worked on the farm, we'd swipe produce when we later delivered fertilizer to the site. After a few close calls, we found out it was best to eat the vegetable as soon as you picked it. In hoarding it, you ran the risk of being caught with the goods. I soon perfected a sleight-of-hand to rival Houdini's.

At night, with the help of the American guard in the barracks, I'd sneak out with several buddies to swipe rice from the warehouse. Using a method taught to us by the Filipinos, we slipped long sharpened bamboo poles between the bars of the window and, working them carefully into the coarse weave of the rice-straw sacks, opened up several bags, allowing the rice to slide down the pole. We liberated quite a bit of rice that way, both in the Philippines and later in Japan.

Usually, when the sacks of rice came up short, the Jap in charge of the warehouse got called in and punished for stealing. Of course, when the sergeant got it, he would kick the corporal at the first opportunity. The corporal in turn hit the private, and the private slapped a POW. That was just part of the game.

For the American POW, going Asiatic could take different forms. One way might be achieved by focusing on an object on the wall, wiping all other thoughts and ideas from the mind, repressing all emotions.

Another might choose to be transported to a different time and place, escaping through the imagination. Dreaming of home and family, letting thoughts of happier days fill the mind and block out the present worked for many. I've heard still others say they designed and constructed intricate things, completely losing themselves in the process.

An infantryman, punished by being imprisoned in a box for a long time, told me that, in order to keep from going crazy, he designed and built an automatic rifle. (No doubt he had a target in mind as well.) One man in solitary confinement said he completely created a grandfather clock from scratch in his imagination, including the works and the chiming mechanism; he'd never done such a thing in his life.

Out of necessity, food became my number-one priority, replacing the practice of chasing women—an earlier passion of mine. Although

I had been something of a Lothario before the war, starvation had a way of completely changing my focus, and (with apologies to the ladies) thoughts of beautiful girls took a back seat to thoughts of new ways to get more to eat. When the going got rough, dreaming up five-course meals became my escape hatch. Except for a few simple things, I didn't know much about cooking, but the gourmet dinners I prepared and ate in my imagination enabled me to cope with the ever-present dangers of life in camp.

Many times in those three and a half years of captivity our training and discipline as soldiers, hardened by the four months endured on Bataan, helped us to use this valuable tool, and whatever way we chose of going Asiatic, the Japs couldn't reach us. It was our way of fighting back when we had no other weapons.

16   Shanghaied

Not long after our surrender in the Philippines, the Japanese began shipping American prisoners to the homeland to be used as slave labor in their industries, replacing the civilian work force drained off by the war. Sometime after midsummer 1943, the Japanese began making preparations to transfer about a thousand of us from Camp Caba-natuan to Japan. Since the Americans were beginning to make real in-roads against the forward movement by the Japs at the time, rumor also had it that they might use us in a prisoner exchange, or as bargaining chips should the Japs lose the war. Laurence (Omasa) and I would be making the trip together.

After weeding out the malaria cases, the Japanese medics gave the rest of us cursory medical exams. They looked down our throats and up our butts and declared us fit for the journey. In fact, most of us were sick as dogs. During the past year in Cabanatuan, I had lost about fifty pounds. I had begun to experience odd aches and pains in my legs and feet, the beginning of what would be lifelong effects of dry beriberi; I also experienced general malaise and lack of energy. Diarrhea was a fact of life, and dengue fever had laid me low for almost a month with chills, a high fever, splitting headaches, and the feeling that every bone in my body must be broken. (It is not called "break-bone fever" for nothing.) Aspirin was all we had to treat this stuff.

After a couple of months back in the big camp, I went blind in my left eye, and later the right eye became affected as well. The vitamins in the Red Cross boxes issued Christmas 1942 helped restore the vision in my right eye, and while I could still see out of the left eye, it had been weakened enough that I would be declared legally blind in that eye after the war. Except for the underground money, which enabled me to buy a little food from the vendors as I went in and out of camp on various details, things would have been much worse.

Before we left for Japan, the Japanese issued us a set of Filipino army dungarees, consisting of shirt, pants, and jacket. A truckload of loose shoes made for us in Manila from carabao hide also arrived in camp, and I got the job of sorting them into pairs. Sitting on a pile of shoes as big as a house, I'd pick up a size 9 or 10, then find the mate for it, tying them together.

Two pairs were specially made for a Canadian in camp who stood six feet, seven inches tall. He wore a size 15 EEEE, making them sort of stand out in the crowd. They had to be the biggest brogans I'd ever seen! Because of his height, he was something of an oddity. Realizing he needed more food than the average man, the Japanese gave him extra rations. But he had a much harder time of it than the rest of us. I don't know his fate, but chances are slim that he made it through to the end of the war.

By the middle of September 1943 everything was ready for the prisoners to be shipped to Japan. Leaving camp, we marched down to the nearby town of Cabanatuan, where two trains waited to transport us to Manila. It took a couple of days to reach the capital, but I don't recall being fed on the trip. The boxcars were crowded; it was mostly SRO. But conditions were not as bad as they had been on that first trip to O'Donnell; at least this time the Japs left the doors open so we could get some air.

We spent the second night in a Manila rope factory, only a block from the harbor and the ship that would take us to Japan. The guards gave us a little rice and water; as we ate, we watched the Filipinos making rope.

Catwalks had been erected across the open spaces of the two-story building. Holding onto long ladders, the men would tie one end of the long abaca fibers to the catwalk and wrap the rest around their waists. Plaiting the Manila hemp—as they called it—into rope, they climbed down the ladder letting out a few feet at a time, careful to keep the line taut. Reaching the floor, they continued to weave their way across the warehouse, depending on the length being made. They could produce a length of rope up to five hundred feet long.

Fascinated by the quick and nimble men, we watched them work for hours. When they left for the day, we staked out places on the factory floor and tried to rest up for the trip. Unbeknownst to us, our worst ordeal was yet to come.

In the morning, after a skimpy breakfast of steamed rice and a half-canteen of water, we boarded a small freighter much like the inter-island steamers that plied the seas in the Orient. I'm not sure about the name of the ship, but it may well have been the *Coral Maru*. It had been sitting at the dock for the past few days, its black hull absorbing the blistering rays of the sun. All the hatches were battened down, making the inside of the hold pitch black and hot as an oven.

As I started down the ladder, a terrific wall of heat slammed into me, hitting me like a sledgehammer. I instantly broke out in a sweat, and in

A typical inter-island steamer—better known as a "hell ship"—used to transport POWs to Japan.
National Archives

a matter of seconds I was soaked to the skin. *My God,* I thought. *This is inhuman. How will we ever stand this?*

But the Japs showed us no mercy. I believe they must have forced all of us into the forward cargo hold at bayonet point. Men piled in upon men until we ran out of space, and still they kept coming until we were so jammed up in there we could hardly breathe. After shoving us inside, the Japs added to our misery and horror by partially closing the hatch, leaving only a section about five feet wide by fifteen feet long open for light and air.

We yelled and pleaded with them to open all the hatches. We should have saved our breath. It did no good. With almost no air, some of the prisoners passed out within minutes; a few may even have suffocated and died right then. Once again, the enemy had reduced us to little more than cattle.

The blood pounded in my ears, and I felt as though I were dying. There seemed to be a heavy weight on my chest. I began hyperventilating, struggling to breathe. I wanted to tear off my clothes, fight my way up the ladder, and jump overboard—anything to get a breath of fresh air and escape the oppressive heat. But there was nothing I could do.

All around me, the equally panicky and now hysterical prisoners stumbled around in that dark, stifling hole, shoving and clawing at each other, feeling with their hands, trying to find a place to sit or lie down. The noise and confusion were unbelievable. I knew I had to get myself under some kind of control, so I beat back the overwhelming urge to break out at any cost. It took everything I had in me to sit tight and wait.

When my eyes finally grew accustomed to the murky gloom, I could just make out the wooden platforms, three decks high, that were erected around the bulkheads and down the center of the hold. The area appeared to be about fifty feet wide by a hundred feet long—not nearly enough room for more than a thousand men. In the crush, we couldn't move at all without sitting or stepping on someone's feet or hands. Ultimately, we would have to work out a plan for sitting or lying down in shifts.

The water situation was as desperate as it gets. While we waited in the harbor to join up with a Jap convoy, they gave each of us only half a canteen a day. Under the circumstances, it was far too little. Dehydrated and dying by degrees from thirst, grown men in agony moaned and cried out in their misery; they cursed God and prayed for His mercy in the same breath. The constant muttering and babbling of the suffering and dying prisoners grew so loud, I broke down and wept. Half out of their minds, many of the men failed to ration their water, foolishly gulping down the little they had until it was gone.

The food situation was no better. The Japs fed us only once a day. As soon as they lowered the large tub of rice into the hold by a rope, complete bedlam ensued, with everyone pushing and shoving to get his share. Rank had broken down; discipline was nonexistent.

Fighting often erupted among the starving POWs, with the strongest prevailing over the weak. In all the chaos, many men got twice their rations—some got none at all. The few officers and noncoms in the hold dared not interfere or try to impose any kind of order in the melee. They would have surely been killed. It was dog-eat-dog and every man for himself. I could see that, without the help of a friend, no one could make it, so Laurence and I tried to stick together, taking turns jockeying for a position close to the hatch to get food and water.

Sanitation consisted of a tub at the foot of the ladder. While we were docked in the harbor, no one was allowed topside, even to urinate; within a couple of hours the bucket was full to overflowing. In fact, more urine ended up on the deck than in the bucket. The Japs emptied the bucket once a day, and it was best to stand clear, since a lot of the contents slopped over the sides when they roughly and carelessly hauled it up by a rope.

The stench of diseased crap and urine, coupled with the sweating, filthy mass of humanity, nearly overpowered us. A few men began to die each day, their bodies quickly decomposing in the hot, dead air of the hold. Unable to dispose of the corpses in port, the smell became indescribable; it permeated my nostrils, I could taste it, and it seemed to ooze out of my pores.

Although it felt like we remained in the harbor for weeks, we probably moved out to sea within a few days. If we had hoped for even a slight breeze once we got under way, we were sadly disappointed. Despite our cries and pleas to open the hatches, the Nips ignored us. They remained battened down tight. The Japs obviously feared we'd take over the ship, given half a chance. They were right.

You get to a point where you don't think it can get any worse, but it does. Then you think you can't stand any more, but you can. As we continued to swelter in the unremitting heat below decks, new woes were added to the list. Turbulent weather marked most of the voyage, especially when we entered the straits of Formosa, notorious for sudden storms.

The small freighter shuddered and vibrated, threatening to come apart at the seams, as she struggled to climb each wave, only to plunge straight down into terrifyingly deep troughs moments later. Gale-force winds, screaming and howling like a banshee, set the rigging to strumming.

As we tried to sit or lie on the crude wooden platforms, the constant roll and pitch of the little ship in the rough seas rubbed raw the thin skin over our prominent hipbones and tailbones. The wild roller-coaster ride emptied out the slop bucket before it was even full. The conditions in the hold were now completely unbearable—the air fetid, the floor wet and slimy with human excrement.

We became paranoid, turning crafty and calculating. With every man almost exclusively looking out for Number 1, we sweated out each other, hoping that by mealtime no one would be able to eat because of mal de mer, and there would be plenty of rice to satisfy our hunger. But we never had enough food in our stomachs to worry about, so no one seemed to get seasick.

Once we put out to sea, the Japs permitted us to bury our dead by unceremoniously dumping the bodies overboard, and they allowed a few of us at a time to go up on deck for one reason or another. Latrines had been set up alongside the railing of the ship, but with that many men it was impossible to answer the call of nature in time. Guys had no choice but to use the bucket or the floor of the hold.

Jap guards checked on us infrequently, coming down a few steps into the hold and no farther. They took no chances with their own safety. I didn't blame them one bit! If you were lucky enough to be near the stairs when they occasionally called for a work detail, you lost no time getting topside.

The first time I went up, the weather was extremely rough. Fierce winds spawned huge waves that continually crashed over the ship, plunging first one rail and then the other under water. I stood there for a moment just filling my lungs with as much fresh air as I could take in. Salt spray stung my eyes and face, and it was better and did more for my spirits than a case of champagne. I could see that we were part of a convoy of about ten or fifteen ships. A destroyer and three or four gunboats accompanied us. Our ship, unmarked and traveling on the outside of the convoy, was vulnerable to the American submarines now active in the China Sea.

The majority of these Japanese freighters were little more than tin cans, old and leaky—past their prime by twenty years. Instead of watertight steel bulkheads, only wooden planking separated one hold from another in most cases. Ours was no different. Put a torpedo through it, and it would sink like a rock! Later we learned that the Allies had sunk at least fourteen of these unmarked prison ships during the course of the war, sending thousands of American POWs to their deaths.

Two of the most infamous cases occurred in December 1944 and January 1945. Americans bombed the *Oryoku Maru*, carrying 1,600 prisoners from Manila. Jap soldiers on shore systematically machine-gunned the survivors of the sinking ship who tried to make it to the beaches. In all, 300 POWs were killed. The Japs crowded the rest into boxcars and took them to another Philippine port to continue their journey, putting them on two ancient tubs, the *Enoura Maru* and the *Brazil Maru*. During the almost two weeks it took to reach Formosa, the prisoners were fed next to nothing. Many went insane in the suffocating heat of the holds and died.

Upon arrival on Formosa, they transferred the naked and starving survivors on the *Brazil Maru* to the *Enoura Maru*. But American planes bombed the *Enoura Maru* while the ship was in port, killing 300 and wounding scores more. The Japs put the remaining 900 barely alive men on the *Brazil Maru* for the final leg of the trip. It took another month to reach Japan; by then, the desperately sick and dying men were suffering from exposure in the freezing northern climate. When they arrived in port, only 450 out of 1,600 had survived.

In another case, only five men on a "hell ship" lived to tell their story. The vessel, carrying 1,700 men, was torpedoed, and when the Japs evacuated they took the only two lifeboats on board. Two destroyers in the area made no attempt to pick up survivors, and 1,695 men drowned in the sea. Through a series of miracles, the five survivors found a lifeboat with a few provisions, water, a sail, and a mast. Blown along by a typhoon, they landed on the only section of coast in China under the control of friendly Chinese troops.

Somewhere between Manila and Formosa, our convoy came under attack by one of our own subs. A loud and heavy blow hit amidships, close to Laurence's bay. He was positive it was a torpedo; fortunately for us, it was a dud. Many of the torpedoes used at that time had been made and stored before the war. A lot of them were unreliable and misfired. Still, the U.S. got lucky and sank a tanker and a freighter that day. I didn't get to see the fireworks, but a few of the fellows on deck said that when the torpedo hit the tanker, it exploded in one big flash of light. Normally, this would have brought a few smiles to the faces of those below; but, dazed and in another world from dehydration, the despondent and apathetic men barely reacted to the news.

Not long after that, a big commotion broke out in another part of the ship. In the near-darkness of the hold, I could hardly make out what had happened. But it seems that several men, shouting and cursing, suddenly attacked another man, beating him so badly that he later died. When the dust settled and some reason returned, we learned that the man, delirious and desperate for water, had gone insane and slit the wrist of his neighbor in order to drink his blood.

This thing had gotten down to the basic elements—either live or die. Life just didn't mean anything anymore. But what really surprised me was that the fellows still had enough energy to beat the daylights out of this man!

It took less than a week to reach the port of Taipei on the northern tip of Formosa. The weather picked up even more the day we arrived, with winds increasing to near-hurricane force. For the next few days, we rode out the storm anchored in the beautiful artificial harbor cut through and protected by the low mountain range bordering the East China Sea.

While it was a great relief to be in calm waters for a change, and not constantly tossed about, we continued to swelter down in the hold with little air to breathe. The water and food rations did not noticeably improve, nor did the sanitation; body lice flourished.

Our death rate remained the same. The weaker ones, broken, spent, and without hope, reached the end of their rope, gave up, and died. I don't know if anyone made an official count of the dead, but every day more bodies were taken off the ship and tossed overboard.

I managed to get up on deck for a few hours to work. Everything was quiet, not much activity going on. We did not take on any fuel and, with the exception of our dead, we did not load or unload anything that I could see. As soon as we left the harbor, it became clear that we had been waiting not only for a break in the weather but for several more ships to join our convoy for the last leg of the journey.

Days and nights had no meaning for us in the dark hold of the ship. Being fed once in every twenty-four hours became our only means of keeping track of the passage of time. All we cared about was air, water, food, and an end to the voyage on this hell ship. I did notice that the closer we got to the home islands, the less chance we had to go topside. A few days before we docked, the Japs wouldn't allow anyone on deck for any reason. I'm not sure of our port of call, but our crossing had taken about sixteen days. It was now the first week in October.

17 Guests of the Emperor

It was dusk on October 5 when I came ashore. The air felt chilly. The temperature might have been in the 70s, but after that hellhole, it was absolute bliss. The Japs counted us, then supposedly sprayed us with disinfectant and insecticide to kill the germs and parasites we had accrued on board. We also walked through a pan filled with a similar solution to delouse us. I could detect no odor in either solution, and I doubt there was anything in the stuff, because we continued to stink; the lice and vermin were as frisky as ever.

Next, we moved through an inspection line to check our baggage. Most of us carried a little musette bag for personal items such as tobacco. About all I had in mine was the little samurai doll "Girocho" and the Japanese fan that I had been given by the sergeant on the Baguio Trail.

Apparently tobacco fell under some kind of restriction in Japan, because all of it had to be stamped. This joker sat at a little table with a rubber stamp and an ink pad and proceeded to stamp everyone's bag of Philippine tobacco as we came through the line. The fact that the pad was dry as a bone didn't seem to make the slightest bit of difference. He went through the motions just the same.

I lost sight of Laurence in the rush to get on deck. When I looked around for him, I saw the Japs dividing the rest of the survivors into two groups. Sadly, we didn't wind up together; I wondered if I'd ever see "Omasa" again.

Besides hunger, the worst part of imprisonment is the uncertainty about what lies ahead. Where were they taking us, and what kind of treatment would we get? Not knowing made us all jumpy and extremely bad-tempered. No one had any patience or compassion for the other fellow; the milk of human kindness had dried up long ago, leaving us hard-boiled. To call us feisty would be an understatement. It didn't pay to look at anyone cross-eyed; he would've knocked the hell out of you!

After everyone disembarked and we carried the dead off the ship, our group of roughly four hundred men, accompanied by heavily armed soldiers, fell in and marched through the dark streets of what looked to be a large city. The bracing night air helped to energize me a little, but I was still weak from hunger and unsteady on my pins. I hoped we wouldn't have far to walk; I didn't think I could make it.

I don't know when I first became conscious of the sound of crickets. It puzzled me; it's not a sound I associated with big cities. The clattering noise got louder as we came to a busy thoroughfare—where the mystery soon solved itself. The peculiar racket was caused by the elevated wooden geta worn by the Japanese men and women as they walked down the street or ran for a streetcar.

At the railway station, we boarded a train; but this time, regular coaches replaced the usual boxcars, letting us sit instead of stand. The shades were drawn in all the cars, presumably to keep us from getting a good look at their towns, industries, or war efforts once we got under way. It was quite late by the time we left the station. Compared to the accommodations aboard ship, the train car felt like heaven, and I think we all fell into an exhausted sleep sitting up, rocked by the gentle motion of the train as we traveled all night.

In the morning, a POW seated across from me addressed the guard standing near us in fluent Japanese. "I have always heard that Japan is a very beautiful country."

The guard seemed very surprised that an American could speak his language. Clearly flattered, he agreed with the assessment by vigorously nodding his head up and down. "Hai, Nihon ichiban!" Yes, Japan is the best (or number one).

"But it's too bad the shades are down and we cannot see if what I've heard is true," the prisoner said wistfully.

The chance to brag about Japan was too great for the guard. Pride in his country overrode whatever instructions he had been given, and he held the shade aside, just a little, so that we could peek out at the passing countryside.

I got the impression of greenness. Of small villages that dotted the rolling landscape. Of houses built close together, with tile roofs and walls of wood and bamboo. I could see that every square inch of ground around the houses had been used to grow food.

Around noon, they handed out bentos, or boxed lunches, similar to the ones sold to travelers in Japan. It consisted of a fair amount of rice, a piece of fish, and a pickle. In my starved state, I considered it to be one of the best meals I'd had since leaving the Philippines.

It was midafternoon on October 6 when we pulled into a siding at Himeji, a good-sized town on the Inland Sea. The guards counted us off and marched us several kilometers down a road to a village called Hirohata (which means "sun flag"), then to the adjacent POW camp by the same name. Although this camp had only recently been built to accommodate our contingent coming from the Philippines, a welcoming committee of about eighty Americans and two Aussies greeted us. Prior to our arrival, they had been transferred to Camp Hirohata from a smaller camp nearby.

The compound had a main courtyard, a guardhouse, headquarters, living quarters for the camp staff, and their bathhouse. The galley stood next to the storeroom, there was a small infirmary, and two barracks, each measuring about a hundred feet by forty feet, housed the prisoners. Two latrines and a bathhouse had been built next to the barracks.

A ten-foot fence, topped by several strands of barbed wire, encircled the camp. All of the wooden buildings had rough, unfinished concrete floors and exposed rafters. Large triangular windows, installed at either end of the barracks' gabled roof, and a few small side windows gave us the only light we had during the day.

Our sleeping accommodations consisted of two rows of double-decker platforms, separated by an aisle; the first level was about two feet off the floor and the second was about three feet above that. Ladders led to the upper bunks.

The guards issued us thin bamboo mats to cover the wooden platforms, along with three blankets made from a rough wood fiber; the weave was so coarse you could see through them. Needless to say, they didn't keep us very warm in the winter. Two of them would have covered the average Japanese, but the blankets were too short for most of the prisoners. The third blanket actually reached all the way to my feet. A little round pillow, the size of a loaf of bread and filled with rice husks, completed our gear.

Two round coal stoves, about a foot and a half in diameter, heated our barracks. Now, that might have been sufficient for a large room in a house, but since most of the heat was dissipated by the twenty-five-foot-high ceiling, we were always freezing. During the severe winter storms, the buildings would get so cold that the water left in our canteen cups frequently iced over. I know there are four seasons a year in Japan, but the bitterly cold winter months remain uppermost in my mind.

We got to keep the clothes on our backs plus our canteens, cups, and mess-kit covers. The rest of our equipment, our mess kits and metal utensils, they took away and replaced with wooden chopsticks. Those who couldn't master the chopsticks carved spoons out of wood, using whatever scrap metal they could scrounge as a tool.

Little covered bamboo baskets, six inches by four inches by two inches deep, replaced our mess kits. We carried our bentos in them, but the skimpy rations we got never filled them up. At least we had plenty of water to drink. It was piped into camp from nearby cold, crystal-clear mountain streams, but the Japanese insisted that we boil it before drinking it to be safe.

The camp administration staff was made up of incompetent enlisted men and reservists under the command of the camp superintendent, Lieutenant Takenaka of the Osaka district. Since Hirohata was a sub-camp, one of many in the Osaka district, Takenaka visited the camp infrequently.

While Japanese soldiers from the army garrison at Himeji patrolled outside the fence and escorted us to and from work, civilian guards held sway over us inside the compound. Without direct army supervision, military discipline and justice, we were at their mercy and constantly subjected to harsh treatment for no reason.

A strict rationing system called *haikyu-seido* had been in effect in Japan for some time. The long, drawn-out war with China, coupled with their expansionism in the Far East, caused severe shortages at home for the Japanese people. The program was administered very fairly. If one hundred families received a ration of one hundred pounds of rice at a time, each family got one pound a piece—no more, no less. Adherence across the board, without exceptions, allowed no cheating whatsoever. Consequently, organized black markets did not flourish as far as I could tell. Prices remained reasonable, and no one ended up with more than his share while others went hungry. *Haikyu* applied only to the average Japanese citizen, however. Those in authority—the army and the guards with access to supplies—were exempt from the system; they played by another set of rules.

The Japanese generally distributed food based on job description, sex, and age. Manual laborers got the most, then office workers, followed by women and children, who got the smallest amount. We American prisoners got the same ration as the women, yet the Japanese expected us to do the work of coolie laborers. If we got sick or injured and couldn't work, the Nips cut our food in half. It was the same old story. "You don't work, you don't eat!" They didn't believe in catering to anyone who was ill—quite the opposite from the way we think and act.

In camp we did not eat in a central mess hall. Instead, we divided up into twenty-man messes, with one man assigned as mess attendant. Prisoners cooked the food in the galley and parceled it out in wooden buckets, then an attendant took it to the different departments and barracks. We ate on a shelf built around the outside of the barracks, sitting side by side and facing the walls.

They gave us two small bowls, one slightly larger than the other. The smaller bowl, no bigger than a tea cup, held rice; the other was for soup. Breakfast consisted of rice and soup. At lunch, we got cold rice and a spoonful of seaweed. Supper was a repeat of breakfast.

The soup was a joke, little more than hot water with a few slices of daikon floating on top. We could see right through it to the Japanese characters painted on the bottom of the cup. They probably read, "Made in Nippon."

As the mess attendant filled and packed the rice bowls, we all stood around, watching him like hawks. If it looked like he had packed a little more rice into one man's bowl than the next, he got jumped right away. We made sure that any leftovers were equally distributed and no one got gypped.

It may sound childish, but shortages became so acute after we arrived in Japan that every grain of rice took on a whole new aspect. While I'm not accusing anyone of being a crook, if a man got the chance to pack his bowl with a little more rice, he usually took it. No doubt, the psychological reaction to one fellow getting just a little more than another was way out of proportion. But just to make sure everyone got a fair shake and no one took advantage of his position, we changed mess attendants often.

We tried to keep a twenty-man mess at all times by rearranging the groups when anyone died. It made it easier for the cooks in the kitchen to distribute the food. It was probably just our imaginations, but getting less than a twenty-man ration seemed to result in smaller portions.

Even so, about the only way we netted anything extra was to continue the practice of holding up the dead for tenko. We did the same thing we had done in the islands, failing to report a man's death in order to get his ration for as long as possible. When his body began to decompose, we left it in his bunk for the guards to find.

During that time of extreme deprivation, a strange phenomenon took hold. Men began to hoard their food. I say "strange" because, to me, if you're starving, saving your food for later doesn't make much sense. I guess those who did it operated under the illusion that eating two or three meals at one sitting would fill up their stomachs.

I tried hoarding a couple of times. But I felt that it got us off the strict rationing the Japanese enforced. In the end, it caused a lot of trouble; hoarding led some men to steal from each other, and to have a day's ration stolen when you were that hungry was a real calamity. It finally broke the men of the practice.

We had been much better off in the Philippines. Here at home, the average Japanese had barely enough to feed himself. They couldn't have given us very much even if they had wanted to. After we were put to work in a steel mill, the kinder straw bosses there gave us extra rice once or twice. And occasionally a civilian worker, taking pity on us as we visibly began to lose ground, would share his meager rations with us. But that was all. We could usually get tea, but while it warmed you in the winter, without sugar or milk, it had no caloric value.

We got so hard up for food that we took to chewing the coal tar we picked up in the area of the mill where they made coke—something I had done as a kid in "coal chute," a section of Morgan City near the tracks where the trains unloaded coal. But apparently the Japs thought it was bad for us. They knocked us around if they caught us chewing it.

Later, we received Red Cross packages containing licorice gum. Assuming we were back to chewing tar when they had expressly forbidden it, the Japs made us open our mouths so they could check. Seeing the black gum, they started in on us again. We had a devil of a time convincing them that this stuff was different. After we did, though, they left us alone. That enabled us to go back to chewing the coal tar when the gum from home ran out.

18 Slaves of the Emperor

The Seitetsu Steel Mill at the port of Himeji was the second- or third-largest steel mill in Japan. It was modern and fairly up to date in design; some of the POWs from steel-producing states remarked that they could walk around the mill blindfolded with no trouble.

Several companies ran the mill. Coal, iron ore, scrap, and limestone were handled by four different concessions, and slag, a by-product of the steel-making process, was handled by a fifth company. Every morning, representatives of the companies came to the gate of our camp to hire the necessary men for the day. The Japanese army leased POWs to the civilian owners to work in the mill; a private got ten yen a day—the equivalent of one cent—and a noncom got fifteen yen, or one and a half cents a day. On the first day of every month, we lined up and presented our ID cards to the paymaster. He stamped the first syllables of our first and last names, in Japanese characters, on the cards. Mine read Jo Po.

No money changed hands (there wasn't much to buy anyway), but the Nips gave us credit in a large ledger. Most of our "pay" was supposed to go toward Japanese war bonds, but that was a sham. Every payday, we got our monthly ration of fifteen cigarettes, if they were available.

Close your eyes and, except for the penetrating cold, you could almost swear you were still in the Philippines; the drill remained the same. We rose at 5 A.M., stood for tenko, the civilian sentries called out "Bango" (numbers), and we'd count off in Japanese. If a man could not count in Japanese, they assigned him a specific spot in line and gave him a number he could remember; otherwise we'd have been there all day. After breakfast, the soldiers took over and marched us two miles to the mill, always arriving by 7 A.M.

Nearly all of the raw materials used to make pig iron and steel sailed into port on ships from the various Asian countries conquered by Japan. Coal and iron ore came in from Manchuria, or "Manchukuo." Large cranes offloaded everything near the mill tracks, and we reloaded the stuff by hand into railway cars or gondolas using a tenbin-bo, a pair of buckets suspended from a wooden yoke carried across our shoulders. From there, the small narrow-gauge locomotives hauled the materials to the conveyor areas feeding the furnace. Although parts of the mill were mechanized, using conveyors to feed the raw materials into the furnaces, everything had to be unloaded by hand from boxcars and gondolas and then put onto the belts.

Working with limestone (which was used as a catalyst in making pig iron) became a preferred assignment because it weighed much less than either ore or coal. Even so, after a day spent scooping it into bamboo baskets (using what looked like toy rakes) and tossing it into the gondolas, only to unload it onto the conveyors, limestone seemed to weigh as much as pig iron.

The work details were hard and backbreaking. When we commented to one of the honchos that with a little more mechanization the cars could have been unloaded directly onto the conveyors, as they were in the States, he told us that the general policy in Japan called for everyone to work. Too much modernization would have thrown the labor-intensive economy out of whack. At any rate, as long as the prisoners held out, the Japs had all the manpower they needed.

At times we worked as stevedores, unloading ships that brought the scrap metal used in the next step of converting pig to steel. When I first arrived on the scene, a massive pile of scrap a mile long, two city blocks wide, and fifty to seventy-five feet high sat on the dock. Every country or island under the domination of the Rising Sun was being systematically stripped of all metals, whether tin, brass, copper, steel, or chrome. Sometimes, sitting on top of the heap and breaking up the larger pieces of scrap for the smelter, we'd come across our own equipment we had busted up just before our surrender in the Philippines. Parts of guns, trucks, and other matériel, easily identified by their serial numbers as made in the USA, had been gathered up on the battlefields by the Japs and were now being used against us. But before the end of the war, the mountain of scrap would be flattened.

To make steel, first pig iron has to be manufactured. The furnaces were charged with a combination of coal, iron ore, limestone, and scrap, and heated to fifteen hundred degrees centigrade. The molten iron produced was then drawn into huge room-sized ladles measuring twenty feet in diameter. Impurities, converted by the limestone into molten rock, or slag, would rise to the top of the ladle. Supported by overhead gantries, the ladle moved along, dumping the slag into pits dug for that purpose next to the tracks in the mill yard.

After the slag, or dross, had cooled for a few days, the men went down into the pits, broke up the rock, and loaded it back into the railroad cars for resmelting. This was not a common practice in the States or other industrial countries, because the little bit of iron produced was not economically worth the labor. But the Japanese were so desperate for iron that they squeezed every drop they could from the slag.

Because so much of their terrain was mountainous and unsuitable for farming, the Japanese had an ongoing program of filling in low-lying areas for development. The land around us had been built up bit by bit, over the years, by hauling in sand, rocks, and debris and dumping them into the shallow spots along the shoreline. Once the "foundation" had been laid, they covered it with topsoil. Before long, houses and farms sprang up where nothing existed before.

After they ran the slag through the process a second time, the molten rock was poured off the ladle into another vessel, then dumped into the sea at the end of the quay. When the hot rock hit the water, it instantly solidified, and the terrific "boom" as a geyser of steam shot into the air could be heard for miles. The Japanese philosophy of utilizing everything they could and wasting nothing had literally converted the worthless slag into somebody's backyard.

To complete the process of making pig iron, once the slag had been dumped, the ladle then traveled on to the next step—pouring the liquid iron into ingot molds mounted on conveyor belts. Showers of water sprayed the cradles as they moved along, quenching the red-hot pigs and cooling the outer edges. At the end of the line, the ingots were transferred from the molds into railway cars—which, over time, became warped and misshapen from the intense heat of the metal.

Down at the quay, we unloaded the six-inch-wide by two-foot-long pigs, dated them, and stacked them for age-hardening. Later, they would be resmelted, adding other alloys, then rolled into steel plate or poured into structural shapes for use in manufacturing ships, tanks, and other war matériel.

So that we could handle the still-hot sixty-to-eighty-pound pigs, with their sharp, jagged edges that could cut a man's hands to ribbons, the company issued us heavy canvas aprons and gloves. We didn't mind the work so much in the winter; at least the heat kept our hands warm. But unloading the pigs in summer was murder. In retrospect, it's hard for me to understand how we did the job, especially toward the end, when many of us weighed little more than the pigs. But I guess having a bayonet virtually up your ass served as a pretty good incentive.

Despite the harsh working conditions, we could always manage to find some fun along the way. A ride through the mill behind the yard billy was always an adventure, filled with enough excitement to more than offset the drudgery.

Whatever detail we happened to be on, whether filling or emptying the cars with coal, ore, and limestone or taking the newly formed pig iron to the quay for storage (perhaps returning with a gondola full of seasoned pig iron for the smelters), we often sat atop our loads, carried along by the small, woodburning engine, driven lickety-split across the congested mill yard without any regard for life and limb of either the passengers on the cars or the pedestrians on the ground.

At a top speed of thirty-five miles an hour, we'd careen through the yards, blowing the whistle for all she was worth. Workers, prisoners, and civilians alike scurried and scattered before our onrushing train. Drivers beat their oxen without mercy, in their haste to get their loads across the tracks in time. That made no difference to us; the throttle remained wide open. We never hit anyone, but it was a miracle we didn't. I don't know, maybe the engineers were kamikaze rejects who got their kicks by scaring everyone to death.

The finale always proved to be just as hair-raising as the ride through the yards, for while the little locomotives had brakes, the railway cars didn't. As the engine slowed (somewhat reluctantly, I thought), allowing the cars to be switched onto the sidings, the brakeman would jump off the train and shove large tree limbs or logs under the wheels to stop the cars before we ran out of track. I was always surprised when it worked and we made it with room to spare.

I never tired of my train trips through the mill. If nothing else, the surge of adrenalin gave me a lift and made me feel more alive. Practically speaking, the kindling produced from the tree limbs crushed under the wheels came in handy during the winter months. The guards usually let us build small campfires in the yards to keep warm.

In the evening we'd repeat the morning's drill in reverse. Around 5 P.M., the mill guards counted the POWs and turned us over to the soldiers for the two-mile trek home. As we entered the compound, we had to goose-step in columns from one end of the camp to the other and then back to the gate. Then the civilian guards took over, counting us again. Nobody really gave a damn whether we were dead or alive, whether we marched in or were carried in, only that the numbers tallied.

On my worst days, when I was filthy from the coal or iron ore, dog tired, and ready to drop, it seemed like somebody always screwed up the count. The more sadistic guards seemed to take a perverse delight in this exercise, particularly in the middle of the night when the watch changed.

Frequently, the new man on duty would throw open the barracks door, crashing it against the wall, flip on the light, and count off the men by striking the bunks with his wooden saber. We would be rudely awakened out of a dead sleep, but growls and curses from any one of us could result in a good whack across the head with the guard's pretend sword.

Just like in the Philippines, our English swear words were usually the first words the civilians in Japan picked up. Even casual cussing, uttered in a moment of frustration, might be misconstrued if overheard by a Jap guard, so most of the men learned to put a lid on it real fast. I was lucky in that regard. Along the way, some of my grandmother's devoutly religious teachings must have taken root in my thick skull. Although I had more than my share of bad habits, cursing was not among them. Unfortunately, some POWs never learned and, more than once, got knocked around when they forgot and let one slip.

After bango, they searched the prisoners before dismissal. We were under constant scrutiny by the sentries, and you'd think that nothing would escape their notice. Not so. Always methodical, the Japanese tended to search over and over in the same places for contraband. Usually intent on going after one thing, they often missed everything else. We joked that, if they weren't looking for it, we could sneak an elephant in undetected.

For the next twenty-three months, in our attempts to survive, we would become very adept at finding innovative ways to fool our hosts. It was amazing how much we smuggled into camp—and right under their noses, too.

19 Gyangus of Japan

By the winter of 1943, we were literally starving to death. For three months, we did not receive any beans, oil, meat, or fish. With no relief in sight, we lost ground every day. When our contingent arrived in Japan from the Philippines, swelling the camp population from 80 to 480, the Seitetsu Steel Company furnished all foodstuffs. Extra portions of rice at noon, courtesy of the different franchises at the mill, coupled with our bentos from camp, helped to supplement our daily rations at first. But this little "perk" didn't last long. Shortly after we marched into Hirohata, food shortages became so acute in Japan that the subcontractors discontinued the extra meal, saying they could no longer feed this new influx of men.

Now, with a 25-percent loss in our daily ration of rice, we figured our daily intake amounted to only nine hundred calories. When they suddenly stepped up our workload by one-third, the honchos at the mill promised, "You work hard, you will be treated well." We believed them and worked our butts off, hoping that someone would notice and give us more to eat before we died. We hoped in vain. By December, almost three hundred men in camp were sick; about sixty of them were confined to bed.

God, I was hungry! And everyone else was in the same shape. I don't mean the kind of hunger that makes your mouth water or your stomach growl at the thought of a thick, juicy steak after a hard day's work. Not even the hunger you feel after missing a meal or two comes anywhere close to my meaning. I'm talking about the kind of hunger that ultimately breaks down the body and destroys the mind. The kind of hunger that would drive you to do just about anything, including selling your soul, for an extra spoonful of rice. We suffered so badly and were going downhill at such a rate, we figured we'd all be dead soon. We had to find a way to save ourselves, and fast!

Ah, but there's also something about hunger that can stiffen a man's resolve to live, sharpening his wits in order to survive. Forced to work while ravaged by the effects of malnutrition, we became like wolves on the prowl, calculating and cunning. Seizing any opportunity that came along, we scrounged day and night for something to satisfy the terrible cravings that never let up. No amount was too big or too small for the taking, no risk too great.

Money meant nothing. A million dollars left lying around wouldn't have fazed us. But anything we could eat, drink, or smoke was another matter. It made no difference to us if we had to trap it, kill it, or steal it, whether it was raw or still hot from the fire. Alone or in packs, once we spotted it, we took it. The guards began calling us *gyangus,* or gangsters, and calling all Americans Al Capone. Hell, we could have taught Al a thing or two!

Large areas of farmland lay between the camp and the mill. The Japanese planted crops throughout the year. Depending on the season, rice, wheat, and vegetables, in various stages of ripeness, grew in fields that ran right up to the road. On the way to and from work, we helped ourselves to whatever we came across. Our starving, seeking eyes missed nothing. We pinched tomatoes right off the vine and ate them green, red, or in between. Onions were snatched up and consumed on the march. When the wheat or the rice reached its peak, we "harvested" it by stripping handfuls from the stalk on the run.

Small knots of angry farmers went to the camp on a regular basis, complaining loudly to the army that our continuous raiding of their crops was making a sizable dent in their quotas. The guards knocked us around, often beating the hell out of us, but they were wasting their time.

Every day, as we followed a honcho down through the mill to our various work details, we constantly looked for food. It was too bad if a

MOTHER:

EVERYTHING O.K. RECEIVED YOURS AND GRANDMOTHERS LETTER, WAS VERY HAPPY. WOULD LIKE TO BE HOME WITH YOU FOLKS.

ALL MY NEEDS ARE PROVIDED FOR AS WELL AS POSSIBLE. WOULD LIKE TO HAVE SOME THINGS WHICH AREN'T AVAILABLE.

NAMELY: PEANUT BUTTER, HONEY, MOLASSES, PINEAPPLE JAM, OLEOMARGERINE, CHOCOLATE MALTED MILK POWDER, SWEETENED COCOA, SOLUBLE CONCENTRATED COFFEE, CONDENSED MILK, BLOCK MILK CHOCOLATE, CHEESE, SACCHRINE TABLETS, HALF AND HALF TOBACCO, CANDY.

SEND ALL IN LARGE QUANTITIES AND OFTEN. TELL GRANDMA, UNCLE JOHN, AUNT GEE, ADELENE TO DO SAME, WRITE OFTEN I WILL BE HOME SOON TAKE CARE OF YOURSELF AND DON'T WORRY

JOHN

（大阪俘虜収容所）

Letter from John Henry Poncio from Camp Hirohata, Japan. Situation: Hungry!

civilian worker had brought a bento to the mill from home and foolishly left it lying beside a stack of pig iron or stashed next to his work station. Eagle-eyed men would peel off from the column right and left and be on it like a bunch of locusts.

The wildly gesturing boss yelling "Modoshite!" (put it back) was always a little too late. By the time the boss noticed the incident, the POW, following the first rule of thumb for survival, had already shoved the food into his mouth. And while the boss fussed and fumed with that POW, someone else would take off and swipe another unattended basket. Working in concert, we seemed to be everywhere at once. In total disgust, the civilians finally had to tie their lunches to their belts. But when one door closed, we opened others.

If you had the guts to do it, the rice warehouse was always a handy target for nighttime raids. Stealing from the one in Camp Cabanatuan had been a snap. But Hirohata's compound, much smaller and more closely guarded, made it harder to leave the barracks and roam around unseen at night. Although no civilian guards patrolled inside the building, they made frequent rounds outside while we slept.

The storeroom, separated from our quarters by just a few feet, also stood across the street from the gatehouse, which was manned around the clock by armed soldiers. The first night we decided to pay the storehouse a visit, three of us lay in our bunks under the blankets, fully dressed. As soon as the Nip guard made his inspection around midnight, we sneaked out the back and quietly made our way to an area behind the kitchen to pick up our "tools," carefully hidden in the tall grass along the fence. Unlike in the Philippines, in Hirohata bamboo grew in only a few places near the coast. The slender reeds chosen for this particular job had been cut and smuggled into camp, where we secretly reamed out the partitions inside and sharpened the ends.

Inside the storehouse, sacks of rice were piled up almost to the ceiling. In an effort to prevent the inmates from stealing it, the Japanese kept the stacks away from the windows, just out of arm's reach. Silently, moving one by one like shadows in the moonlight, we sneaked around the buildings, alert for any movement in our direction by the guards. We saw two Japs standing at the gate, their rifles propped against the fence, smoking and talking quietly in violation of their own rules.

One of our trio reached the back of the hut first and waited for us to join him. While he stood watch, I carefully guided my six-foot-long bamboo pole through the bars of the window and over to where I thought the bags of rice were stacked. The end of the pole struck something solid—a box or crate—bending the pole and nearly breaking off its tip. I almost dropped the pole; catching it just in time by thrusting my other hand through the bars, I drew it back out. We soundlessly moved to another window on the side of the building, where the moonlight now exposed us to anyone coming around the corner.

Again, I guided the rod through the opening, aiming for the sacks that were visible from this angle. My hands were shaking, making it hard to keep the rod steady, but this time I hit the jackpot. Gently probing with the point, I made a small opening in the bag by slowly working the grass fibers back and forth as the Filipinos had taught me. In just a few seconds, the rice began filling the mouth of my "fishing" pole and trickled into our waiting sack.

The whole job, the first of many raids on the storehouse, took about twenty minutes. Shrewdly, we kept this activity a secret, never stealing very much at one time. Unlike at Cabanatuan, in Hirohata we didn't want to get the Nips in trouble. That wouldn't have worked anyway; the civilian guards were a law unto themselves. Our goal was simple: an extra source of food, as accessible as possible, for as long as possible, with no reportable shortages. Luckily, it worked; they never caught us. And we continued that little operation right up to the end of the war.

The ships bringing the raw materials and scrap metal into port for making steel also brought food and supplies to the city. Those of us who were lucky enough to work as stevedores, offloading everything from soup to nuts, always took advantage of any opportunities to pilfer.

Many of the freighters were Chinese, and sometimes their crews, who didn't like the Japs any better than we did, went out of their way to slip us a little food or some cigarettes. Chinese or no, however, the majority of the ships' personnel were too afraid of the Nips to befriend us, and they watched us closely. In those cases, we waged total war, helping ourselves to any and everything we could carry off the ship.

Protected by gunships, the transports traveled in convoys. Since the docks could only accommodate five at a time, the other ships had to remain anchored out in the harbor as their goods were transferred onto barges.

As a rule, the Japs made an eight- or nine-man detail responsible for unloading the entire contents of a ship. At any given time, there might be as many as sixty or seventy prisoners on board the freighters; if it took as much as a week to finish each job, that gave us ample time to relieve them of a few supplies.

Once we boarded a ship, the first order of business was to case it for anything we could use. On the pretext of going to the latrine (or head), a few of us would spread out and wander off to check on the layout.

All of the ships were constructed somewhat alike. The galley, open to port and starboard, was on the fantail next to the cold storage. Naturally, we'd hit this area first, using a scam we had down pat. One man would enter the galley, swipe some food, and run. The cook, who was usually alone, would take out after him. This would be the signal for the rest of us to get down there on the double and grab whatever we could.

Running in one door, we'd steal rice right out of the pot. And man, if there's one thing that's hot, it's boiling rice! Sometimes we scooped it into our canteen cups, but often we just reached into those big pots and grabbed a fistful, juggling it in the air as we raced out the other door.

One morning, our decoy entered the galley from the starboard side, pinched a daikon from under the cook's nose, then whipped through the port entrance without breaking stride. The cook picked up another daikon and, waving it overhead like a sword, chased after him, yelling and screaming Cantonese curse words, threatening his very life. As he rounded the corner, the prisoner slipped on the rain-slick open deck and went sprawling. Before he could scramble up, the fat little cook, breathing hard and mad as hell, caught him. Swinging the daikon with all his might, he hit the prisoner in the head with the foot-long vegetable. The daikon broke, and two-thirds of it went sailing through the air.

Another POW, who must have been a wide receiver for Notre Dame, saw his chance. With split-second timing, he jumped up, snatched the daikon in midair, and took off in the opposite direction. As he disappeared down the passage, we heard him exclaim, "Oh, boy, manna from Heaven. Thank you Jesus!" When it came to food, the men never missed a trick.

Much of the foodstuffs brought in by ship had been loaded into the holds in bulk. When we got below decks, we'd always feel around the overhead beams and supports for any fallout. Competing with the other rats on board, whatever we ran across we either ate on the spot or hid in our clothes to cook later. On one occasion, a man remarked, "Boy, look what I found! Ain't they pretty?" He held out a handful of large, flat, shiny speckled beans for our inspection.

"Yeah, what are they?" we asked.

"Heck, I don't know," he said, as he popped one into his mouth. Then he smiled. "But they ain't half bad. In fact, they taste pretty good."

Reaching up, someone else grabbed a fistful. "You're right," he agreed, smacking his lips. "They're quite tasty."

Not completely sold, we watched those two guys like hawks for the next few minutes. When neither one keeled over, the rest of us swept up handfuls of the beans, eating them like popcorn. We munched on them all day long, and at the end of the day we still had enough to take back to camp to share with our friends.

The next morning, we were sick as dogs and had no friends! Everyone woke up with severe stomach cramps and a bad case of the runs. Of course, you had to be half dead before you could stay in camp. A little case of diarrhea was no big deal. In spite of feeling lousy, we had to finish unloading the ship, but we spent more time in the head that day than we did working. It had been some time since we had had diarrhea (there never being enough in our stomachs at any one time to cause a problem), so we figured the beans were to blame. But how?

The guards, along with some of the crew on board, knowing our garbage-can mentality, must have put two and two together and guessed that the gyangus had helped themselves to a little of the cargo in the hold. Every time one of us suddenly made a break for the head, they pointed and cackled like a bunch of hens. All day long they razzed us, implying that they knew what ailed us. Then they'd slap each other on the back, howling until the tears rolled down their cheeks. I guess we were a little slow that day, because we still didn't get it, and they wouldn't let us in on the joke for the longest time. Finally, wiping their eyes, a couple of the Jap guards told us that the main shipment on board was castor beans, which were used commercially in Japan for making engine oil for airplanes.

Unknowingly, we had given ourselves large doses of castor oil. We were damned lucky that our ignorance didn't kill us. But even that experience didn't cure us. As soon as the effects of our self-administered laxative wore off, we were hungrier than ever and looking for something else to steal.

Whatever we did manage to smuggle into camp we hid, more often than not by shoving it down the legs of the long drawers we wore in winter. The Japanese issued us unbleached cotton underwear with a drawstring around the waist and at each ankle. Drawing the "tie-ties" tight held the stash safely in place. With our uniforms on top, we brought in a good bit of contraband with no one the wiser. We got away with it for almost a year and a half before anyone thought to search us.

We smuggled in rice, beans, peanuts, and occasionally soybeans. It was a rare treat when we could get our hands on rock salt, because the Japs never gave us salt for our food. It didn't come free, however. Chunks of the abrasive mineral, bouncing above our tie-ties as we walked, serrated the thin, tender skin on our scrawny legs, burning like fire as it rubbed into the cuts. But we had been without the luxury of even a little salt for so long that it was worth the price we paid just for the sheer pleasure of tasting it again.

Other places of concealment were somewhat limited by our circumstances. Still, we came up with some lulus! We hid things under our hats, in our shoes, beneath our shirts, even under our tongues. We hardly ever hid things in our pockets; they always looked there first. But because most of us stood head and shoulders above the average Japanese, and they seldom searched there, we sometimes concealed small things in the hoods of our raincoats—things like metal for shivs, palmed from the scrap pile despite camp rules and, after hours, honed to a razorlike sharpness.

A shipment of iron ore came into port from Manchuria, and the Japs sent me out on a work detail to unload it. For the next several days, I helped shovel the crumbly clay (which stained everything red) into big nets that they lowered into the dark, airless hold.

When we finished hauling all the ore up to the surface, much to our surprise we found another cargo down there. Hundreds of grass sacks lay exposed, stacked up against the sides of the compartment. Ripping into one of the bags, we discovered a bonanza too good to be true—beautiful, large peanuts, already shelled and almost ready to eat!

They were green and raw, but who cared? We ate 'em until we were about to pop. We stuffed them down our drawers, and this time we broke our own rule, shoving them in our pockets, stashing them in our bento baskets, even filling our canteens. When we got back to camp, we posted a couple of guys as lookouts and roasted some of the peanuts on the little coal stoves in our barracks. For two days, we sneaked in so many peanuts that all the men in camp got a share of the bounty, restoring our reputations to their previous levels.

Well, as usual, anything rich eaten in large quantities made us sick. We had cramps, diarrhea, the whole nine yards. But no one minded. We hadn't eaten anything that tasted so good in a long, long time, and we ate peanuts until every last one was gone.

It wasn't long before the ships' officers, unhappy with hordes of Yanks stealing them blind, set up such a racket over our escapades that the camp commander stepped up the search of prisoners and instituted harsher punishment for those caught. The sailors cracked down hard and stopped us from going to the head in groups, making us go one at a time. We beat them at their own game. When one guy got back from the head, another took off, so that there was a continuous stream of men going to and from the toilet. On the way, we somehow managed little excursions, scouting for whatever we could find.

Many of the ships calling at Himeji were American-built and so old they had been sold to Japan for scrap before the war. Economically strapped when the United States seized her assets in 1941 for invading Indochina and Vietnam, and slapped with a steel and scrap iron embargo to boot, Japan was forced to press them into service.

By 1944, these old rust buckets were in such poor shape that we had to literally watch where we stepped. We dodged holes and weakened areas through which a man could put a leg if he wasn't careful. The wooden bulkheads made it a piece of cake to break into the compartment next to the one we were unloading. Now and then we got real lucky.

For some of the prisoners, fifteen cigarettes a month, if they could even get them, just didn't cut it. To them, tobacco ranked up there with food, and many gladly traded their rations for a few butts. At one point, things got so bad, our ranking marine sergeant had to get tough with these men for their own good. As warrant officer, he meted out physical punishment when necessary to control the practice.

I liked my smokes as much as the next man, but if I had to choose, it was no contest. I missed food even more. However, after we stumbled upon the ship's supply of cigarettes in the next hold, thanks to a "loose" board in the bulkhead, we couldn't look a gift horse in the mouth. We found a couple of cases in there, and carted out every one of them in our drawers. That day, we brought in at least two thousand cigarettes. Our popularity in camp hit an all-time high; everyone considered us heroes!

There was, however, one small hitch. These Chinese cigarettes had a more distinctive odor than the Japanese brand. Unfortunately, when they discovered the theft, the ship's captain reported it to the camp authorities, and our jailers went looking for anyone smoking the "superior" brand. The minute they saw anyone light up (we could only smoke in designated areas in the barracks) the guards would approach us, sniffing the air for the telltale pungent smoke. After a couple of the men got hauled in and beaten for possession, we had to save the Chinese smokes for the mill or out in the open when the guards weren't around.

In situations where the object of our affection was a scarce commodity or a little large, we'd wait until just before the ship pulled out to take it. Although this ploy didn't always work—as in the case of the stolen cigarettes, which were reported to camp by ship's phone almost as soon as the ship left the harbor—it still made sense. So it was a red-letter day when two of us, looking through a knothole in the wooden bulkhead, spied what must have been the crew's supply of rice in the next compartment. We stared at each other in amazement. Calling out to the other seven men in our work party, I nearly shouted, "Hot damn, you won't believe what we've found." They all came running to help us remove a few more boards. Looking around, we counted about twenty-five or thirty sacks of rice.

A few of the guys, automatically slitting the bags open and filling their pants legs, stopped when someone said, "Hey, don't bother with just a bag or two. We've got to take as much of this back to camp as we can."

"Are you crazy? How are we gonna do that?" one of them asked.

"Take it easy! Let's think about this for a minute. We'll be through unloading by five o'clock tomorrow. The ship is due to leave tomorrow night. If we could get it off the boat just before she sails, would you try it?"

"Damn right!" we all agreed.

Warming to his subject, excitement making him look young again, the first man continued, "You know the old saying 'You can't always see what's right under your nose'?"

When we all nodded, he went on, "Well, what if each of us took a sack topside a little before quitting time tomorrow and walked off the ship with it, as though this was an ordinary work detail?"

"Now I know you're nuts!" someone sneered.

"Look, I know it sounds insane, but never in a million years would the Japs dream we'd have the balls to pull off a stunt like this. You know how these Nips are. If they're not looking for something, they don't see it. It's so simple, it can't fail!"

"Okay, let's say we get it off the ship. What then?"

"Man, that's the beautiful part! Why not haul the rice behind the bento hut and hide it under the pile of lumber stored in back? That way, we can sneak a little at a time into camp every day."

For a long time, nobody spoke. We constantly risked our necks, never thinking twice about stealing anything we could lay our hands on. But to actually carry whole sacks of rice off the ship, right out in the open, was just plain suicide. Men had been shot for a whole lot less!

By now, we had run out of time. We had to make a decision one way or another and get back to work. Out of the dark recesses of the hold, someone finally spoke up, "It may be risky, but what choice do we have? If we don't get more to eat real soon, we're gonna die anyway, so it ain't as though we got a whole helluva lot to lose."

His words, left hanging in the air, mirrored my thoughts exactly. Even so, sleep didn't come easily that night. I kept waking up in a sweat from a recurring nightmare—something about a firing squad.

The next day, no one had much to say. We didn't need to talk. We were all thinking the same thing: this could blow up in our faces. It wasn't too late; we could still change our minds. The only problem was, no one wanted to appear yellow by being the first to back out.

The light was fading when we finished unloading the ore in the hold. It was almost five o'clock and time to go topside. One of the men walked over to the bulkhead, pried away the loose boards between the two compartments and, shoving them aside, stood there looking at us. We hesitated for a second or two, fully aware of what would happen if we got caught, before we wordlessly entered the next hold and picked up our sacks of rice. One by one, we fell in and climbed the ladder to the main deck, lining up in full view of some of the crew. Then, with the sacks over our shoulders and our hearts in our throats, we filed off the ship and down the gangplank.

A few Japanese soldiers, sent to escort us back to camp, stood talking on the dock, waiting for the whistle to blow. We marched past them, fighting a strong inclination to break into a run, and continued smartly down the wharf until we reached the shack where they locked us up every day at noon. At that point, one of us dared to look back. He reported that no one was paying us the slightest bit of attention. Outwardly calm but inwardly quaking, we walked behind the shed and deposited our loads underneath a pile of wood and debris.

We had done it! We had actually gotten away with it! And for the next few weeks, we hauled every bit of that rice into camp in our drawers. But stealing was never without an element of danger, and this proved to be no exception.

During inspection a few nights later, I noticed a little pile of rice beginning to form beside the foot of the man standing in front of me. Apparently, the tie-tie around his ankle had come loose, spilling the contents of his long johns.

Oh Lord, I thought, breaking out in a sweat despite the chilly wind off the sea. *If he gets caught, we're in for it! They'll shake us all down, then they'll take at least nine of us off to be beaten—or worse.*

That evening, it seemed to take longer than usual to get the head count right. Someone in the back screwed up his number, and we had to start all over again. While the seemingly endless procedure went on and on, I tried hard not to stare at the rice, but I couldn't help it; I watched in morbid fascination as the tiny white hill grew to about two inches high. Any minute now, the guard patrolling our line would glance down and see it, too. Looking heavenward, I made a silent plea for help. It was a simple request, straightforward, to the point: *Just get us the hell out of here!* The prayer had barely formed in my mind when they gave the command to march back to camp.

Fortunately, the prisoner must have felt the rice trickling through the opening. As they moved us out moments later, I heaved a huge sigh of relief and thanksgiving when I saw him kick the rice away, scattering the evidence far and wide.

20 Donald Duck and Company

I never asked him, but "Joe" must have been a thief in civilian life. The lock he couldn't pick didn't exist. Even when confronted with the huge Japanese locks—often the width of a man's two hands—he cracked them in seconds. He maintained that the bigger the size, the easier the job. Small wonder he became our most valuable asset in camp.

Joe was especially in demand aboard the ships. First off, he always checked out the contents of the cold-storage compartments, normally kept locked. Nine times out of ten, they were disappointingly empty, since the oriental diet usually consisted of little more than dried fish, rice, and seaweed. Nevertheless, we kept trying on the off chance we might get lucky.

One morning nine of us, including Joe, were assigned to unload a freighter that had arrived the night before. Following the routine we had mapped out, Joe asked to visit the head as soon as we boarded the ship. This time, however, he was gone longer than usual. At least twenty minutes passed, and we began to worry that something had gone wrong.

When he finally joined us in the hold, without meeting our eyes or saying a word, he grabbed a shovel and went straight to work, pitching coal into the big net. Only the slight smirk on his face gave us any reason to hope.

Lunchtime came, and the guard escorted us to the little shack on the docks to eat our bentos. Almost before the door was closed, we all jumped him. "Well, you son of a bitch, did you or didn't you find anything in the reefer?"

The corners of his mouth twisted up in the familiar, sardonic way that, for him, passed as a smile. "What if I told you I saw a hindquarter of beef hanging in the locker?"

We stared at him without any comprehension whatsoever. He might as well have been speaking Greek. Did he say hindquarter? Lord, I couldn't even remember what beef looked like!

"Are you serious?" someone demanded.

"I'd say you was dreamin'," drawled another.

"Hey, if you don't believe me, take a stroll through the joint yourselves. The padlock's in the hasp, but it ain't locked," Joe replied.

"Man, if what you say is true, we've got to have that!"

"And how!" we all agreed.

"Wait a minute, you guys," one of the men objected. "Before we get too excited, it ain't gonna be all that simple! Takin' a hindquarter of beef's not exactly like takin' nine sacks of rice outta thirty. They're bound to notice the minute it's gone."

"Not if we take it right before she sails."

"Well, so much for that idea," the objector said in disgust.

"What do you mean?"

"The damned thing'll be gone in a week!"

"Not necessarily," Joe argued. "I doubt they'll eat it all by then. We may not get the whole thing, but maybe they'll leave us enough for one good meal. Look, this is Tuesday. We'll probably be finished unloading her in five or six days. Now, if we can time this thing just right, we can smuggle the meat off the ship Sunday evening. Let's say it leaves the next day; maybe they won't discover the theft until she's well out to sea."

"Yeah, but suppose they do? Guess who'll get the blame."

"No problem." I shrugged, always ready with a solution. "The minute we get it into camp, we hurry up and eat it! No evidence, no proof."

Motivated as always by extreme hunger, and emboldened by our recent success with the sacks of rice, we settled on a plan to relieve the Japs of the problem of how and when to serve the beef.

The following Sunday morning, Joe swiped a large butcher knife from behind the cook's back and unlocked the reefer one last time. Looking smug, he reported that there was still plenty of meat on the bone.

All day long, on the pretext of going to the head, each of us sneaked into the locker and hacked off a chunk of beef. We hid it where we normally hid the bulkier items we stole—in the waistbands of our long johns, tied securely with the drawstring. By the end of the day, all that was left of the hindquarter was the glistening white bone. We'd have taken that, too—it would have made a dandy soup. Unfortunately, it wouldn't fit in anybody's drawers.

That evening when we entered the gates of the camp, the Nips made us goose-step as usual up and down the compound. The whole time we marched, my hunk of meat threatened to work itself loose and drop into my pants leg. I could just see it shooting past the tie-tie above my ankle, becoming airborne. Thankfully, that didn't happen.

After the parade, we assembled in the courtyard for inspection. You could feel the promise of snow in the frigid night air. The guards, satisfied with just a cursory search that night, found only a few lumps of coal on a couple of men. (The damned fools should have known better than to hide it in their pockets!) Anxious to get back to their warm guardhouse, they roughed up the guys a little, then quickly dismissed us.

It was bath night in camp. Most of the men returning from work immediately took advantage of the privilege and headed for the bathhouse for a chance to soak their tired and frozen bodies in the hot water. But that night we skipped the routine.

Several men lay in their bunks as we slipped into the barracks. We hurriedly posted a watch and, untying the meat, laid it on some bamboo matting.

When the others got wind of what we had, they fell on it like a bunch of thieves. They pushed and elbowed each other, grabbing for a piece of the booty. Climbing up on a top bunk, I warned them in a stern voice, "Pipe down, you jackasses! If the Japs hear all this commotion, they'll come running, and no one will get even a taste!" They had to admit I was right, but, still sore, they grumbled as they got in line for their share. We carved up the beef with our homemade blades, dividing it equally among the men.

We had no real place to cook it. Matches were strictly forbidden in camp, and anyway, a fire at that time of night would surely have been spotted. We used the only resource we had—the little coal stoves in the barracks. They worked like a charm. As each man filed past a stove, he slapped his portion of the meat up against the white-hot sides, just barely searing it before having to move on. Normally, I liked my steaks medium-well, but I couldn't complain. They tasted just like home. For the first time in a long time, we went to bed fully satisfied.

I must have been dreaming when the door suddenly burst open, the lights came on, and several Jap soldiers stormed into the barracks. As we tumbled out of our bunks, they forced us to assemble in the aisle.

A soldier motioned us to step forward as he barked out nine POW numbers. My number, 102, was the second one called. The room was very cold, but it was nothing compared to the chilling fear that gripped me when the rest of the men who had unloaded the ship joined me, one by one.

The Japs always posted the numbers assigned to us on the work rosters. That way, if anything went wrong or turned up missing, they knew where to come looking. Although our numbers seemed to link us to the theft, could we still get away with it? By now, the odor of frying meat had evaporated and the grease and juices had been burned off by the intense heat of the stoves—the meat itself was well on its way to being thoroughly digested. We believed the Japs had no real proof. We were wrong.

The guards herded us into the brilliantly lit courtyard dressed in nothing but long johns topped by our undershirts. Using their "reform bats"—heavy, four-foot-long sticks made of oak—they "persuaded" us to form a ragged line. We stood at attention for a long time, shivering in the frosty night air. A fine, cold rain driven by icy winds off the sea soon turned to sleet, peppering our faces and bodies, covered only by the thin, damp cotton of our underwear.

We were damn-near frozen by the time one of the camp staff, bundled up in a heavy overcoat and boots, came out to address us. Through an interpreter, he accused us of stealing the hindquarter and ordered us to strip. I reached down with numb fingers, barely able to loosen the tie-ties above my ankles, fumbling with the string at my waist, before I finally managed to peel out of the stiff drawers.

My heart sank as I looked down at the red stains on my waistband, then at the long streaks of blood, dried and encrusted, running down my legs from the butchered meat. They had us!

Large cisterns made from concrete culverts, measuring six feet square by five feet deep, stood on cement slabs at all four corners of the barracks. They were always kept filled with water in case of fire—the thing the Japanese feared most next to earthquakes. During the cold winter months in Japan, the tubs often froze to a depth of several inches. They had a dual purpose, however. Some sadistic mind had concocted a way to use them for torture.

When our POWs violated some minor rule or were caught stealing, many times the Jap guards would beat them until they were unconscious, throw them into the tubs to be revived, then repeat the procedure. While the men were in the tanks, no one could go to their aid until the Japs released them. The only way to keep from drowning was to hook your arms over the sides and hold on. The veterans who had lived through this ordeal preached the drill to us over and over. Tonight we would get a taste of this kind of punishment, and one man would die.

They started in on us, beating us over the head and across the shoulders, ramming their bats into our ribs; the sickening sound of heavy wood on human flesh and bone was punctuated by the screams of the men.

Two of the guards began working me over. One of them punched me in the face. The impact sent me reeling. I felt a trickle of warm blood slide down my cheek. The other Nip struck me in the back, and as I lurched forward, the first one slammed his stick into my midsection. I clutched my stomach, doubled up in agony, and got sick all over the guard's shoes. As I took in great gulps of air, trying to get my wind back, the tears in my eyes helped to blur the terrible scenes taking place all around me.

They hit me again, this time in the back of the knees and across the kidneys. I almost blacked out from the searing pain. Everything was fading; the cries of the other men seemed to come from far away. Just as my legs buckled, I received a stinging blow to the buttocks, and I landed on my face in the frozen mud. Before I could lose consciousness, the guards roughly jerked me to my feet. When they saw that I couldn't stand, they dragged me over to the tank, and one of them broke the ice with his bat.

They threw me bodily into the frigid water; the shock was so great my heart nearly stopped. Gasping for air with my mouth wide open, I swallowed huge amounts of water instead. Almost paralyzed from the beating and the numbing cold, I struggled to stand and fell because my limbs wouldn't support me. Again and again, I tried to regain my balance, but nothing worked. Exhausted, I began to sink.

With my face below the surface of the water, I was unable to breathe; fear and panic took control. I couldn't think. Uselessly, I thrashed about in my mind while the water slowly closed over my head. I knew I was drowning, but I couldn't do anything about it. The little strength I had melted away; with no fight left in me, I simply gave up.

A strange feeling of peace descended, enveloping me in a sort of cocoon. I floated in space, where nothing was real; it all seemed to be happening to someone else. I could feel my life slipping away. I wasn't cold anymore. I had no cares and no pain—only freedom. Dying didn't seem so bad.

Only God knows what happened next. I suppose that when I relaxed and let go, my head and shoulders rose above the water before I could actually drown. I came to with my face smack up against the rough concrete of the tank. I was coughing and gagging, my lungs on fire. Suddenly, the CO's instructions on tub survival popped into my head. The will to live kicked in, and I somehow hooked my arms over the sides of the tub, hanging on for dear life.

The Japs shoved Joe into the tank with me. Waves of water laced with ice doused my head and shoulders and threatened my tenuous grip on the wall. Joe fell several times and, like me, inhaled gallons of water before regaining his footing. He lunged for the edge of the cistern and clung there, choking, puking, drawing air in ragged breaths. His face, so close to mine, was a peculiar shade of blue. It contrasted sharply with the bright red blood oozing around the edges of a deep cut over his eye. One of the Jap's heavy bats had laid the skin open, exposing the white bone underneath. Weak and barely alive, Joe tried to speak, but the gurgling sounds he made didn't sound human.

Two other POWs in equally bad shape joined us in the tank. They floundered around, attempting to save themselves. Half dead from exposure and torture, they operated on instinct alone, heading for the sides of the cistern and life.

A similar process was being staged across the way for the benefit of the rest of the prisoners. They had to watch as the other five men, systematically beaten into a semiconscious state, were tossed one by one into the icy water.

The Japs left us in the tanks for thirty minutes before they let us go. When the time was up, the other prisoners, looking on, helpless except for making the most basic preparations, dragged us out of the water and carried us into the barracks. Pale, hardly breathing, our blood pressure down around zero, we were near death. I barely remember the rest, but since all of us had been in on countless rescue parties before this, we knew the drill by heart.

Inside the barracks, the men coaxed the dying embers in the little potbellied stoves back to life. Some of them warmed their blankets in front of the blazing fire and made pallets for us next to the heaters. We had no tea or coffee, but canteen cups of steaming water waited atop the stove.

They quickly wrapped us in the blissful warmth of the blankets and laid us on the makeshift beds. Two men went to work on each of us, vigorously rubbing down our arms and legs to restore the circulation. The warm water they made us drink was better than nothing, I guess, although a shot of booze would've been more to the point.

When the blood began surging through our veins again, we moaned and cried out from the excruciating pains shooting through our limbs. I felt like someone was stabbing me with a sharp knife. But at least I was alive.

I got pneumonia out of the deal, but the rules said that injuries or sickness resulting from punishment couldn't be treated for forty-eight hours. For the next two days, I received no medical attention. (This strictly enforced regulation also applied when a Japanese soldier was overzealously disciplined. Under the circumstances, we POWs couldn't expect any better.) For the next two days, I received no medical attention.

I lay in my bunk, somewhat delirious, alternately burning up with fever and shaking from the cold, too sick to care whether I lived or died. I felt like one of those sixty-pound "pigs" from the steel mill sat on my chest. Thick, stringy mucus blocked my air passages, and the rales from my breathing kept everybody in the building awake. The coughing made me so weak, I couldn't stand.

When the forty-eight hours were up, Dr. Sidney Seid, a pediatrician in civilian life and the only doctor in camp, did what he could for us. About all he had in the dispensary was a little aspirin, something to stop the runs, and vitamin B, none of which helped us much.

Unfortunately, one man died from exposure soon after. Someone else suffered a broken arm from the ordeal and remained in camp for several weeks. The rest went back to work within a few days. Despite heavy colds, bruised and swollen faces, and possible internal injuries from the vicious beatings, the Japs forced them to limp back to work.

They cut my rations in half, as expected. But I got by, thanks to a few brave souls who shared what they had, risking their necks to smuggle some food in to me.

There was no such thing as "enjoying poor health" in camp. The minute I showed some improvement, the Japs put me in charge of the glove detail. Although pleurisy made it tough to sit up, I had to salvage the usable parts of the gloves and replace the worn areas in the canvas with patches. The sharp edges of the pig iron ate up the gloves in record numbers. By the time a pair was discarded, we had sewn patches on top of patches—a constant assignment for those on sick call.

As I gradually got better, the Japs found other odd jobs around the camp for me to do. About a month later, the day came when they considered me fit enough to go back to work. The pneumonia had left me much thinner and very weak. I probably weighed all of 115 pounds.

Somebody was always getting caught and punished for stealing food—an ongoing operation. In the summer, either we got whipped with slender bamboo rods that stung like fire and raised welts on the skin, or they beat the hell out of us with their truncheons. The next day, we'd go right back to stealing the eyes out of their heads. Even if they'd gone to the extreme of pumping our stomachs, I don't think it would've had any effect on us. We battled for our very lives, locked in a life-and-death struggle for survival.

The younger guards gave us a much harder time than the older combat soldiers. The slightest excuse furnished them with a reason to knock a few heads. We figured it stemmed from the fact that when the captain handed down their brand of discipline to the sergeant, and so on down the line to the private, the private had no one else to hit, so he targeted the POW. We'd experienced it hundreds of times. Although we avoided privates like the plague, we weren't always successful.

I remember a particularly nasty little character in camp we called Donald Duck. He was short, with a fiery temper—a mean little rascal. He spent most of his time rounding up men who, he said, had violated one or more of the 101 house rules, many of them ridiculously childish and of no consequence. When he had collected his quota for the day, he'd make the prisoners form a single line in the courtyard and read them the riot act.

Just about all of the POWS were taller than Donald Duck. To level the playing field, the Japs had positioned a box off to one side of the line for Donald to stand on. When we stepped forward and sidestepped to the right, we'd be eyeball to eyeball with him. Not big enough or strong enough to knock anyone down with his fists, he'd chew us out in Japanese real good and pop us a few times with his "equalizer."

As prisoners of the Nipponese for the last three years, we had learned to endure the slaps and kicks without trying to take the little bastards out, knowing full well it would mean the death penalty if we killed one of them.

Donald, however, did not seem to inspire hatred in the men. Unlike the other guards we could've cheerfully murdered, penalty or no penalty, we thought Donald was funny. Instead of intimidating us, he made us laugh.

It would start out the same way every time. The sight of Donald standing on the box usually made some guy snicker. We'd put our heads down, trying our damnedest to keep a straight face. But it was a losing battle. As soon as the shoulders of a prisoner standing in front of us began to shake in amusement, that was enough to get the rest of us going. The chuckles, loud enough for him to hear, would break out up and down the line, making him furious. The more we laughed, the madder he got, and the harder he hit the man in front of him. Working himself into an absolute frenzy, his already high-pitched voice would fly into orbit, making him sound just like the cartoon character. By the time our laughter had turned to outright guffaws, he was wild. Swinging his bat with all his might, at times tottering dangerously close to the edge of the box, he'd almost lose his balance and fall off his perch. We always said that if he ever got mad enough, he'd screw himself right into the ground!

We really felt sorry for the last poor devil in line because he always took the brunt of Donald's rage. But since that guy was usually doubled up in hysterics, I wonder if the glancing blows even registered with him. Although Donald Duck became a huge joke, we would teach him a lesson in good old American humor that he'd never forget.

Ishidasan, or "Whiskey" as we called him, was one of the more seasoned soldiers in Hirohata and had seen a good bit of combat in his time. He had fought the Chinese in Manchuria for years. Now too old for the battlefield, the veteran of many campaigns had been made camp-supply sergeant. He drank, and when drunk he could be both unpredictable and dangerous.

We nicknamed him Whiskey for two reasons. Late at night, when he had a snootful, you could hear him all over the compound, singing at the top of his lungs in his old whiskey voice. You could never tell when, tipsy and feeling no pain, he might take it into his head to wander into our barracks and entertain us with his crazy antics or perform a Japanese ditty or two. The stories he told about fighting in China were funny—a lot of them ribald and pretty earthy stuff.

"In Manchukuo, snow all the time," he'd say. "High, high snow. Easy to tell man track from woman track."

One of the GIs would bite. "How's that, Whiskey?"

"Woman reeve two track. Man reeve three track."

Laughing like a banshee and slapping his knee, he'd start coughing.

"In Manchukuo, all time hammer and pliers hang on wall in benjo."

Always ready to play the game, some dumb-ass would ask, "Why the hammer?"

Grinning like an ape, he'd say, "All time so cold, when man pee, his piss freeze all way to ground. He use hammer to break off."

"Whiskey, that explains the hammer. What about the pliers?"

"Pliers for woman."

Encouraged by the laughter, and reminded of more tales, he'd light up another cigarette and be off and running again.

But he wasn't always so jovial. He had an ugly side as well. After February 1, 1944, when the Japanese army resumed its care and feeding of the POWs, Ishida occasionally took a few of us to the garrison in Himeji for supplies. I know food was scarce; the authorities enforced strict rationing throughout Japan for both native and prisoner alike. Yet I don't think the army meant for us to starve the way we did.

After picking up the food and provisions for the week, Ishida would make a few stops at the geisha houses along the way to drop off a few sacks of rice, beans, or cooking oil. This happened every time we'd go for a truckload of supplies. No doubt he made points with the ladies, and no doubt he later cashed them in.

Holding two fingers up to his lips, he'd warn us, "Don't you dare say anything about this back at camp, or I'll bust your heads." He could be a mean son of a bitch when he got the notion; since he held full sway over the food supplies, he had used his position in the past to punish us by shorting our rations. He was definitely capable of making good on his threat.

In the few instances when we got fresh beef, the camp staff took the best cuts, then Ishida would select the choicest parts left for his own personal use. When we drew the tobacco ration, he was notorious for taking large quantities of cigarettes—to the tune of five hundred packs each month. All the civilian guards knew he stole things right and left.

But while Ishida's generosity with our foodstuffs extended to the camp staff, he had given strict orders that the guards were not to receive so much as a grain of salt from the kitchen. The guards were angry at being prevented from having a part in the scam, and a feud developed

between them and Ishida. They often urged the American camp leader
to report him to the *kempei,* or military police. However, we POWs had
no guarantee they would act on any charges made by us, and there was
every chance we'd get it in the neck.

Ishida had a terrible temper and was easily provoked. At the drop of
a hat, he would knock some POW silly for no real reason. Men were
beaten on trumped-up charges of not saluting properly or having a
"bad attitude." He and his cronies often ganged up on and brutalized
the prisoners so badly, they had to be hospitalized in Himeji.

I never saw it happen, but I heard stories about how Ishida gave our
men the so-called water cure. After severely beating a POW, he'd force
another American to run a hose into the mouth of the victim until he
became insensible. If anyone tried to stop him, he turned on that man,
charging him with insolence, and clubbed him to the ground. This happened to Dr. Seid several times when he dared to protest on behalf of
our men.

At first we reported Ishida's cruelties to the camp staff, but since they
were in cahoots with him, this backfired. As soon as Ishida got wind of
the complaints made by the doctor or our CO, he found a way to make
our lives miserable. Although we all secretly called him a first-class
chickenshit, we learned the hard way to keep our mouths shut.

Our CO was a first sergeant in the Marine Corps, about thirty years
old, stocky, with a pugnacious manner. Frankly, I didn't like him; I
thought him arrogant. Although Dr. Seid outranked him, the Japanese
army put the marine in charge of the POWs and made him liaison officer between them and us.

I'm sure that he, along with the help of other senior noncoms, de-
served credit for saving lives by insisting that we all strictly adhere to
the rules and regulations in camp and by making sure all food got divided equally between the prisoners. But he wasn't particularly thanked
for it. Maybe because he lived apart from the rest of the men or because
he didn't have to work outside the camp—I don't know, but others felt
this way, too.

We spent just about all our energy on stealing enough to eat or getting even with the Japs. But on the rare occasions when we fought
among ourselves, this self-appointed warrant officer administered the

discipline, which in some cases took the form of beatings. He kept an especially tight rein on the men who sold their rations for tobacco, often at the expense of their very lives.

By the time we reached Japan, friendships were not the same among the prison population. Losing a buddy to death every time you turned around cost you. When they divided up the services with constant movement, they almost conquered us. Now, except in extreme cases, when we banded together it was usually a means to an end or a way to present a solid front against the Japs. For the most part, we considered softness or pity a weakness, a dangerous indulgence. We had become a sweet bunch.

During the time of hoarding that first winter in Japan, men stole from other men in an attempt to stay alive. Stealing from a fellow soldier was considered the worst possible crime a man could commit in prison camp, but none of us was immune to the temptation.

In an incident where one man squirreled away a day's ration and another man got caught stealing it, the sergeant was called in to settle the fight that broke out in the barracks. After a brief investigation, with testimony from the men who had witnessed the whole thing, he hauled the accused into the compound.

In front of the entire company, the CO began to whip him using a big leather belt that looked like an old-fashioned razor strop. As we watched, he lashed out over and over, the thick leather wrapping itself around the man's body, cutting deeply into his skin. The beating of one of our own by one of our own made us very uncomfortable. Every man standing there had, at one time or another, entertained the thought of stealing from his neighbor. It was a terrible offense, to be sure, but this kind of retribution was too cruel, even for that.

When the man fell to the ground under the continuous assault by the marine, we looked at each other in alarm, shuffling our feet in embarrassment. "That's enough," a few voices muttered. The sergeant—grim-faced, sweaty, seemingly unaware of the restlessness among the men—kept beating the prisoner long after he was down. The POW cried out for mercy and tried to escape the escalating blows by rolling first one way and then another.

"That's enough! Let him go!" someone shouted. But the sergeant, caught up in the role of dispensing justice, ignored the growing protests and flogged the POW even harder.

"God dammit," yelled another man. "We said stop it!"

And with that, several of us rushed forward, pulling the marine off the seriously hurt prisoner. Dazed and breathing hard, the CO looked puzzled for a moment, then fell to his knees and buried his head in his hands.

The prisoner lay there bruised and bleeding, sobbing, with his face in the dust. A few men gathered around him, speaking softly. After a while, they helped him up, supporting him until he could stand. Looking around, the soldier spied the CO sitting a few feet away and, shrugging off any further help, staggered over to him.

He stood there for a long minute, staring down at the marine, his dirty, tear-stained face distorted by pain and rage. Then, drawing a deep breath, his eyes narrowed in pure hate, he said, "You did this to me today, you son-of-a-bitchin' bastard, but if I ever get back to the States, I'll find you, and if it's the last thing I ever do, I'll kill you with my bare hands!"

The sheer impact of his words, uttered coldly, between clenched teeth, shocked everyone around him. This was no idle threat; he meant every word he said. The CO didn't answer. He made no sign that he even heard the soldier, but apparently the message registered. It was the last time I remember him using such forceful tactics on anyone.

The two men avoided each other from then on, and nothing more came of the incident. I lost track of both after the war, but I've always wondered if the GI ever met up with the sergeant and evened the score.

21 Rules of the Establishment

The fellows billeted near the entrance to the barracks had to be on the ball at all times. If a guard came in and one of the prisoners forgot to take his cap off before entering the building, for instance, he'd get knocked in the head before he knew it.

Of course, the minute the guards started slapping anyone around, we'd all look over to see why. If the crime was "hats on inside," those of us wearing hats shed them real quick, because for the next few minutes the guard would concentrate on headgear worn in the billets and nothing else. Another man might be smoking in his bunk or somewhere else besides the designated smoking area, and the Nip might not even notice.

Strangely, the Japanese often operated in this methodical, single-minded way—zeroing in on a minor infraction of the rules on one hand, while ignoring an obviously blatant violation on the other. Naturally, we took advantage of this quirk whenever possible.

They had a thousand little silly rules about "hats on outside" and "hats off inside," rules calculated to keep us in line by enforcing strict order and absolute obedience twenty-four hours a day. They weren't necessarily playing favorites; they ran their own civilian prisons this way, as well. Rules to govern, organize, and even provide for the safety of the men were important, but they carried this thing too far. Trying to keep up with it all drove most of us nuts.

Every button and hook of our clothing had to be fastened. A miss-

ing button posed a problem, since we had no spares in camp. While the
Japanese made us *keirei* (salute) the officers and senior men outside, or
when passing the guard room and the outside sentry, we didn't have to
salute or bow to the guards patrolling inside the camp. The lights came
on at 4 A.M. and went off as soon as it was light or we left for work. They
came back on at 6 P.M. and not a minute before, forcing us to grope
around on dark days or winter afternoons until they were turned on.

As for their own regulations, the Japs operated in the same rigid
manner. On a certain day in the fall, they exchanged summer uniforms
for winter uniforms, even if the temperature outside was a hundred degrees. It might be weeks before the weather turned cool enough for
heavy clothes, but as soon as the orders came down from Tokyo, they
implemented them the next day.

Lieutenant Takenaka of the Osaka district, who was in charge of the
Hirohata subcamp, set the standing orders and posted them for all to
see and observe. Schedules were religiously adhered to, starting with assembly and meals, which were announced by playing two G blasts on
the bugle. (A long G note sounded the alarm.)

The Japs spelled out everything for us in minute detail. We had rules
to govern the arrangement of kits and even how to line up our shoes
under the beds with the toes pointing outward. Some of the rules for
cleanliness were puzzling, such as: "The woodwork in the closets will
be scrubbed with water daily, using hot water obtained from the cook-
house twice a week." Rules for behavior (no whistling or singing),
money owed to us, and breakages of bowls or other items kept us in
line.

The list went on and on, and Lieutenant Takenaka ended it with a
dire warning for breaking out of the mold:

> You are warned that, during the alarm, the camp is surrounded
> by large numbers of Nipponese Army, Gendarmes and Police. Ac-
> cordingly, should you commit a rash act, you can be certain that it
> will have an unfortunate result for you.
>
> Nipponese usually looks gentle but in case of accident, they get
> out of temper, and some might inflict an injury on you; therefore,
> even should you be in the right, it is necessary to prevent any mis-

understanding, to avoid direct action absolutely and deal only with the officer or official in charge.

I shall investigate all such cases fully and settle the trouble on a basis of what is right and fair. Your minds can be easy in this respect.

I accept no responsibility for any unfortunate incident arising out of disobedience to Nipponese Army orders. On your way to and from your working place:

1. You will be under Nipponese Leaders' supervision, and comply with all orders.

2. Especially, you should mark the behavior of the Nipponese at large, and just as at the working place, you should make every effort not to get into trouble.

The part about our minds being easy when it came to settling trouble on the basis of what was right or fair was a joke. A better bet would be to follow rule number 2 and make every effort not to get into trouble. But toward the end of the war this proved difficult. With the stepped-up bombing of Japan, their hatred of us escalated, and they took their fears and frustrations out on the prisoners on a daily basis.

Some of these regulations—such as not being able to talk or make contact with the civilians at work—would have made it impossible to do our jobs, so we had to find a way to circumnavigate that order. Rules about "no stealing" and "no possessing metal objects" we just totally ignored. Since the Japs couldn't meet our basic needs, stealing food was not an option; we stole or we died.

And maybe knowing our constitutional rights as Americans made us throw caution to the winds and arm ourselves to the teeth. The scrap pile provided us with a rich treasure trove of weaponry—everything from bayonets to broken knives to pieces of metal we could fashion into shivs.

We didn't limit this operation to small items. One day, while the Japs were looking the other way, we managed to smuggle into camp a section of steel plate measuring two feet by one and a half feet. We used it to make a griddle for frying seaweed. (Someone was always trying to vary or disguise the food on the menu, and we had learned to appreciate two or three kinds fixed that way. Our "hosts" liked it too, and would order a mess of fried "greens" from time to time.) At any rate, the scrap pile supplied our every need, and if they had ever shaken us down, the guards would've found a ton of that stuff in camp.

The Japs were funny about fire. In winter, they ignored the camp-fires we made from the splintered wood produced when tree limbs and logs were shoved under the wheels of the speeding yard billies to stop them. In the summer, however, we got in trouble if we tried to build a fire, making it virtually impossible for us to cook anything we stole during those months.

They gave us a weekly ration of sixty kilos of coke for the two little stoves in our barracks. Since this amount barely heated the drafty, barn-like building for more than a couple of days, we stole coal from the mill, bringing in a lump or two every night. But unlike coke, which burned cleanly, the black smoke from the coal would have been a dead give-away, so we burned the coal after dark, reserving the coke for the day-light hours of our rest days.

The guards rarely caught us hauling in that little bit of coal and never quite figured out how we could stretch our fuel like we did. The bastards knew damn well we couldn't make it on 132 pounds of coke a week. We showed 'em!

We could have slept a whole lot warmer at night, if we had been al-lowed to double up by putting three blankets belonging to one man on the bottom and covering with the other three. Naturally, that was strictly forbidden. Nor would they let us sleep with our heads under the blankets. Our heads had to be visible and turned toward the aisles, in order for them to count us.

The guard coming on duty, paranoid about taking the word of the guard going off duty, would count us again. Often, he made a game of miscounting. Pounding on the platforms with his stick, he'd haul us out of bed to "get it right." But basically, the guards checked often to see if someone had managed to escape and rigged the numbers by arrang-ing two shoes to stick out from under the covers. Had we been able to escape, the fact that as tall, mostly fair, Americans we would have stuck out like sore thumbs among the Japanese populace never seemed to occur to them at all.

22 A Matter of Life or Death

Bad diet, harsh working conditions, accidents, beatings, diseases brought in from the tropics (still very much alive and active in our bodies)—all came together during that first severe winter in Japan to produce emaciated men who staggered around on toothpick legs. At least one man fainted in line just about every day at tenko. This brought swift and sure retribution from the Japs. They'd hit him with rifle butts and reform bats, or kick him, to make sure he wasn't malingering.

At the mill, the honchos similarly struck men who couldn't make the quota or collapsed under the workload. Every night, when we carried in these prisoners from the job, we received another beating.

Upon mustering in the courtyard at 6 A.M., those of us suffering from beriberi had to strip to the waist and "massage" our skin, using brushes supplied by the Japs for that purpose. They said this would increase the circulation, thereby aiding the healing process.

They would have none of that "lying around camp bit" on our rest days; besides the usual drills and exercises, we had to run two miles to the river and back to help "cure" the beriberi. This was worse than working. The exercise required of us on those days almost finished off some of the really sick guys.

Beriberi caused diarrhea and frequent urination, but the Japs whipped us for going to the toilet more than once in the morning or for asking for permission to do so. Coming back to camp in the evenings, sometimes we just had to relieve ourselves by the side of the

road, and we suffered the penalty for it, even though the Jap guards answered the call of nature whenever and wherever they felt like it.

No one except the CO and Dr. Seid was exempt from the workplace.
In violation of international law, the Japs wouldn't allow the four navy
medical corpsmen to stay in camp and tend our sick. Exhausted and
often ill themselves, the corpsmen willingly volunteered their off hours
to care for their fellow inmates. These guys operated out of a small
dressing station where they dispensed the few drugs supplied by the
Japs.

In addition, there was a twenty-bed infirmary for men who either
needed constant monitoring by the doctor or had to be quarantined for
contagious diseases such as meningitis. The medics could set broken
bones, and if we had an accident at the mill or aboard the ships, they
could clean the cut or wound with something akin to iodine. They also
performed some routine dental work but not much else.

In the case of an operation or a difficult diagnosis, we had access to
the hospital at Kobe, which was staffed with an adequate U.S. medical
team and Red Cross medicines, or the large Seitetsu Hospital, which
was maintained in the steel mill. Most of the doctors at the mill hospital were women. I heard that our POWs who were admitted there got
the same quality of care as any Japanese civilian.

A good example of how the Japanese treated the sick—whether
among us or their own people—was brought home in one instance
where a prisoner suffering from mastoiditis and a high fever had to walk
to the hospital three miles away. He was operated on by the mill doctors and hauled back to camp on the back of a bicycle. Apparently the
doctors did a good job, and the boy recovered, but the Japs didn't believe in coddling the sick, theirs or ours.

The majority of the POWs in Hirohata were far too weak to work
that first winter. Doctors sent from headquarters in Osaka visited the
camp to investigate matters and report their findings. They took one
look at us and said we were starving. They recommended better food
and more rest. As soon as they left, however, the local camp-staff member, acting as medical corpsman, disregarded their orders almost entirely.

The camp staff, under constant pressure from the Seitetsu author-

ities to send more men back to work, used every method they could devise to harass, punish, and inconvenience the sick men, hoping to make
their time in camp so miserable that it would drive them back to the
mill. They wouldn't permit us to rest and regain our strength.

To be exempt from work, you had to be either delirious, unconscious, or dead. They conscripted those who could barely walk or get
around into a twenty-man detail called the sanitary orderlies. We had
to sweep, mop, or hose down the barracks and latrines. (A guy with a
crutch under one arm learned to hobble around while slinging a mop
with the other.) The detail also picked up trash and debris outside the
billet and generally kept the grounds neat.

In Japan, unlike the burial details in the Philippines, when one of
our own died we cremated the body. Usually someone on sick call
tended the fire in the crematorium.

Later, when they came up with several schemes to enrich our diets,
sick men were roped into projects that never came to fruition. Everyone else who was not ambulatory labored on the never-ending glove
detail or performed odd jobs for the Japs, such as shining their shoes
or mending their clothes.

Shortly after the doctors' visit, two Japanese enlisted men, Privates
Miyazaki and Tsujino, took up the duties of medical corpsmen in camp.
They vowed to reduce the sick list by any means necessary.

The "system" they set up allowed no more than six men to remain
in camp. Men with broken bones or serious job-related injuries that
prevented them from working always took precedence over the rest. All
other cases were ranked according to how much fever a man had. For
instance, if I was the sixth man to report to sick call in the morning,
and I had a 103-degree temperature, but the seventh man had 104, he
stayed in camp and I went to work.

Often Miyazaki and Tsujino arbitrarily changed Dr. Seid's diagnoses,
ordering POWs in terrible shape back to the mill. At times, Tsujino
flatly refused to issue medicine to sick men and, although he had no
medical training, "examined" the patients with a stethoscope to prove
that they were well enough to report to the mill.

A cocky little bastard full of a sense of his own importance, Tsujino
was always sucking up to the camp superintendent and trying to im-

press him with his efficiency. A snappy salute given to Tsujino—rather than the type or degree of one's illness—often determined whether a sick man stayed in camp or worked.

Tsujino also refused to allow a blood transfusion for one of our men even though the prison doctor said the man's life depended on it and another POW with the same blood type volunteered to give it. This ignorant Jap said that the man was going to die anyway, and he forbade the procedure. Dr. Seid and our medics decided to ignore Tsujino, despite the severe punishment they would suffer if caught.

Later that night, after the guard had made his rounds, the medical team secretly drew the donor's blood. Several prisoners posted at the windows served as lookouts, alert to any movement in our direction. Except for those on duty, the Japs soon retired to their quarters. When the lookouts judged it safe, they gave the all-clear. The doctor lost no time hooking up the apparatus to administer the transfusion to the dying man.

The next half-hour crept by, as the life-giving fluid slowly flowed into the young prisoner's veins. The rest of us looked on, nervous and jumpy. An unscheduled inspection by a guard at any time of the day or night was always a distinct possibility. It wouldn't have surprised me to see all our careful preparations turn sour, especially the way our luck had been running.

But this time we got lucky—or maybe it wasn't luck at all. Maybe Someone else was directing events that night. For once, everything went smoothly and according to plan.

The next day, the patient showed improvement. Thanks to extra rations donated by others, he continued to grow stronger each day, and by the end of the week Dr. Seid pronounced him out of the woods. His life had been saved by a fine and truly dedicated medical officer assisted by five equally brave and heroic comrades.

Tsujino and Miyazaki apparently liked playing doctor. One day they persisted in this farce by calling all the American Indian POWs into the dressing station. There were about nine or ten Native Americans in camp, most of them from New Mexico. The Japs kept them corralled nearly all day.

Curious as cats, the rest of us speculated all day long about the nature of the summons. We just couldn't figure out what they were doing in there. That evening, when the men finally came back to the barracks, they were plenty hot and on the warpath!

I knew several of the fellows pretty well, and I asked the one we called Chief what the hell happened.

"Aw, shit," he grumbled. "They have the bright idea that in ancient times they may have crossed the Bering Strait and then migrated across and all through North America, settling and populating the continent as they went. They want to prove they're our ancestors."

That broke up the barracks, but it was just the beginning.

"All day long, they poked us and prodded us," Chief went on. "They looked up our noses to see if we had hair in our nostrils, then they looked under our armpits. Because we have very little hair on our chests, they say this is a good sign their theory is true. They opened their shirts to show us how smooth they are in that department."

Shoving his hawklike nose in my face, Chief demanded, "Now, I ask you, with a schnozzola like mine, do I look like a Jap to you?"

After the laughter died down, I agreed he had a point.

"The part I hated the worst," another man broke in heatedly, "was when one of them touched my skin, examined its color and texture, and claimed theirs looked the same as mine. I almost lost my head and punched his lights out!"

"Yeah," piped up a young lad who had suffered the same humiliation. "When they compared the size and shape of my head with some of their men's and came up with similar measurements, they got all excited, as though that meant something. They got shit for brains, if you ask me, and they don't know their ass from a hole in the ground!"

Alternately laughing our heads off or shaking them in amazement, we listened for the next few hours to their indignant accounts of the outrageous scrutiny they had undergone at the hands of the corpsmen. Whether or not the Nips ever "proved" their theory, it was as plain as the nose on Chief's face that these guys definitely wanted no links to the Japanese!

Although our rations improved after the Japanese army took us over in the spring and summer of 1944, we still didn't have enough to eat. Then, before we knew it, winter struck again—it seemed as though it was always winter in that place. Nothing had changed. With food scarcer than ever, our next meal became an obsession. And talk about sad looking! The average POW dropped about sixty pounds. Others, unable to work because of accidents or pneumonia, and put on half-rations, lost a good bit more.

We ate polished rice in Japan. Old and musty smelling, invariably full of weevils, it lacked the vitamin B1 that prevents beriberi, which was by now the most prevalent condition among us. We got an injection of the vitamin about every six months—not enough to keep us healthy. Just getting around became increasingly difficult and painful.

To keep the rest of the POWs from succumbing in droves to the disease, our medics stepped up the pace of vitamin-B shots. Drawing their supplies from the bottom of the box, they refilled the empty bottles with soapy water to mimic the appearance of the vitamin, hoping the Nips wouldn't notice. Fortunately, the war ended before they ran out.

A funny thing—the Japs always gave us shots in the chest. Observing that they injected their own people the same way, I was curious to know why. They told me it kept our arms from becoming sore. After all, a sore arm might make us miss a day's work or keep us from performing our jobs at the usual rate. They thought of all the angles.

After the cistern incident, in which I had nearly drowned and subsequently developed pneumonia, I was never the same. While I recovered from the pneumonia, I couldn't seem to pick up any strength in the months following the winter of 1944–45. That's when the beriberi that I had contracted in the Philippines began to affect the nerves in my back and legs.

One morning around 4:30, I fell down at tenko and stayed down. The Japs made sure I wasn't goofing off before dragging me back into the barracks to be examined. The Japanese medic came in and stuck me with a needle, then rubbed me with a brush. When he didn't get much of a response, he agreed that I must be suffering from beriberi. Of course, from the time they diagnosed a man as having the disease, injections of vitamin B ceased immediately, so that ended the vitamins for me.

Although they knew better, the Nips began subjecting us to an excruciating procedure said to cure beriberi. They ignited half-inch pieces of punk and placed them directly on the affected areas. This process, called "moxibustion," was based on an old superstition; it was supposed to drive the evil spirits out of our bodies.

I don't know about evil spirits, but it burned like hell! We had to lie there and endure the searing pain and the smell of our own smoldering flesh. Needless to say, I don't know of anyone who got up and walked after that. If we could have walked in the first place, we would have made tracks long before they gave us the treatment. All it did for me was leave scars on my hips and back.

All this time, the Red Cross was trying every trick in the book to get the Japs to allow them to inspect the conditions in the POW camps and get more food and medicines to us. The Japs not only refused the requests, they put strict limitations on the amount of supplies the Red Cross could ship.

Worse, when they received the boxes that the Red Cross sent us, the Japs broke them open and doled out the items one at a time. In a show of generosity and good will, they usually parceled out our "Christmas boxes" around November or December. But we weren't fooled. Along with the box that had been issued to me in the Philippines, I may have gotten three more boxes in Japan.

We knew that the guard Ishida and camp-staff members such as Tsujino made off with most of the stuff. Not only did he steal enormous amounts of Red Cross medicines to sell, but whenever Tsujino took part in inspections, he confiscated personal effects and supplies, such as the little bit of soap, cigarettes, and food we did manage to get from the Red Cross. While the Japanese army wouldn't have generally condoned stealing from the POWs, they failed to enforce their own rules in these matters. As a result, the local guards knew they had us by the throat.

The year before the war ended, I received my first box from home. The minute Mom was informed that I was alive and a prisoner of the Japanese in the summer of 1943, she went right out and, following the rules governing mail and packages to POWs, sent things she thought I might need from a list provided to the families by the War Department.

She addressed it to me in the Philippines, but by the time it arrived several months later I had already been shipped out to Japan. Somehow or other, this box followed me all the way from Cabanatuan to Hirohata, catching up with me seven or eight months later in the late spring of 1944. I can only imagine what kind of route the box took and the weather conditions it must have undergone before it reached me in Japan after all that time.

When I opened it, the vitamin pills and the malted-milk balls had fused together from the heat and humidity of the ship's hold into one shitty-looking, stinking mess. In addition, there were khaki shirts and pants, pillow slips, a pipe, soap, shaving gear, gum, one package of dried vegetable soup, handkerchiefs, playing cards, underwear, pencils, and a toothbrush. Oh yeah, she also included socks, three washcloths, two scapulars (one promising the wearer eternal life, the other a prayer to St. Joseph), a box of toothpicks, and even some pecans.

I wrote to thank her for the box. What I didn't tell her was that I had traded everything except the gum, soup, pecans, and scapulars to a Japanese civilian guard in exchange for something to eat. After I got home, I told her how good the clothes she sent had tasted. She looked at me as though I was crazy and said, "What do you mean, the clothes tasted good?"

When I explained, she shook her head sadly, and spoke of how my whole family would have gladly used their ration stamps—doing without items in short supply at home—to send me things like sugar, coffee, chocolate, and canned meats. But the Red Cross had said that the Japanese restricted the number of parcels a family could send to a POW to one a year. The Red Cross had also assured her that we were getting enough to eat. Mom said she didn't really buy that, but she couldn't do anything about it.

Not until the war was almost over did the camp staff try to get rid of the evidence of their cruelty—undelivered packages piled up in the warehouse—by distributing more food and supplies to the men from the backlog of boxes they had withheld. At that time I received one more box from my family.

But even as late as the night after Japan surrendered, Tsujino sneaked large portions of the Red Cross food out of camp. That food had been set aside for the sick, but Tsujino took it, leaving only spoiled and moldy fruit for the prisoners. His greed, however, also proved to be his undoing. I heard that after liberation he met with an unfortunate "accident," and I doubt that he survived.

That last summer of 1945, the Japs finally allowed the Swiss Red Cross to inspect the camp at Hirohata—for all the good it did us. The Japs ordered the prisoners to spruce up the camp for the arrival of the delegates.

I never saw any grass growing in the yard in Japan. With that many men tramping around, anything green and growing would have had a difficult time of it. So we swept the dirt and raked it smooth in the Japanese manner, cleaned up the barracks, and hosed everything else down. When we finished, it looked neat and presentable. The camp authorities made sure most of us were at work during the inspection. Although we didn't see them, I'm sure the inspectors were duly impressed. Too bad they didn't get to visit us during the previous winters. Greeted by filthy, flea-bitten, hollow-eyed, and freezing men, sick from disease and starvation, their report might have been very different.

23 Time Out

The Japanese people embrace a work ethic calling for personal sacrifice in order to achieve their national goals. During World War II, their total energy and focus for living centered on winning the war. They gave their all to the state and to the emperor, and they rationed, measured, and counted everything toward that end.

The authorities expected the average person to work until he or she dropped. They expected no less from us. The Japs kept us so busy working from sunup to sundown, there wasn't much time for leisure activities. Our days in Japan as prisoners of war were marked by hard labor and very little rest.

Every other Sunday was supposedly set aside for resting, but since they filled our morning with the usual drills, exercises, and footraces, that left only the afternoon to spend as we chose. Mostly we chose to spend it lying down. The guards laughed at us. Like the ones in the Philippines, they called us lazy. They couldn't understand why we didn't want to play games or engage in physical recreation. They kept asking us, "What do Americans do on holidays or vacations? How do you spend your free time?" Their standard reaction to our standard reply "Take a nap!" was to shake their heads in disbelief. But what did they expect? I didn't see them putting in killer days in the mills or staggering under loads of ore or coal as their old men and women workers had to do. If it hadn't been for the POWs, the guards would have had little interest in fun and games on their day off; we took their places in industry as coolies.

In order to survive the grueling regimen, we developed a philosophy of "us against them." Basically it boiled down to living hour by hour, making the most of every opportunity that came along, and taking our fun when and where we could find it.

More food remained our prime goal in life; we spent a lot of time planning the next heist. Getting even with the Japs in a million different ways kept things interesting. When we managed to pull off some little job successfully, morale soared.

Ishida, the Japanese mess sergeant we nicknamed Whiskey, had a monkey. The little fellow had been the old guy's constant companion ever since his days in the field on Borneo. We wondered if Whiskey's wife didn't like the monkey and refused to allow Whiskey to keep him at home, because he had become a fixture in camp. The monkey could always be counted on to brighten your day and was good for laughs when we had nothing else to laugh about. As clever as any kid, friendly, and always into some kind of mischief, he won us over with his antics. He scampered around, showing up here or there, often by hitching a ride on a GI's shoulder.

Ishida taught him how to bathe in a bucket in the kitchen, his favorite hangout. It's funny, but none of us begrudged him the little food or scraps he managed to pinch or beg. We considered him more than a pet. He had a definite human quality about him—more human than some of the Japs. Maybe we thought of him as one of us! We did have a few things in common.

A favorite with the prisoners, the monkey wasn't so popular with some of the Japanese staff and guards. More than once, they chased him out of headquarters or the guardhouse, screaming and yelling, sometimes threatening him with a broom. The little guy, too quick for them, usually left them in the dust as he made his getaway. Climbing up high, well out of reach of those below, he'd sit there scolding them in high-pitched squeals, ears flattened against his tiny head and teeth bared in a show of bravado.

He frequently stole a guard's hat—one of his favorite tricks—and ran up the grille surrounding the smokestack on the galley roof. He'd dance around up there with the Jap's hat, chattering away, now and then coming down just close enough to tantalize the guard before running back up. This, of course, infuriated his victim even more. It was a regular show, comical as hell, and sure to create a crowd of onlookers.

The Japs had absolutely no sense of humor about the whole thing and always chased the onlookers away. Ishida, the only one able to do anything with the monkey, would end up having to coax him down by trading a bit of food for the hat.

Toward the end of the war, when our bombers were making hundreds of daily raids over Japan, with a heavy concentration in our area, tensions ran high in camp, and one day the monkey pulled one trick too many. He sprang onto the shoulder of one of the Japs and tried to snatch the cap off his head. But this guard was faster than most; he caught the little fellow before he could run away. Taking out all his fears and frustrations on the innocent animal, he viciously broke the monkey's neck before anyone could stop him.

The news spread through camp like wildfire. This was it—this time the Japs had gone too far! Everyone rebelled. Hard-bitten men, no longer sentimental about much, whose humanity had seemingly grown cold, who called everybody else "sonuvabitch"—were hopping mad! We loved that little monkey; we identified with him. Watching the spunky little creature scavenge for food, harassing his captors and driving them nuts every chance he got, made us comrades at heart. Besides, he meant no harm; he was just playing. That bastard had no right to kill him.

Shouting, yelling, cussing, defiant, and unafraid, we stormed into the courtyard, ready to riot. The heavily armed soldiers responded quickly by surrounding us, threatening to shoot the first man who made a run at them. They didn't scare us! We stood in the middle of the compound, shaking our fists at the Japs, telling them in no uncertain terms how we felt, first in English, then in Japanese.

In the end, our show of bravado panned out like the monkey's. We really couldn't do anything about it. The Japs had the upper hand. We had no choice but to disperse before they shot us. But I believe that for a moment—just for a moment—I saw fear in the eyes of the guards who faced us.

Although nearly every religious denomination was represented in camp, we had no chaplain in Hirohata. Under the circumstances, we did the best we could. An enlisted navy man held a Protestant worship service once a month and another led a Catholic prayer group once a week. For the most part, each man had to come to grips with his beliefs in his own way.

Brought up as a Roman Catholic, I somehow managed to hang on to the Christian medal I wore around my neck throughout the war. The Nips did not confiscate the rosary, issued by my Catholic chaplain, when they captured me. Although my coveralls hid the medal and the rosary remained in my pocket, I really didn't try to hide them. On Luzon, when my clothes finally wore out and I had to wear a G-string while driving a truck, the medal, worn on a chain with my Japanese dog tag, was plainly visible to everyone.

The only comment I ever got from the Japanese was when occasionally a man would point to my chest and say, "Christo?"

"Hai," I'd reply. He would nod, as if he understood who Christo was and what He meant to me.

I thought it was kind of peculiar that they never poked fun at me or threatened to take either the medal or my rosary away. They seemed to tolerate all religions, yet they permitted only two Japanese clergy—a Catholic priest and a Protestant minister—to hold two services in Hirohata.

On the day the priest came to say Mass, GIs of every faith crowded into the barracks. Roman Catholics stood next to Baptists, Methodists, and Lutherans. Everyone forgot their religious differences—if they even existed at this point—and united together in worship and prayer, realizing that we needed all the spiritual help we could get.

Father stood on a bench to say Mass, and he spoke to us in excellent English. He kept his sermon short and based on a real hope and trust in God. Then he announced, "Although I am forbidden to hear the individual confessions of the Catholics in the room or to have any personal contact with you men, I will now grant you a general absolution so that you might receive Communion." We bowed our heads to receive his blessing and then filed past as he distributed the Elements of the Eucharist.

The authorities never allowed the Vatican to send representatives to the prison camps, but they managed to get us a few musical instruments. I remember that we received a guitar, a trumpet, and even a trombone at one point.

For some reason, we never put on any skits or plays in Japan as we had in the Philippines. Maybe our camp staff didn't allow such goings on, or maybe we were just too worn out by that time. But sometimes, just before lights out, someone would pick up an instrument and begin to play.

The sweet sound of an American song, played on a lone trumpet, touched us at times when nothing else could. The thought of being free, of going home to our families and loved ones again, was a physical yearning that never left us. I don't think any of us ever doubted that someday, somehow, this war would end, and we'd all be together with our families again. While that hope kept us going, it didn't pay to dwell on it. That was dangerous. It kept your mind off the job at hand—staying alive.

Whenever the Japanese celebrated their religious feast days, they excused us from work. In the fall of 1944, we witnessed an elaborate ceremony, held in our area, honoring their rice god. The authorities, not above using our captivity as a morale builder for their people, invited the civilians living nearby to come into the compound as part of the festivities. They ordered the barracks cleaned up in anticipation of the special occasion. Normally, we looked forward to having a day off, but I was not especially enthusiastic about being on public display, as though we were animals in a zoo. Also, word of the bombing raids on the home islands began to trickle in, and it made us nervous about rubbing elbows with the locals and their possible reaction to us. We needn't have worried. The whole affair proved to be a break from our deadly-dull routines and was really quite interesting.

In the distance, the delicate tinkling of bells, borne on the autumn breeze, signaled the start of the festival. We rushed through the gate, thrown wide by the guards to allow us to watch the spectacle as it came into view. The sights and sounds, so foreign to most of the men, held us all spellbound.

Black cotton sashes crisscrossed the chests of the drummers, who set the pace for the dancers. As they whirled and pranced along the road, the brilliant reds, greens, golds, and blues of their exotic costumes fused together in a wonderful kaleidoscope of color. The mournful wailing of the pipes wove a strangely melodic background for prayerful chants and songs of thanksgiving; the music was punctuated by loud crashing cymbals and the deep resonance of brass gongs.

Dozens of men, swaying in measured cadence to the beat of the drums, followed behind the musicians and singers, their headbands wet with sweat as they struggled under the weight of an elaborate platform supported on long poles carried on their shoulders.

In the center of the colorful, intricately carved wooden structure, a statue of one of their Shinto deities sat in splendor on a golden chair, his overhead canopy draped in yards and yards of blazing red silk. His terrible face, made up and rouged like a woman's, inspired awe and wonder in the people. He was richly dressed in layers of jewel-toned brocades that glimmered and sparkled in the sunlight. Garlands of flowers encircled his feet and twined around the columns of the shrine, spilling over the edges in a cascade of vivid blooms. Yellow sheaves of rice had been placed in his arms as an offering of the "First Rice."

Hundreds of Japanese peasants, dressed in their best kimonos, respectfully followed the procession. All along the route, farmers and their families lined the road, bowing low as the wonderfully gaudy, noisy pageant passed by. Then they, too, joined the long line, taking their places behind the rest. When the parade drew abreast of the camp, it turned in at the gates and entered the compound.

Anxious not to miss a thing, we joined the crowds pushing their way through the entrance. Inside, seeing our eagerness to join in the fun, the civilians made a path for us so we could have a clear shot of the entertainment.

Swaying, gyrating in step with the tempo of the music, the celebrants slowly made their way around the courtyard. "Boy, this is just like Mardi Gras!" I said. These strange but splendid and ancient rituals were not a whole lot different from the annual parades I had enjoyed so much in New Orleans. Caught up in the carnival-like atmosphere, I almost yelled out, "Hey, throw me something, mister!"

Although I recognized a few of the people who lived nearby and worked in the mill, many of the civilians had never seen a Westerner before. Surprisingly, they were not hostile. They eyed us politely, plainly curious about the "round eyes." The GIs frankly enjoyed watching the graceful Japanese women twirling their lovely painted parasols as they swooped and bowed, balanced on the wooden geta we never mastered, their tiny steps confined by their slender skirts.

Trying to absorb everything I saw, I attempted to engage one fellow in conversation to learn what I could about the meaning of the festival. But between his nonexistent English and my halting Japanese, we didn't get very far. He frowned, concentrating on my words, but the more I talked, the more confused he became. Finally, bowing three or four times, he backed away, escaping with relief.

In the end, we had to rely on some of the camp staff for enlightenment. All Japanese are proud of their heritage, the history of their country, and they would talk about its customs at the drop of a hat. The guards, used to our lingo, more or less supplied us with a rundown of the harvest festival.

After the people had paraded around the courtyard a few times, they drifted on down the road to the next village, taking the mood of gaiety and merriment with them. Most of the villagers from Hirohata left as well, except for a few men and boys who stayed to hoist their kites into the afternoon wind from the rice field across the way.

The guards shut the gates, cutting off our view. But the party wasn't over yet. Closed gates and a high fence were no obstacle to the high-flying kites. All eyes in camp traced the progress of the beautiful, intricately constructed works of art that seemed to come in every color of the rainbow, in all shapes and sizes—some even cleverly designed to look like birds flying overhead.

We found places on the ground and, for the rest of the day, quietly watched the show against the backdrop of purple mountains in the west; a cobalt-blue sky gradually turned to crimson as the sun went down and then to navy blue as the light faded completely.

April 29, Emperor Hirohito's birthday, was always observed with great joy and happiness by the Japanese. For the past four years they had marked the occasion in the camps with extra rations all around, and for that reason it became a great favorite with us, too. In addition, we could take the day off—a definite plus in our books. However, when they hauled out the baseball bats and balls, organized races, or made us play games, it was enough to take the wind right out of our sails. These people just couldn't relax! We came to the conclusion that their makeup differed vastly from ours and—even without a war to complicate things in the future—would probably always lead to strained relations between the two races.

We became convinced of this when, some time later, a few of the guards proposed a fishing trip for the prisoners. Fishing was never my bag; I had always been interested in other game. But some of the guys thought it might make for a change. So when they passed the word, "Everyone who wants to go fishing, get down to the gate," a large crowd assembled there in no time. I think the prisoners envisioned sitting on the bank of a quiet stream, leaning up against a shade tree, and taking their ease while they patiently waited for the fish to bite.

The Japs chose the first ten men they saw, leaving the rest extremely teed off. Back home, fishing had been a passion for most of the guys, so they returned to the barracks with long faces. "Of all the rotten luck," they griped. They spent the rest of the day nursing their disappointment, imagining the great fun the others were having, not to mention the tasty fish fry they would enjoy when they got back.

What is it about Americans? Are we unusually gullible? We never seemed to learn that the Japanese had their own way of doing things. We should have known things would somehow turn out differently from what we pictured. When the ten "lucky" fellows returned that evening, the expressions on their faces registered complete and total disgust.

"Hey, what happened? Where's the fish?" we asked as they slunk into the barracks. They looked terrible—hot, exhausted, dirty, and wet.

"Jesus, what did you guys do, fall in the damn creek?"

"Aw hell," one of them answered. "That's the last time I go fishing with a Jap!"

That caught our attention! Amid all the questions, we finally got the story. It seems that after they had picked ten men for the expedition down by the gate, the guards took them over to headquarters. The Americans figured they'd pick up their fishing poles and buckets for the outing. They got the buckets all right, but no fishing poles. Instead they got shovels.

Puzzled, but still enthusiastic about getting in a little fishing, they followed the guards down to the little creek a half-mile from camp. What they found when they got there, though, was not exactly what they had in mind. Our hosts had managed to screw up yet another thing as simple as a fishing trip. Oh, yeah, the picturesque little mountain stream was there, a nice tree overhung the water, and there was even a cool breeze blowing. But that's where the fantasy ended.

When the would-be fishermen caught sight of the Japs' recent handiwork, they guessed the reason for the shovels and buckets, and every bit of joy and enthusiasm went straight out of them. I mean, it just died right there!

Where rushing water once cascaded over stones polished smooth over time by the swift current, rocks, dirt, and debris now blocked the middle of the creek. The Japs had dammed up a section, diverting the flow into a small lagoon, and had taken the prisoners there to bail it out.

No one got to sit in the shade and dangle a line in the brook. Far from it! They spent the day hauling water out of the pool bucket by bucket. The sun was low in the sky by the time they got down to the bottom. Their reward for all that hard work? A few paltry fish flopping around in the mud.

"If that's what the Japanese call fishing, the hell with them," the men declared. "We don't go fishing anymore."

And it was the first and last expedition of its kind.

24   Life in the Hirohata Hilton

In the tropics, a man can make do with just a loincloth. In Japan, clothes turned out to be almost as important as food. The cheap blue-denim Filipino uniforms issued before we left for Japan, wore out quickly in the steel mill and provided very little protection from the cruel, razor-sharp winds off the Inland Sea that first winter.

The Japanese army began issuing clothing salvaged from the bodies of our dead servicemen in other camps. A mixture of army, navy, marine, and air corps uniforms were shipped in and distributed to us according to size and availability—not according to the branch of service we belonged to. You couldn't tell who was who anymore.

Thrown together, our service language got all mixed up, too. Half the time I talked like a dogface, the other half like a swabbie. Around the barracks, we spoke of going to the latrine. When unloading ships in the harbor, we called it the head. Walls became bulkheads. Quitting time was either oh-five-hundred hours or five bells, depending on who was talking.

After a while, even our American-made uniforms were getting shabby, full of holes and tears. The camp authorities switched us to Japanese work uniforms made from wood fiber. They looked pretty nice—sort of a shiny, greenish color with a herringbone pattern. But they turned out to be like our blankets—stiff, scratchy, and uncomfortable.

Although the outfits didn't keep us very warm, that was the least of their drawbacks. Getting too close to a stove or furnace while wearing them could be risky. The wood fibers scorched real quick, and sparks from the fires we built in the winter burned holes in the uniforms, sometimes setting them ablaze.

We always seemed to be in hot water with the Japs over the clothes. We should take better care of the suits, they said. "They are supposed to last four or five years, and here they are, wearing out in less than a year!"

If clothes were a problem, shoes were impossible. The steel mill ate up the carabao-leather shoes made for us by the Filipinos. We patched, glued, nailed, and sewed, trying to salvage what we could, until they were no more. The Japs told us we'd just have to wear wooden geta because that's all they had. Japan had run out of leather, too.

If we didn't look like a bunch of clodhoppers, walking around trying to balance on four narrow pieces of wood turned sideways! I found out real quick that it's one thing to wear geta while driving a truck and another thing to wear them in the role of a coolie laborer. I spent a lot of time with my toes sandwiched in the thongs on top, my heel on the ground, and my instep painfully astride the edge of the hard sole.

Working in a steel mill in that kind of footgear was challenging, to say the least. We balanced our loads while teetering around on high heels like a bunch of guys in drag.

Trying to "walk the plank" up into the gondolas with a "ten-bo" full of limestone slung over our shoulders was no picnic either. Our female co-workers laughed as we stumbled and fell up the ramp. They giggled even more at the colorful words we muttered under our breath. It would have been funny if it hadn't been so awkward and even dangerous.

Winter was worse. When it rained or snowed, the Japanese people wore really tall geta. They must have been four or five inches high. They kept your feet dry, if you could stay on them, but the GIs never got the hang of it. For most of us, the snow piled up underneath our insteps as we walked to work. Soon we were slipping on the icy "innersoles" and sliding right out of the mini-stilts. More trouble than they were worth, we'd end up taking them off and finish the trip barefooted. Now, brother, that was cold! It's a wonder we didn't end up with frostbite.

The Japs, realizing the clumsy Americans would never feel at home on the geta, finally furnished us with *tabi*, a kind of split-toed tennis shoe, somewhat resembling a mitten, made out of canvas and fastened with clips up the back. While they were a slight improvement and far more practical, they hurt our Western feet so much, we never got used to them. Before the end of the war, the Japs would replace them with a plain-toed version, making life more bearable.

Bathing in camp was a luxury that was permitted every other Sunday. The standard bath setup in Japan looked like a small indoor swimming pool. It measured about fifteen feet square by two feet deep, with a coal-fired unit built into the side. Sixty kilos of coal at a time was all the fuel we could have to heat the building and the water—again, not enough for the job.

Although we had a day off every other Sunday, bath day did not necessarily coincide with our rest day. If it did, we had all afternoon to schedule baths. But if bath night fell on the Sunday we worked, it was best to make a deal with one of the honchos to work a little harder and finish up early, in order to beat the crowd. Otherwise you were exposed to a tub full of water that had taken on an evil-looking color, depending on which detail hit the bathhouse first. The guys unloading coal immediately turned it black; the ones working in limestone that day endowed it with a light gray film that floated on the top, coating everything it touched; and the stevedores unloading iron ore turned it a muddy red. By the time we all had a shot at bathing, the water had turned a shade that's not even in the spectrum.

The trouble was, we didn't follow the Japanese method of bathing. All the enclosed bathhouses were constructed with cement floors that sloped to a drain, allowing the people to use small wooden buckets to rinse off outside the tub, soap up, and rinse off again before stepping into the pool to sit and soak. Since they were nicely scrubbed down by then, the water in the pool remained clean. Not us! No matter how many times the Japs instructed us in the proper way to bathe, we insisted on jumping right in, straight off.

"Americans are not civilized!" they'd fuss and fume. "They are not cultured, have no finesse, and don't even know how to use a bathtub!"

Without question, we needed a bath, but thawing out was the main

Bath night in Camp Hirohata, Japan.

Illustration by Lauren Y. Pursley

reason for diving in and skipping the preliminaries and a good way to warm up in a hurry in that hostile winter climate. Unfortunately, by the time you began to feel halfway human again, there were usually so many others in there with you, it was next to impossible to get clean. Sometimes I couldn't tell whose feet I was washing, mine or the fellow's next to me.

Despite having to shovel out three inches of brown muck left in the bottom of the pool the next day, we never changed our minds about the art of bathing, and the Japanese finally gave up, saying we were hopeless.

Not being able to bathe more than two or three times a month, coupled with the inability to wash our clothes in hot water, resulted in fleas, fleas, and more fleas. An influx of sixty-five extra souls was added to the equation in June 1945 when for some reason the Japs took about 170 men out of the Number 2 barracks and transferred them elsewhere—destination unknown. The remaining men got thrown in with us; we now had three hundred men jammed together under one roof.

Pretty soon, under these conditions, lice—big as grains of rice—began to flourish along with the fleas, making our lives even more miserable. If the authorities had only let us take our clothes down to the mill and boil them in the slag pits, we might have kept the problem under control. But the Japs didn't see it that way. The only means we had of combating the lice was to sit in the light and inspect the seams in our clothes, killing the things one by one.

I got used to the lice, and after a while they didn't bother me so much. But I hated the damn *nomi* (fleas). They left tracks—red welts that marked their trail over my skin.

A little scruffy white dog belonging to one of the Japanese civilian guards liked to hang around with us. The guard's American counterpart, a marine responsible for keeping tabs on the men who went to the latrine after lights out, often made his rounds with the pooch tied to his belt. This was a feeble attempt to collect as many fleas on the dog as he could before brushing them off outside. Since the mutt spent the days with his master while we worked, the Japs were soon bothered with as many nomi as we were.

Things got so bad, the camp staff ordered a big house-cleaning on our day off. We stripped down the barracks and hauled every bit of clothing, bedding, and equipment down to the little mountain stream. We dumped it all into the ice-cold water and secured everything with heavy rocks to drown the little buggers. Later that afternoon, when everything had been washed clean by the swift current, we spread our belongings in the sun to dry.

Back at camp, we fire-hosed the barracks from top to bottom, flushing out fleas by the jillions. Swept away in torrents of water, they looked like black sawdust coming out of there. Our efforts paid off for about a week; then the little SOBs were back, full force!

The different concessions were supposedly paying for our services all this time, although no money ever changed hands. We'd been in Japan for almost a year and a half, and decided we must have a small fortune accrued on the books. Maybe it was time to go shopping.

On the first of the month, we would sign the register or payroll book before getting our allotment of cigarettes. We tallied up what the Japs said we had coming (about three thousand yen) hoping to buy some food or extra cigarettes. After all, you can promise your mind, but you've got to deliver to your stomach, even if it's only cigarette smoke.

Since both food and cigarettes were on *haikyu,* which meant they were rationed and not for sale, the Nips offered us a list of other things that we could purchase—things like chopsticks, wooden buckets, geta, bento baskets, and . . . nomi powder. "Hey now," we said. "Flea powder is something we can definitely use!"

Most of the stuff on the list was issued to us on a regular basis, so a representative group of men from our barracks held a brief meeting. Everyone agreed to put the whole three thousand yen on flea powder. We notified the camp commander, who wrote up the requisition and sent one of the guards into town to buy it. When he came back, each man got four tubes of the stuff.

None of us could read the Japanese instructions printed on the package, but we could see that the hollow cardboard cylinders were made in two parts, with one smaller than the other, designed to slide back and forth like a pump. As we worked the simple mechanism, it sprayed a fine, tan-colored powder out one end.

"Hot dog!" we declared. "Maybe we can't buy more food or smokes, but at least we're gonna get rid of the fleas and sleep good tonight!" And we went to work spraying the devil out of our bunks. We broadcast it under the platforms, up and down the aisles, and even dusted the dog with it. Choking clouds of flea powder hung in the air when we were done.

That night, things were worse than before. It seemed like the fleas came from all over Japan to our place. No one got any sleep. Everyone grumbled and swore while they clawed their skin the whole terrible night long. In the morning, I could see my bunk was more alive than ever with the jumping little bastards. My arms and legs looked like one big red welt. Exhausted, I said to myself, *This makes no sense. What in the world happened?*

As we assembled in the courtyard for the count, the guard who bought the flea powder the day before asked one of the men how we spent the night. "Nomi powda wuk velly good, ne?"

"Good?" the sleepy prisoner growled. "It was terrible!"

"Wha' hoppen?" asked the surprised Nip.

"I don't know. We can't figure it out. We sprayed everything down with the stuff; we didn't miss a thing, but it didn't work. Last night was the worst night I've ever spent in my life. Today, we have more fleas than we had yesterday."

"You put powda in bunk?" he frowned.

"Well, yeah, of course we did."

"No, no, you not put in bunk!" the guard said excitedly. "You must put Japanese powda for nomi away from bunk. Nomi reeve bunk, go to powda!"

Grinning from ear to ear, the guard turned and said something to another sentry. They began to laugh. A couple of soldiers came over to see what was so funny. After that, it didn't take long for the story to spread throughout the camp. Pretty soon, everyone was pointing and laughing at the itching, scratching dummies standing in line.

That evening, we swept everything down and shook out our bedding, hoping to get rid of what turned out to be flea bait. It didn't help. For the next month, the fleas seemed to multiply. The Japs weren't about to let us forget our mistake, either. Within a day or so, the mill people were in on the joke. From then on, every time the word *nomi* was mentioned, they roared. It got to be the biggest doggone joke of the war. And, in a way, I guess it was.

If fleas and lice bothered us, earthquakes bothered the Japanese even more; they didn't like them one bit! The first time I felt one in the Philippines, I knew what it was without being told, even though I had no experience with that sort of thing. There's a peculiar noise that comes from the bowels of the earth; to me it sounded like a giant bowling ball gathering momentum as it speeds down the alley.

In Japan, there might be a mild tremor or two every week. The buildings would shake, things would swing and sway, but it only lasted a minute or so. Some quakes were rougher than others. Belongings fell off the shelves or "walked" across the floor when the ground shook and rippled in waves. While it could be unsettling, most of us took it in stride.

They didn't. The temblors really worried the Nips. Japan has a history of violent earthquakes. In fact, the Japanese word for earthquake is *jishin*—which roughly translates as "people die." In 1923, fires following a major quake practically destroyed Tokyo and Yokohama. The memories of total devastation left everyone afraid that another of the same magnitude might occur at any time.

One day a particularly strong one struck the area, making believers of us all. It was a work day, so the barracks was empty except for me and two other men on sick leave. Suddenly everything began to vibrate and shake as though a column of tanks was rolling by. The unmistakable sound, produced by volcanic rocks slipping below the earth's crust, grew loud and ominous. I don't know what it would have measured on today's Richter scale, but it may have been a seven.

Our metal canteen cups danced across the shelves. Overhead drop lights swung in circles. Up on the roof, concrete shingles snapped and popped like corn. The heaving floor shifted under our feet, and the windows rattled so hard, many of them shattered. The barracks' structural timbers, twisting first one way then another in what felt like a figure eight, creaked and groaned in protest, making me think the walls would fall in on us next.

Although my mind signaled flight, I couldn't move, so I just hung onto the bunk uprights for dear life. Although it probably lasted for only a few minutes, the quake seemed to go on and on, building to a rafter-shaking crescendo before finally leveling off.

When it was over, we congratulated each other on being alive. Bits of glass, sprinkled over everything, sparkled like diamonds in the dusty sunbeams streaming through the now paneless window. It crunched underfoot as we tentatively surveyed the scene. Nothing was left on hooks or shelves; our belongings and equipment lay heaped on the floor.

Outside, all the water had sloshed out of the fire tubs on the corners of the buildings. Miraculously, most of the damage was cosmetic. Except for smashed windows and plenty of shingles on the ground, everything else appeared largely intact.

That night in camp, the men at work talked excitedly about what they were doing and how they coped when the tremor struck. Like us, everyone was amazed at the little damage done to the camp and the mill, thanks to the flexible construction methods used by the Japanese.

For the next few days, a series of fairly strong aftershocks caught everybody off guard, sending us scrambling for safety. We weren't as nonchalant as we thought; I was as jumpy as the Nips.

But the earthquake taught me a lesson. When Mother Nature got into the act, she quickly reduced us mere mortals to a common denominator. For a short time at least, we were neither Americans, Brits, nor Japanese. We were just human beings, all in the same boat, afraid of dying.

25 Friendly Faces

The Japanese army had devised a rotational system of conscription, requiring a man to serve in combat for one year, be put on reserve status
for another year, then return to civilian life for the third year, usually to
work in industry. When his civilian year was up, unless physically im-
paired, he was called up to fight again in the field. If young enough, he'd
repeat the whole process.

Most of the Japanese honchos, in the military at one time or another, presently served in civilian roles. A few had been wounded and
declared unfit for duty, while others were old and past their prime. The
red armband they wore signified their full authority over the POWs.
Some of them ignored us. Some of them hated Americans so much,
they constantly used their positions to impose harsh punishments for
the slightest excuse, and generally gave everyone a hard time just for the
hell of it.

While these honchos could be tough, most of them just tried to do
their jobs. Getting the maximum work out of us made them look good.
Not meeting their quotas often spelled the difference between being
boss one day and coolie the next.

Then there was Pop, as we called him. Eighty-five years old and blind
as a bat, he would split his last cigarette with you. He worked the gang
on the scrap pile. It was a good detail, if you could get it. We'd sit up
there all day, supposedly breaking up the larger pieces of metal that had
to be sorted into like kind for catalyst in the furnaces. Since the pile

measured a mile long and two city blocks wide in the beginning, it was impossible to check on the work we actually did. As long as we banged away, and the old man thought we were hard at it, he was happy.

He carried a big, old-fashioned pocket watch in the pocket of his blue uniform, often referring to it during the day. He could barely see his hand in front of his face, but every now and then, one of the guys would call down and ask, "Hey, Pop, what time is it?" as though we had an appointment in town or a hot date to keep. He'd pull out his watch, hold it up in front of his eyes, and tell us the time, religiously.

Next to the scrap pile sat two warehouses where women workers separated the different metals or glass into big trays. We had to empty the trays into sacks then haul them over to the conveyors in the mill. The honcho in charge was usually busy overseeing both warehouses and frequently left us unsupervised. As long as we kept up with the women, that's all that mattered to him.

He didn't even mind if we spoke to them while doing our jobs, making this one of the more pleasant work details. But he warned us about talking when other Japanese honchos were around. He needn't have worried. If any mill boss came by, well, we appeared to be on the ball!

The women usually treated us well. One young girl, around seventeen or eighteen (Japanese babies were considered a year old at birth), sometimes shared a little of her rice with me. She always made sure I had tea, and we became friendly, making small talk—me in my bad Japanese, which made her giggle. Noticing that I smoked a pipe, she had her little seven-year-old brother pick up cigarette butts and save the tobacco for me.

Mariko told me that she came from a small village near Himeji but now lived with her parents and brother in a barracks that had been built for the mill workers. For a short time, she made a big difference in my everyday existence. If I landed a job in the sorting shed, I didn't mind going to work so much. At least I could look forward to seeing her sweet face and ready smile.

Frankly, I was sick to death of a world filled with rough men who smelled bad, acted crude or cruel, and looked just plain ugly. Judging from all the chit-chat in the shed between the prisoners and the women workers, the other men felt the same way. What a rare treat to speak to a female again! The fact that they were kind, recognizing we were human beings too, impressed us. We would never forget them.

By the time the war was nearly over, a lot of the civilian guards in camp were almost as hungry as we were. A few of them let it be known that they would help us get some of the larger foodstuffs into camp if we'd split the food with them fifty-fifty. A buddy and I worked up a private deal with one of the sentries. Since the guards never examined him as he was going into or out of camp, we'd make the switch as we went through the gate but before they searched us. He'd haul our take into camp on his bicycle, and we'd collect our half later.

He proved to be a valuable ally. He was never caught with the fish or other foodstuffs we stole off the ships and smuggled into the compound. For many of us, his help probably spelled the difference between life and death, increasing the odds that we'd live long enough to see the end of the war.

During the year and a half I spent in Japan, all of us worked for nearly every concession in the mill. We put in several months at the coal company. When lunchtime came, we'd head for the little shack to eat our bentos brought from camp.

One of the women workers had the job of preparing the noon tea. The Japs gave her this "easy" assignment because she was pregnant. Every day she hauled the water into the shed and cut wood for the fire. Despite the hard work, she never failed to be polite. She always made extra tea so that after the Japanese workers had been served she had plenty left over for us. We appreciated this, knowing she didn't have to do it.

As she got farther along in her pregnancy, we all began to take an active interest in her. Acting like a bunch of surrogate fathers, we'd ask, "When's the baby due?"

She'd duck her head, answering shyly, "Maybe three more months."

Watching her struggle with heavy buckets of water or split logs with an axe almost as big as she was, we felt sorry for her. It just didn't seem right that she had to work so hard in her condition, so we started helping out when we could. We took turns. I'd chop the wood one day while someone else hauled the buckets of water to the shed. The next day, other POWs would take over. She always seemed so grateful. You could tell this kind of attention was new to her; it surprised and pleased her. It made us happy to be of service.

The birth of the baby became a much-anticipated event in the lives of the work detail. The potential papas pestered her with questions. Was this her first baby? Did she want a boy or a girl? Would she go to the hospital, or have the baby at home? Did she plan on coming back after the baby's birth, or was she staying home permanently? If not, how soon would she be back?

Mamasan, as we called her, good-naturedly satisfied our curiosity. This would be her second child. Her husband wanted a boy, but it didn't really matter to her. The baby would be born at home, like her first. Women usually worked until the baby came—and yes, she planned to return to the mill immediately. She would have one day of maternity leave—the day the baby was born. Laughing, she said she hoped it would come on a Saturday so she could have Sunday (her usual rest day) off as well. This floored us! It wasn't fair! Surely she needed more time off than one day. American women certainly did!

Amused by our concern, Mamasan said it was their custom for pregnant women to work in the fields or factories until their time came, go home, have the baby, and return to work the very next day with the baby tied to their backs. They had been doing it that way for more than a thousand years.

Nevertheless, we were amazed to find Mamasan making noon tea in the bento shack one Monday morning with a tiny infant strapped to her back, its little head, covered with shiny black hair, rolling back and forth while she worked. The baby girl had been born on Sunday, her mother's one day off.

26 The Man in the Top Hat

A network of canals, running north and south, had been dug near the coast for hauling goods to market by barge; we crossed several of the canals on the way to the mill every morning. One day I was startled to see an old but immaculately kept black Packard parked on the bridge, with an elderly man dressed in a morning coat, striped trousers, and silk top hat sitting in the back seat. A manservant with a white linen towel over his arm stood nearby, tending a pot of boiling water on a hibachi. *Is he about to take tea?* I wondered.

Several weeks later I saw him again, this time leaning over the railing as a barge approached the overpass. The Japanese barges were not like the big covered vessels that plowed up and down the mighty Mississippi River back home. These looked more like gondolas—narrow, open, flat-bottomed boats with pointed prows and sterns, propelled by poling with a single oar.

The cargo in this barge was foul-looking and stunk to high heaven. As he drew near the bridge, the bargeman extended a long dipper full of the goo up to the old man to sample. Reaching down, the elegantly groomed fellow stuck his fingers into the cup and rubbed them together for half a minute. Then he turned and rinsed them in the bowl of hot water held out respectfully by the faithful retainer.

For the next few nights, I racked my brain trying to figure it all out. The third time he appeared on the bridge, I had to admit that my powers of observation had failed me. Bowing politely to one of the soldiers who marched us to work every morning and spoke a little pidgin, I said, "Sumimasen, anokatawa donate desuka? (Please excuse me—who is that gentleman?)"

The haitai gave me a big, toothy smile and replied in elementary Japanese, "He is one of the richest men in Japan."

Interesting, but I had pretty much worked that out already. Plumbing the depths of my sketchy knowledge of Japanese I asked, "What is his occupation?"

"He is fertilizer merchant, and he is checking the barge for purity of product," said the soldier.

"Fune niwa naniga?" I asked. "What's in the barge?"

"Japanese fertilizer—the best in the world."

"Do iu imi desuka?" I said. "I don't understand you."

"Very rich is Japanese benjo daiben [shit] for growing crops."

"E! honto desuka?" I said. "What! Is it true?"

"Hai. Yes. After collecting, it is sometimes shipped by barge from Osaka to merchants who buy it then sell to farmers."

Baloney! I thought at first. But wait a minute—it might explain the stink coming from the barge. Maybe the story was just crazy enough to be true. I pressed the soldier for more details.

"When the bargeman comes near the bridge," he told me, "he must dig down deep and fill his ladle by scraping the bottom of the hold before lifting it up to be examined."

"Naze tashikameru no desuka?" I asked. "Why feel it?"

"Each load he buys will be inspected to determine whether dirt or sand has been added along the way," said the soldier. Putting his thumb and forefinger together, he slowly rubbed them back and forth to illustrate his point. "If smooth to the touch, it passes the test. If gritty, he knows they are cheating him."

I stared at the soldier for a second, trying not to laugh. Surely he was kidding; the Japanese loved their little jokes, after all. But my time had run out. The guard, impatient with my questions when he noticed that we had fallen behind the rest of the men, roughly waved me on.

Still intrigued by the man in the top hat, I hated leaving before I had all the answers, so I sneaked a look over my shoulder at the transaction still taking place on the bridge. Well, whaddaya know! The haitai must have been on the level after all. The old man had finished washing up and was drying his hands on a fresh towel. Smiling, he seemed to okay the deal with a quick bob of the head before turning to leave. The cargo of crap must have come through with flying colors.

With this bit of business apparently over for the day, the driver of the ancient automobile snapped to attention, ceremoniously holding the door open for his master. With a show of dignity that belied his profession, the royal merchant of manure settled once more into the back seat of the car. Watching him slowly drive away like he was first cousin to the emperor, I said to myself, "Well I'll be damned, I guess I've seen everything!"

During my extended visit to the Far East as an imperial guest, I discovered that the crap merchants were the wealthiest men in the Orient. Manure was certainly big business in Japan. By adding liberal doses of

The Man With
the Top Hat

"The Man with the Top Hat": Japanese fertilizer magnate checking the raw material.
Illustration by Lauren Y. Pursley

"night soil," or human waste, to the thin layer of dirt covering their landfills, the Japanese transformed these barren places into fertile farmland.

Since no sewer systems existed in the country, every house had a benjo, or outhouse, with a clean-out access in the backyard. Once a week the people lined the road with containers, in much the same way that milk cans once lined the roads early in the morning in rural America. Only these weren't milk cans, and they weren't waiting for the dairyman to make a home delivery. These cans held crap from the benjo. The "honey merchant," as he was nicknamed, came around in his ox-drawn cart with a wooden tank mounted on the back to collect it, paying his customers so much a can.

Farmers dug big pits out in the fields to store the stuff while it aged. Two such vats sat out in the middle of the rice paddy across from our camp. Low retaining walls had been built around them to keep people from accidentally falling in—although every now and then a POW, making a sudden detour into someone's field to snitch a turnip on his way to the mill, managed to find a way. Once the contents were well seasoned, they were used to fertilize the adjacent farms several times a year. "Honey" was a valuable commodity, and the businessmen who dealt in it made a killing off the farmers.

All around the camp, the landscape was dotted with two-acre plots where families lived and cultivated their crops. The ever-efficient Japanese in this area of Honshu grew two crops a year in their fields. While the wheat grew in the winter, they sowed rice seedlings in cold frames. After harvesting the wheat, they flooded the paddies and planted the seedlings, which were now about five to six inches high.

In the fall, when the rice was full grown, they cut it, shocked it, and put it alongside the road to dry. Meanwhile, wheat had been started in beds, and as soon as the fields were drained, they repeated the whole process.

The farmers did everything by hand, using a long hoe or sickle. But in spite of these old-fashioned methods, they got more yield per square inch than we did back home because of their brand of fertilizer. I saw fields where I didn't think grass would grow, let alone tomatoes, turnips, and radishes three times the size of those harvested in the States.

This was potent stuff in more ways than one! The fields down south had a fresh, earthy smell during plowing season. Springtime in Japan smelled like something else. Although it was beautiful, with its brilliant green rice fields neatly bordered by dikes and set against a backdrop of smoky mountains, the whole countryside was permeated with an awful odor, almost like someone had pushed over a giant johnny house!

There's no doubt the Japanese had a different outlook on this human manure bit than our country did. Since they utilized every scrap of available land for agriculture during the war, they expected the prisoners in Hirohata to do their share to help feed themselves. We had several rows of radishes and carrots growing next to the road; anyone who was sick, but still able to get around, worked the patch.

I injured my hand one time, and I couldn't lift anything heavy. Of course, this didn't prevent my tending the little garden outside the prison gates. Hoeing away one morning, I saw an old man coming up the road pushing a small cart. As he drew even with me, he carefully maneuvered his wagon to one side of the highway, parked it, and crossed over to my side.

I stopped working, straightened up, and looked at him, expecting him to say something or ask me a question. He bowed politely, and I returned the bow. Then he walked over to the row I was cultivating, straddled it, pulled down his pants, and proceeded to crap right on my vegetables.

I couldn't believe my eyes! When he finished, he pulled up his trousers, then bowed again before resuming his journey. Watching him steer the cart on down the road, I thought to myself, *You know, that old son of a bitch thinks he did me a favor. But if he pulled a stunt like that in someone's garden back home, he'd get shot. Not only that, when the case came to trial, the farmer would get off scot-free!*

We often experienced such culture shock, especially when it came to their latrine practices. In Japan, men and women used the same facilities without any apparent embarrassment. The outdoor benjo at the mill was not segregated. It unnerved us to be using the urinal along the wall and have a woman walk right in. While she would politely knock on the door of an occupied stall before going in, she would stand there and watch us pee into the trough until the occupant of the stall came out. We Americans found it hard to adjust to that kind of thing. Nine times out of ten, what they considered normal was abnormal for us. But forced to live and work among the Japanese, you got with the customs sooner or later.

Unlike the benjos behind the houses, the latrines in the prison camp and at the mill did not empty into a single pit. They built them in such a way that solids collected in one tank while liquids from the urinals drained into another. The army had contracted with one of the manure merchants to sell the stuff for so much a bucket. Every day the man called at the gate with his wagon to pick up a tankload.

We smelled more than just crap in the air! The gyangus, ever alert to any potential business deals floating around, sensed a quick profit to be made, especially after learning that the camp got less money for urine. We approached the wholesaler with an offer he couldn't refuse. For certain considerations, we told him, if one of us happened to be in camp when he came calling, we would act as lookout or divert the guards' attention while he went about filling up his cart.

I guess there's a little larceny in everybody's soul. Quick to see the merit in our proposal, the wholesaler kept nodding and saying, "Dai jobu," or "Okay," over and over. He was more than willing to go along with our idea and leave the camp with a mix containing far more solids than he'd paid for. He always compensated us for services rendered with a handful of cigarettes.

Knowing there was a stiff penalty for stealing that stuff in Japan, I thought to myself, *What a hell of a note it would be, if I got my head chopped off for aiding the honey merchant in stiffing the army.* I could just see the letter to my mother: "Dear Mrs. Lombardo, we regret to inform you that your son John Henry lost his head for stealing crap from the camp."

I entertained that distinct possibility for about two minutes, until I saw the wholesaler's cart come rumbling into the courtyard. Mentally donning my top hat, I took off across the compound. Nihingo no renshu ga hitsuyo da (it was time to go practice my Japanese) with the guards on duty.

27 Skinning the Cats

Despite their use of "night soil," Japan's ability to produce enough crops to feed her people could not keep pace with the demand. One of the country's main reasons for going to war in the first place, the confiscation of additional land to increase crop production, had failed. By 1944, the nation's food supply was dwindling with each passing day. As a result, the "honey" became much poorer in quality. Because the fertilizer business was so important to Japan's economy, we figured we'd win the war that way, if no other. In the meantime, we got busy doing our part to hasten the day.

If stealing food was the number-one, all-consuming passion for the POW, sabotage had to be a close second. The same amount of attention we gave to planning our little "jobs," we gave to taking some of the sting out of the Japanese war effort. Our revenge took many strange and bizarre forms.

Knowing the importance of the fertilizer business gave us the upper hand in a few instances. The Japanese army wasn't the only one to profit from the crap we "manufactured" in camp; the steel companies also derived an income from the honey merchants. So if the camp staff did us dirty for any reason, we chose a unique way to get even—a way that was guaranteed to get a rise out of the Japs. We'd simply wait until we got to the mill in the morning to do our business. When the expected volume of crap at the camp fell off, and the profit picture took a dive, the army camp commander would get all excited, and we'd get this big lecture at tenko.

"You must always use camp benjo in morning! It is not permitted for you to use benjo in mill!" the interpreter would yell. "All prisoners will obey commander in this! Anyone caught disobeying order will be severery punished!" And so it would go for the next thirty minutes. Try to keep a straight face under those circumstances. Never hoppen!

For a while after we arrived in camp, the Japs themselves worked the winches that transferred the ore, coal, limestone, or scrap from the ships to the dock. Anyone who has worked as a stevedore knows that, for maximum safety, once the net has been loaded, the operator of the crane must bring the huge steel net straight up out of the hold, being careful not to swing it from side to side; otherwise it could injure or kill the loaders down below. But the Nips didn't give a damn how they swung those babies. We had any number of suspiciously close calls due to their criminal negligence.

When they finally succeeded in crushing a few of the men against the hull one day, killing two and maiming several others, we rebelled and went on strike. We threw down our shovels, sat in the hold, and refused to fill another cargo net. We told them, "You either let us man the cranes, or forget it!" We had to be pretty desperate to make such a demand. The Japs didn't usually put up with much static from us, but the way we figured it, if they were going to "accidentally" kill us anyway, we might as well make a stand right then and there.

Short of shooting us all, the army didn't have much choice. They agreed to let our navy guys take over, provided we didn't slow down or lose time on the job. We felt a lot safer after that. At least if somebody got hit, it wouldn't be because an American-hating Jap had dropped a steel net on us.

Only five ships could be accommodated at the dock, so when another convoy steamed into the harbor, it had to anchor in the stream. To keep it from being tied up too long, the Japs hauled extra crews out there to unload the cargo onto barges. This gave our saboteurs the perfect chance to do a little dirty work.

It's funny how we suddenly had a lot of trouble with the equipment. Those navy boys became real experts at jerking the controls on the winches while swinging the fully loaded nets so that the cables snapped at just the right moment—when the cargo hung between ship and barge—sending everything (including the steel-mesh net) to the bottom of the channel. The water was very deep there, making the recovery of said cargo virtually impossible.

The Japs would get furious, raise hell, and knock heads, but we'd plead innocent. It was always due to the dilapidated condition of the machinery, we'd say, or the rusty cables that were ready to break. This was partly true, of course; the Japs couldn't argue much about the outmoded equipment. Our guys also took care not to overdo these accidents, but in the course of nearly two years, I imagine we dumped a good bit of stuff, already in short supply due to U.S. submarine activity in the area, overboard.

The Japs utilized the POWs' skills wherever possible. This also worked to our advantage. If you know how something works, you can fix it so it doesn't.

After the war, I ran into American POWs from another camp on the train to Yokohama and the staging area for the trip home. They told me of their work in the shipyard a few miles up the coast from us and the many hours spent secretly carving wooden "rivets" to destabilize the Japanese ships being built there. They successfully installed a number of them in the hull plates of the ships. Once the fake bolts were painted, they easily passed inspection.

I'm sure the Japs had plenty of trouble with those ships thanks to American "engineering." Some might even have sunk. At the very least, the shearing stress would have caused the wooden pegs to break off and the plates to come apart shortly after they put out to sea, making them leak like sieves.

On the ship going home, I learned that the POWs who worked at a munitions factory near the steel mill at Himeji had also been active in the sabotage business. "The 105-mm shells the Nips manufactured were shipped in separate crates from the boxes that held the fuses," one of the inmates said. "There was absolutely no way we could dump the shells overboard, so we came up with a way to make them ineffective. When loading the ships, we simply palmed the fuses from their boxes, later getting rid of them without much trouble. We could just picture the Japs' faces when they tried to arm the shells in the field—and no fuses!"

Japanese "talent scouts" raided camp Hirohata to replace their technical manpower drained off by the war. Our Navy Seabees were in constant demand to do any machining needed. They set up a machine shop down at the steel mill to manufacture gears for airplane propeller hubs for the Kawanishi Airplane Factory at Himeji. This was a direct piece of armament going into the fight against our own. Even though the prisoners had no choice in the matter, they felt like traitors. "There ain't no way we're gonna do this!" they agreed among themselves. Finding a way around the problem took some thought before they hit upon an idea.

To do the job, the Japs gave our men micrometers and calipers—delicate instruments used to measure the gears during machining. The Americans knew these tools were costly, in short supply, and not easily replaced. So much the better!

Under the guise of working away on the new parts, our guys carefully honed down the face of the spindles on the micrometers and the jaws on the calipers—just enough to produce slightly oversized gears. The tolerances were such that the hubs could be assembled, but they would be either a little too snug or a little too loose. During flight operation, the hubs would overheat or vibrate, causing the propeller assembly to self-destruct (rather disconcerting at ten thousand feet).

The prisoners counted on the Jap supervisors to follow their usual procedures in overseeing the work, and they weren't disappointed. Why carry around an instrument when a perfectly good one lay there on the lathe? Without fail, the inspectors would pick up the machinist's own micrometer to measure the dimensions of the finished gear against the specs. Naturally, the new gear always checked out.

After shipping out thousands of these imperfectly made gears, complaints from the factory began to roll in fast and furious. The parts didn't fit, Kawanishi's management said, and the propellers malfunctioned. They either jammed or flew apart, while all the other component parts seemed okay. The management insisted that the trouble had to be with the gears and the shoddy workmanship of our POWs at the mill.

To save face, the mill honchos were forced to repeat the same routine over and over again. Up and down the aisles of the shop they'd go, performing random inspections, stopping here and there to measure the gears in production. Their report never varied. "The problem does not originate here. All gears are perfect. Go look somewhere else."

The thought that maybe something was wrong with the instrument itself never seemed to occur to these guys. The Seabees lost track of how many times this happened; luckily, the Nips never pinned anything on our men.

There must have been about ten or twelve of these little shops and warehouses in a row where they also made spare parts for the mill. While I was there, they used no Japanese civilian labor, other than the honchos, in these shops; only the American navy personnel in camp had the skills needed for this precision-type manufacturing.

While working in the scrap-sorting shed, I got the job of keeping our twenty or so boys supplied with metals to fabricate different items. The plots hatched by these cagey characters, who were supposedly serving the emperor and the Imperial Japanese war effort, had more twists than Lombard Street in San Francisco. Watching them in action was a privilege!

As the Japs expanded their forging capabilities, another row of shops went up across the street. Only fifty feet separated the new complex from the old. Prison laborers mixed the concrete by hand. If they were in the middle of pouring the foundation or working to level the slab, they couldn't always leave right at 5 P.M. Making my deliveries for the next day's orders late one afternoon, I witnessed the "burial" of quite a bit of hardware. When he thought no one was looking, a Seabee called softly to one of his friends pouring concrete, "Hey, Rick, put this in your mix."

"Sure thing, Bob. Pitch it over."

Bob threw his micrometer to Rick, who neatly fielded the gadget and dropped it into the wet cement, deftly leveling it off in nothing flat.

Another Seabee standing nearby laughed quietly and asked, "Do you have room for another?"

"No sweat," Rick replied as he caught the second. It disappeared as fast as the first.

"Watch it! The honcho's coming back from making his rounds of the other shops," whispered a third man. Shortly after that, the whistle blew and we lined up to go back to camp.

I couldn't wait to get back down there the following afternoon. Around 4:30, I hauled in a couple of sacks of brass scrap and hung around on some pretext to see what would happen next.

What I saw was a lot of expensive precision implements, tools and pressure gauges that were hard if not impossible to get, tossed one by one at intervals by the machinists leaving for the day to the fellows across the road, shoved into the still-soft foundations, and quickly smoothed over before you could blink an eye.

Every morning, you could hear these same sailors griping and complaining to the bosses. "Look here, somebody must have come in and taken my instrument; it's gone!"

"Yeah, mine, too. It was here when I left yesterday. Jesus Christ, how do you expect us to get the job done without any tools? We're not magicians, you know!"

The honchos would go into a frenzy searching the POWs, always the first to be suspected. Then they'd go over the premises from top to bottom hunting for the tools gone astray. When they couldn't find anything, they'd hightail it over to the barracks and turn the place upside down; they just knew that we were somehow responsible for the thefts.

Since the evidence lay under now-hardened concrete, nothing ever materialized. The honchos caught hell from management, and we caught hell from the honchos, but they never solved the mystery of the missing instruments.

Three things are fairly certain: One, thanks to the diabolically imaginative Seabees and the slick operators next door, the manufacturing of airplane gears and spare parts for the mill ground to a virtual halt. Two, more than one enemy aircraft probably crashed. And three, if those foundations still exist today, that's the most expensive concrete in the world!

Of course, we committed just as much daily sabotage in the steel mill as anywhere else. Anything to cause a delay, actual work stoppage, or disruption in the routine, no matter how insignificant, was SOP (standard operating procedure). We were an unruly, recalcitrant bunch of guys who couldn't be controlled in any real sense of the word. Technically speaking we might have been POWs, but we broke out of the mental imprisonment imposed on us by the Japanese every chance we got. The constant harassment of our jailers was food and drink for our spirits; we lived on it. Hell, it probably kept us alive! Now we had a reason for getting up in the morning. Each new day provided us with a thousand and one little ways to get even.

The slag pits alongside the tracks down at the steel mill took several days to cool after the molten rock was poured off the big ladles. The Japs sprayed water to cool the steaming trenches so that we could safely get in there and break up the dross and load it onto gondolas for its second trip to the smelter.

Yama in Japanese means hill. When the Japs said they wanted a yama of slag on a gondola, they meant, "Stack a rail car so full, it forms a hill on the top."

Japanese women worked this detail with us. They could haul heavily laden tenbin-bo up the planks into the cars at a rate that filled one car in the morning and another in the afternoon. There was no way we could keep pace with them, even if we tried, which we didn't. In the first place, we were too weak; in the second, goofing off was the name of the game.

Basically, we kept losing our balance under the loaded tenbin-bo that bounced with every step we took. When the unstable boards leading up into the cars also sprang under the weight of the loads, the opposing motion threw us off every time.

This frustrated the honcho in charge to such an extent he'd hit us on the head or across the shoulders with his club. Day after day, we failed to meet the quota of two cars a day. Day after day, he beat us. Not until he became convinced that what he expected was just impossible (especially during the winter months, when we had to wear the geta due to a shortage of shoes) did he finally let us try another way—two men, with a single basket suspended on a bamboo pole between them, walking up two adjacent planks. This system worked much better, plus it got us off the hook of filling two cars a day.

We didn't stop there! Down in the pit we learned that if we broke out the slag into the thinnest possible layers, they looked okay viewed from the top but weighed far less than you'd think at first glance. We got real good at playacting, grunting and groaning our way up the ramps. When we stacked the sheets in the gondolas, leaving plenty of hollow spaces between them, our carefully staged yama appeared legit.

But the minute the rail cars were coupled together in the evening, the subsequent jolt, traveling the length of the train as the cars rammed into one another, collapsed the whole damn thing like a house of cards. Instead of a full load, the honcho would end up with only half. He'd be chewing nails, but by then the prisoners were gone for the day.

Although the boss in the slag pit went through a new crew just about every day, looking for a bunch of men who might be natural acrobats, he had no luck. His complete lack of success in meeting his daily quota by getting an honest-to-god yama out of the men drove him up the wall and caused him to routinely remark, "I'll be glad when this war is over and you guys can go home. Then I can go home, too, and back to my old job in the rock quarry."

28 Dogs Eat Dog

The slag pit at the mill was an ideal place to work in the winter, if we could swing it. The intense heat radiating from the molten dross kept us warm when bitter winds swept in off the Inland Sea. We tried to maneuver our assignments so that all the prisoners got a crack at it. Unfortunately, because of the Japanese system, that wasn't always possible.

On those bone-chilling days, the lucky ones working in the pit boiled water in their canteen cups on the glowing-hot rocks that sometimes took a week to cool down, and pretended they were drinking tea. Hot water seemed to be the standard beverage around there; somehow, it was comforting. I suppose it gave us the feeling of taking a tea or coffee break.

One month after we arrived in Hirohata, I was on a work detail down in the pit, chipping out slag to be loaded onto rail cars. Somebody in the group remembered it was Armistice Day and asked the honcho if we could pause for a few minutes to pay tribute to those who died in World War I. Since Japan had been an ally in that war, the boss agreed. At 11 A.M. on November 11, 1943, twenty-one men, including the boss, faced east and silently prayed for our comrades who had fallen in battle long ago.

At the time, the different concessions still furnished an extra bento for lunch. Every day at noon, we tramped over to the shack, where the cook gave us tea and an extra ration of rice, in addition to the bento we had brought from camp.

The boss, of course, ate in the warm shack, but not before feeding his large black dog. We noticed that the animal, about the size of a re- triever, not only got a bigger portion than we did, but his owner usu- ally served him while we waited in line. We found this rather insulting, so a couple of times, the minute the boss was out of sight, we beat the pooch out of his lunch. Then somebody got the bright idea to go a step farther.

The thought of eating dog meat didn't faze us. The Filipinos ate it all the time. I'd had my share of stray canine at Cabanatuan and been glad to get it. When you're hungry, it tastes pretty good—sort of like deer meat, a little tangy, maybe, but not bad.

Even though I love rice and never tire of eating it even now, a steady diet of nothing but rice gets old. As we got hungrier and hungrier for some real food that first winter in Japan, the mutt began to look better and better; every time I saw him my mouth actually watered. We started dreaming about how good he'd taste in a stew or a soup, and we soon hatched a plan. Basically, it boiled down to simple dognapping the minute his master turned his back.

Watching the dog run around the shack as we ate our bento one day, the ranking man and ringleader of the group suggested, "Let's get him tomorrow."

"Suits me," I said. "How about the rest of you jokers?"

"We're ready," they all agreed.

Someone raised the question, "Who can skin him?"

"I'll do it. Shouldn't be much harder than a squirrel or a cat," said a man who had been a frequent rider of the rails during the depression and, as a result, was a connoisseur of campfire cuisine.

"Will he be ready to eat in an hour?"

"Maybe a tad on the rare side, but I think so," he answered.

The next day dawned cold and miserable with the threat of snow in the air. Our blood was still a bit "thin" from having been in the tropics, and the pit felt good after our two-mile hike to work. That morning, as the dog followed his master around the job, twenty pairs of eyes stalked him greedily while weighing him mentally.

At noon everyone headed for the shack and our usual fare. The Jap fed the mutt his bento first off, but he never had a chance to eat it. As soon as the honcho went inside, three guys at the head of the line whisked the rice right out from under the dog's nose.

The minute we got our rations, we used the dog's own rice to lure him back to one of the freshly poured areas of the trench that felt like hell itself. He never knew what hit him. Working fast, our man had him skinned, gutted, butchered, and roasting on the searing, white-hot slag in no time flat. The rest of us formed a protective circle around the barbecue, shielding it from view. While sitting there savoring the aroma, with one eye on the feast and the other looking over our shoulders, I rubbed a little rock salt (hoarded for just such an occasion) into the meat.

Oh, man, it smelled good! As the meat began to brown crisply and curl slightly around the edges, I could hardly wait to taste my share of it. Everyone tried to be patient, but it was hard. Thirty minutes under those circumstances seemed like hours. Finally we couldn't wait any longer and dove in.

Lord, it was even better than I remembered! We smacked our chops over the goodness of the meal and gnawed our way clear down to the bones. By the time we got through, there wasn't a shred of meat, fat, or gristle left. Unfortunately, one forty-five-pound dog (minus head, fur, and frame) divided among so many didn't go very far. Nevertheless, we all agreed (being careful to pitch the joints and ribs into the fire) that it was great while it lasted.

At five o'clock the boss got us out of the pit and lined us up for bango. He called Fido a few times, snapping his fingers, whistling for his dog. When his sidekick failed to materialize, the honcho shrugged, probably thinking he'd gone home, and moved us out to join the other prisoners for the walk back to camp.

Maybe the boss lay awake all night worrying about his dog's whereabouts. Maybe the loss of sleep put him in a bad mood. No doubt he arrived at the mill in an even worse temper for having to walk to work without his old buddy. But when he climbed into the pit that morning to inspect the area we'd be working in and spied the dog's skin and head lying where we had foolishly flung them the day before, he was beside himself.

"Amelicans are without principles, they are like savages," he cried, holding up the animal's pelt when he first caught sight of us. "You killed my dog, then you ate him! What kind of people could do such a thing? A poor, innocent creature that never hurt anybody! You are criminals! I will kill you myself!" he screamed at us, almost in tears.

I'm sure all of us could have kicked ourselves every way from Sunday. How could we have been so stupid? Especially when getting rid of the evidence would have been so damn simple. Some areas of the pit reduced everything to ashes in seconds.

The honcho tried to take his pain and rage out on us by working everybody over with his bat, but that didn't seem to help his spirits much. We had done away with his old pal, and he wasn't going to forget it any time soon. He spent the day glaring at us, generally making things as rough as he could. I don't believe we got any tea or bento from him at noon. He was plenty teed off. He was also not finished with us by a long shot.

That evening, he turned us in to the military guards for our crime. It looked like we were in big trouble again. Back at the camp, the commander personally greeted us and officially accused us of killing and eating the boss's dog. There was no point in denying the charge, since our ID numbers appeared on the work roster.

"Japanese do not eat dogs!" he declared. "Why did you eat that man's pet?"

"Because we were hungry," our leader replied.

He should have known better than to say that. The Japanese people never openly admitted to being hungry, cold, or in want—particularly in wartime. They certainly didn't allow us to complain. To do so amounted to criticism of the emperor and of their ability as a nation to provide for the people and their captives. It was a matter of pride. By saying we were hungry, we had caused them to lose face. They wouldn't take it lightly. And they didn't!

For our punishment for telling the truth, we had to stand at attention out in the courtyard for the next six hours, dressed only in our Filipino denims. Naturally, it began to snow. They permitted no one to bring us extra clothing, blankets, or anything to eat or drink—not even hot water. Every now and then, one of us fell down from the effects of the numbing cold and exhaustion. The guards made us pick him up and stand him on his feet again.

Around midnight, they dismissed us. Frozen men, some semiconscious, half-walked or were dragged by their buddies into the barracks. We crawled into our bunks and fell into a dead sleep for the few hours remaining before tenko.

From then on, whenever any of us worked in the slag pit, the honcho down there gave us a real hard time, exacting every bit of work he could from each man, using methods of intimidation that included yelling and screaming, threats of punishment, and beatings. To him, Americans were unredeemable, sorry excuses for human beings. The only damn thing we were sorry about was that his pal hadn't been bigger, and that he didn't have more dogs at home!

Someone was always coming up with a harebrained scheme to raise more food. Very few ever panned out, although the plan to raise rabbits seemed like a good one to us. Sometime in the spring of 1945, the guards brought six pairs of rabbits into camp. The responsibility for their care was entrusted to José and Frank, two sheep-herders from New Mexico who had been permanently disabled by injuries suffered at work.

I never knew rabbits could exist without water, but the Japanese in charge of the project wouldn't let the men give them any. He maintained that they got enough moisture from their diet of greens and clover. He must have known what he was doing because those rascals went to town and started multiplying at a pretty good clip.

The Japanese said that three hundred pairs of rabbits were mandatory before we could even begin to eat them. By my calculations, if everything went according to plan, it would take about six or seven months to reach that goal. Fortunately, the war ended before the magic number of rabbits was achieved.

Silkworms were reported to be nutritious. At least that's what Cookie said the day they appeared on the menu. He assured us that the protein in a six-inch-long pupa equaled the protein in a good-sized steak. I sat there looking at the critters in my bowl, swimming in soy sauce, and uttered the one word that said it all: "Shit!"

Old Whiskey laughed when he heard the griping and grumbling from the GIs as the mess attendant ladled the silkworms into their bowls. "Umai! Delicious," he said, reaching over to pop a couple into his mouth. "Japanese delicacy," he mumbled between bites. "You eat, you like!"

I watched him smack his lips with obvious relish over the crunchy little tidbits that reminded me of brown beetles congregating under the movie marquee on summer nights back home. Either he was faking it or he really liked the taste. Maybe I was missing out on something, after all. *What the hell,* I thought. *If he can do it so can I.*

I cautiously bit into one. Not bad. They tasted sort of like Cheez-its. I tried another one. "Well, I'll be," I said to the skeptical-looking fellow sitting next to me. "Now if only I had a cold beer to go with this, wouldn't that be nice?"

We considered ourselves lucky to get silkworms a couple more times. Ishidasan was right. They tasted a whole lot better than some other meals I can recall. Since *haikyu* strictly controlled all foodstuffs in Japan, I assume the silkworms had come out of some warehouse in the district, but I never learned for sure. We really didn't care where the food originated or how we came by it. Just as long as we got enough, we weren't too picky. We ate things that I couldn't possibly stomach today. Silkworms would probably be among them.

The summer of 1945, things got a bit more lively. The constant bombing raids knocked out the power in Himeji, and the fish and meat rations stored in the large commercial freezers in town began to go bad. The authorities had to quickly dispose of everything, so they handed it out to all and sundry. They didn't forget the inmates at Hirohata.

Trucks delivered transparent pink fish in crates to the gate. Half were rotten and already crawling with maggots. The other half, warm and smelling pretty ripe, appeared to be in better shape. Cookie made a gruel with some of it for dinner, adding some curry powder to disguise the taste, and we managed to eat it without a whole lot of complaining. The rest of the fish we spread out on the roof of the barracks to dry. Someone coming back from the latrine after supper ran into the building to report that the roof was glowing in the dark. We rushed out to see a strange phenomenon. The funny-looking fish were phosphorescent, lighting up the tiles like hundreds of miniature neon signs.

Christmas 1944 was the saddest Christmas I can recall of all the ones I spent as a prisoner of the Japanese. Four hundred men from the Philippines had been in Japan for almost a year and three months. Amazingly, of a total camp population of about 480, only 17 had died so far from starvation, disease, and accidents—a testament in part to the courage, perseverance, and yes, pure cussedness of men determined to survive no matter what.

But we were tired. Tired of holding out, of being brave, of living by our wits, moment to moment, and of having to cope with hunger, cruelty, and sickness. So we could hardly believe it when the mill bosses told us they had gotten together to give us a hog for Christmas.

The day they delivered the pig, a good-sized one weighing in at about 175 pounds, was cause for celebration. We immediately went to work and built a pen for it back of the galley. Every day we checked on our pig, watching his progress with great interest as he filled out a little from the slop Cookie fed him. For a while, that's all we talked about.

We spent hours planning how we'd handle him when the time came; we would use everything but the squeal. The army would get the skin; they always got any kind of hide. That was all right; we didn't have any use for it anyway. But we could start by boiling the head to make hog's head cheese. The feet would be pickled, of course. Barbecued pork ribs were on everybody's mind, and visions of fresh ham, roasts, chops, and sausages danced in our heads.

Christmas Day, 1944, fell on a Monday. Since Sunday was our only day off, we would have to celebrate a day early. Friday, the kitchen crew slaughtered the hog. Japanese soldiers arrived from the garrison and took the skin, as expected, then helped themselves to the hind legs and most of the loin as well. When I got back from work that night, one of the guys in the galley greeted me with the news.

"Did you hear what those sons of bitches did to us today?" he asked.

"What now?" I said.

"The soldiers from the garrison came in here and not only took the skin, but half the damn hog itself!"

"Aw, hell! I might've known." Punching the air and wishing I had a Jap to hit, I stalked off, vowing revenge.

News of the theft ran through the camp in a matter of minutes. The mood of good will, good cheer, and anticipation instantly switched to one of sharp disappointment, anger, and extreme frustration. "Those lousy bastards." "They've done it to us again!" "It's not fair!" "That was our pig!" "Boy, if I could lay my hands on a gun, I'd shoot the dirty little bandy-legged rats right here and now!"

Downhearted and bitter at being cut short, but finally resolute about our loss, we figured, "Well, hell, we'll just have to make do with what's left."

What we didn't count on, though, was having to stand by and watch the envious civilian guards make off with both shoulders the next morning. That struck the final, devastating blow! We wound up with the leavings—the head, the fatback, the belly, and the tail. We all knew that a whole hog would barely make the rounds. But this—what could we possibly do with this?

Our spirits took a nosedive. What had been given to us as a gesture of good will by some had been stolen by others who hated our guts. Our plans for a Merry Christmas suddenly vanished along with our pig.

Sunday, December 24, dawned just like any other winter day—dark, dreary, and cold. The sun had abandoned us, too. Until the Japs turned on the lights at 6 P.M., there was nothing to do except lie in our bunks and stare at the ceiling. In anticipation of the feast, no provisions had been made for breakfast. We would have to wait a few more hours for the only meal we'd get that day.

Someone tried to play a Christmas carol on the harmonica. I think it might have been "Silent Night." Halfway through, he broke down. He didn't try any more songs after that. A fight broke out. I don't remember why. No one bothered to stop it. After a while, the two participants lost interest in their argument and went back to bed. Several of the men started a card game, but that didn't last very long. I heard one of them throw his cards down saying, "Crap! Who the hell can see anything in this light?" Morale was as low as I'd ever seen it, even in the first few days at Camp O'Donnell after the surrender. It would take a bloody miracle for the dejected, morose men to snap back.

Twelve o'clock came; time for lunch. It wasn't the lunch we'd had in mind, but it was the best the kitchen staff could produce under the circumstances. What was left of our hog—mostly fat—had been chopped up and boiled with rice. For once, no one cared about food, especially when we sat down to eat the gelatinous goo they dumped into our bowls. We couldn't even find a single string of meat in the whole batch! The sound of spoons scraping the sides of the bowls took the place of the normal babble usually heard at mealtimes. After lunch I went back to bed.

I must have been dozing, drifting in and out of sleep, when a little stir in the barracks woke me. Something was being passed from man to man. I couldn't make it out exactly, but I could feel the atmosphere in the place rapidly changing from one of gloom and despair to hope and cheer. Wait a minute. It didn't seem possible! Catching a glimpse of a familiar-looking object, I sat up and rubbed my eyes, but it was still there! How in God's name had the soldier managed to keep it all these years?

My turn came, and I carefully took it in my hands. The soldier had made a staff from a sliver of bamboo. From it hung an American flag, our flag, the Stars and Stripes, Old Glory! Everyone had his own name for it. Even in the semidarkness, the small scrap of silk shone with all the brightness of the future, just like our hopes and dreams. Just seeing and holding the little symbol of freedom again, so pretty and brave, gave us all a tremendous lift and made us feel a little closer to home. It gave us a sense of renewal of faith, in ourselves and in our country. It also reminded us of the reason we had stubbornly refused to give up and why we doggedly fought on.

29   Ashes to Ashes

The relatively small number of POWs who died in Hirohata, compared with the thousands who perished in the Philippines, were cremated instead of buried. Although the method of disposal in Japan differed from that used in the islands, the routine remained the same: our sick performed the rites of passage for our dead.

The crematorium we used was in a cemetery about a quarter-mile from camp. You could see the tall brick chimney of the furnace poking up from among ancestral monuments scattered around the grassy area. A rough iron firebox and oven, separated by a metal grate, had been built into the base.

On the morning of a cremation, civilian guards escorted the usual crew of three POWs, who had drawn the unpleasant but necessary duty, to the crematorium. Two men carried the body, while the third man would stay to tend the fire. We shoved the corpse into a half barrel in a crouching position and tied it with rope. This was the baby's position in the womb before entering the world; therefore, according to Japanese tradition, he should go out this way as well.

After we put the barrel into the oven, we shut the heavy double doors and started a fire with coal and kindling. Then, for the next eight hours, the third man fed the intense blaze continuously with coke to render it hot enough to consume the deceased. Late in the afternoon, the guards would return for the prisoner and the ashes, which had been scooped into a plain wooden box tied with grass rope.

Dr. Seid inscribed the names of the dead on the lids of the boxes, then placed them on a shelf in the infirmary. After the war, we took them to Yokohama and turned them over to the American authorities for their final journey home.

Following the frozen-tub incident, I was too weak to carry the dead to the site, but the Japs gave me the job of stoking the flames a couple of times. It was bitterly cold the day I cremated a man who was too tall to fit into the usual barrel. Someone built a special coffin for him, and it reminded me of the Canadian soldier in Cabanatuan whose feet measured 15 EEEE. Sadly, the bigger the man, the more he suffered in camp. Although the dead man was pitifully thin, we still had to fold him up in the fetal position to get him into the box and the three-foot-square oven.

That same afternoon, a Japanese family came by to pay a visit to an ancestor. The Japanese always honored their dead; they never forgot them. Not only did they believe them to be actively involved in the affairs of the living, but they thought they were also present in the graveyards and household shrines, especially on the anniversaries of their deaths.

I watched Mamasan, Papasan, and their two children bow low and pray at the foot of an obelisk. They had brought the usual offering of rice as a token of their respect. After they left, I lunched with the spirits, helping myself to the rice and some wild onions springing up around the little stone memorials.

It's true I was hungrier than usual, still somewhat sick and on half rations, but I have always liked to think that what I did probably went a long way toward strengthening the family's religious faith. Imagine their surprise when they returned later and found that their offering of food was gone!

A Japanese soldier who died in combat was cremated in the field and his ashes transported home in a white wooden box about twelve inches square. The funeral procession for the fallen hero was a solemn occasion for the family. A white sash was wound around the box of ashes and the neck of the soldier bearing it. Behind him, for all to see, military guards carried a picture of the deceased draped in black and white, along with his medals or awards for valor. Chanting priests from the temple gave the ceremony an air of reverence.

But the Japanese soldier who failed to commit suicide and allowed himself to be captured alive, or who voluntarily surrendered to the enemy, suffered total disgrace. If a soldier dishonored himself or his regiment in battle, the Japanese executed him for the crime, burned his body, and shipped his ashes home in the same unpainted box, tied with grass rope, that they reserved for their captives or others held in contempt.

They loaded the remains into a cargo net, then dumped them unceremoniously onto the dock. No procession of uniformed and spit-polished haitai escorted the little box to a place of honor. The father of the soldier collected the plain, unadorned symbol of shame, then he often went home and committed *seppuku* or *hara-kiri* (literally, "cutting one's belly").

Because his son had dishonored him and the emperor, the father stood a good chance of being shunned by the people he knew, making it very difficult for him to hold up his head in his village or his neighborhood. Custom seemed to demand that he repay the debt owed to the nation by his son. Under those circumstances, he might feel that he had little choice but to take a short-bladed sword, plunge it into his stomach on the left side, draw it across to the right side, and then pull it upward. Now, the debt was canceled. Bushido (death before dishonor).

One thing always seemed to amaze and puzzle the military doctors and psychologists who checked us over after we got home: the surprisingly small number of GIs who went insane or tried to commit suicide while imprisoned by the Japanese.

I can recall only one legitimate case of attempted suicide among all the men I knew in the camps. He was a young fellow, very sensitive, not physically strong. Things seemed to affect him more than the others, but everyone genuinely liked the boy. While many of us were not much older, we sort of took him under our wing.

The Sunday he tried to take his life dawned nasty and miserable. At least we didn't have to run stupid races or play ball. We spent most of the day in the sack, trying to stay warm. The sound of the rain dripping off the eaves was soothing; just about everybody was dozing.

A fellow drowsing in a lower bunk at first thought the roof was leaking. Except the droplets falling on his face felt warm and sticky. Then, too, shouldn't the guy in the top rack be raising hell? But there wasn't a peep out of him. *Crap,* thought the fellow in the lower bunk. *I'd better check.* Rousing himself, he threw the blankets back and sat up. Another drop fell. He looked at the dark spot on his sleeve, then up at what had become a thin, steady stream of blood.

He sprang up and gave a shout, catapulting all of us out of our bunks. "Get the Doc, quick!" he yelled.

It was usually best not to panic at the first sign of trouble. Any sudden activity on our part would bring the guards running, for sure. The Japs considered suicide a serious offense, an attempt to escape prison, and they exacted a stiff penalty from any man who tried it. Although we wasted no time in summoning the medic, Dr. Seid acted as though he had simply decided to stroll over to our building for a game of cards. Once inside, though, he went straight to work.

Even in the half-light, the lad was the color of his straw mat. He had cut the arteries in both wrists. His pulse was faint, but he was conscious. His bunkmate had quickly applied pressure bandages to staunch the flow of blood. While Dr. Seid worked over him, we tried to comfort the patient and get him talking.

"Hey, kid, look—things aren't that bad. I mean, you're gonna get out of here. We all will. It won't be long, now."

"I'm so tired of fighting. I just can't anymore."

"C'mon now, don't give up. You can make it. Just try to hang in there a little longer."

But he closed his eyes and shook his head, unconvinced.

"You know, this thing can't last forever, you'll see," someone said.

"Yeah, we can't let the bastards whip us," I added. "Besides, if you check out now, you'll miss the fireworks when we bust outta here! Man, our day's comin'! We're almost there."

"John, you always make me laugh," the young man said, smiling in spite of himself.

"Hey, that's the spirit! You stick with us and you'll make it. Keep telling yourself you have your whole life ahead of you and everything to live for. That's reason enough to go on. Someday, all this will seem like just a bad dream."

Putting his hand on the young man's arm, his bunkmate added, "And from now on, kid, if you get low, don't keep it in. You go talk to the Doc, or to one of us. Maybe we can help you see things differently."

The boy turned his head to the wall, but not before I saw a tear squeeze out onto the pillow. Quiet for a few minutes, he was trying hard not to cry. When he was able, he looked at all of us hanging off his bunk and grinned. "You guys are something else, you know that? I must have been crazy to want to leave a bunch of pals like you behind."

The next few days were crucial. The Doc made up some excuse to the camp staff about why the youngster couldn't work. Somehow, he made it stick. The kid's long sleeves concealed his bandaged wrists long enough for the wounds to knit. Someone took his bloody mat and burned it, and scrubbed the stains out of the blankets.

We held a powwow, and each man volunteered to kick in a portion of his rations to help get the kid back on his feet. The corpsmen pumped him full of vitamin B. Cookie sneaked in a few extras from the kitchen, and one of the men contributed his store of vitamins from the last Red Cross box handed out.

The kid bounced back quickly. Everyone kept an eagle eye on him for a while, making sure someone stuck close to him most of the time, but we really didn't have to. He never made another attempt.

One character in camp, however, a real manipulator who always had some deal going, saw this incident as a chance to milk the guys for all they were worth.

Several weeks later, on another sloppy Sunday, this joker I'll call "Max" climbed up on a top bunk, threw one end of a grass rope over the rafter above his head, tied it off, fashioned a noose on the other end, put it around his neck, and threatened to end it all. "I can't stand it," he announced to the room at large. "I'm going to kill myself."

I opened one eye and there he was—one foot on the edge of the platform and the other poised in midair, as though ready to jump off into oblivion. Others were watching the show, too.

"Look at that son of a bitch, he's gonna take a powder."

"Aw, who cares? Let him. Good riddance, I say."

"I'm not kidding," said Max with a sob in his throat.

"Go ahead and jump, man, I ain't never seen a hangin' before. Whatcha waitin' on?"

"You guys don't believe me, but I'm really serious," Max declared amid all the laughter.

"If you're gonna do it, just do it. Only shut up about it. I'm trying to get some sleep," said someone, rolling over in his bunk.

Either Max's temper finally got the best of him and he deliberately jumped, or his foot accidentally slipped. In any case, he fell and was left swinging at the end of the flimsy rope, about four feet off the floor.

"Well, I'll be damned. He's gone and done it now!"

"Shoot, he didn't mean to. He's a born manipulator."

"Yeah, I'll bet all he wanted was for us to feel sorry for him and give him extra rations and treats from Cookie."

"And the shyster wouldn't have to go to work, either."

Max clutched at the rope around his neck and tried with all his might to swing his body back over to the bunk so he could hook his leg around the wooden upright, but he wasn't having a whole lot of luck. He couldn't get up enough momentum without suffering even more pain, and his foot wouldn't quite reach that far.

"Boy, he must think we're stupid or somethin'. I seen my share of his kind, and they're all the same, only interested in one thing—what's in it for them."

"Well, I can tell you, from the looks of him the only thing he'll get out of this, if he's lucky, is a rope burn on his neck."

"Hey, Max, you hear that? You'd better stop screwin' around up there, man. You're gonna end up hurtin' yourself!"

Max wasn't making as much noise now, and his face had gone from a dangerous shade of red to more of a purplish hue. Still, no one moved to help him. An almost casual conversation continued between two men.

"How 'bout that? The son of a bitch is turning blue!" the first one observed.

"Yeah, you're right," said the second man. After a long pause, he continued. "Y'know, he's not a favorite of mine, see, and ordinarily I wouldn't care if he killed himself, but maybe we oughta get him down before the guard walks in and finds him."

"Cut him down if you want to, but count me out. Never liked the bastard."

"Me neither, but just the same, don'tcha think the commander will get a little bent outta shape when he hears about this?"

After a long pause, the first man reluctantly said, "Oh, hell, much as I hate to admit it, you're probably right. The rat's not worth the beating we'll get if he succeeds in hanging himself."

Taking his time, he fished around in his Red Cross box, got out his homemade blade hidden among his prized possessions, ambled over to the bunk, slowly climbed up the platform, then scrambled onto the rafter and reached over to saw through the cord that was choking off Max's air.

"Boy, you know something, this grass rope musta been stronger than I thought," he remarked as Max fell to the floor.

"Naw, he's just full of hot air," the second man said.

30   Hamming It Up

It's a funny thing, but whatever a man's traits, they became more pronounced in prison. If naturally patient and kind to start with, his stint as a POW usually made him more so. Under the grueling regimen and the pressure of living as a captive, some of the men became veritable saints. Conversely, if a man was a first-class son of a bitch, chances were excellent that he wouldn't improve with time. Somehow these types never seemed to learn much from their experiences in camp, and I expect they had a hard time of it after the war.

José and Frank, two Mexican Americans from New Mexico, were able to take whatever life dished out without complaint. Both had suffered injuries right after they got to Japan; Frank's back was hurt down in the hold of a ship, and José's knee got crushed at the mill. Although both survived their ordeals, they were left with permanent disabilities: Frank couldn't stand up straight, and José walked with a bad limp.

Neither worked on the docks or at the mill after that. The odd jobs around camp fell to them—sweeping up, hosing down, feeding the rabbits or the Christmas hog. Whatever the need, these two good-natured men managed it between them.

Then there were the Italians. Even though word of Italy's surrender to the Allies in September 1943 reached us via Cabanatuan's underground, it surprised us to see Italian POWs show up in Hirohata so soon after our arrival in October. The day the twelve of them marched into our neck of the woods caused quite a stir. They were dressed in distinctive naval uniforms, and even before they opened their mouths I had them pegged as Italians by their lively, animated manner. They reminded me of my gregarious family when they got going real good. Not one of them could hold a conversation without using their hands—or their whole bodies, for that matter.

The new POWs weren't allowed to mix with us. The guards kept them in a small compound back of camp headquarters. They didn't have to work as laborers, either. Maybe that was because Italy was a former ally of Japan, and Mussolini still headed up the opposing government-in-exile in northern Italy. Whatever the reason, during the day, the haitai took them off somewhere else. The only time we saw them was when they exercised or played ball in the courtyard. But they were fed from our mess, so messages were soon being passed back and forth in the food buckets between those GIs fluent in Italian and some of the Italians who spoke English.

They told us in their hastily scribbled notes that after Italy surrendered, the Japanese seized their destroyer in the port of Yokohama as a prize of war. Part of the crew, still loyal to Mussolini, went to work with the Jap navy in the shipyards. They, on the other hand, by naively making it plain that they were squarely on the side of the newly appointed prime minister Badoglio, were taken into custody as enemies of Japan. But before leaving the ship, the defiant dagoes scuttled it and sank it right in the harbor.

Their leader looked just like an old uncle of mine. Short, squat, and balding, he was the spitting image of Uncle Leonardo, and he hated the Japs worse than anything. I'd watch the feisty little guy out in the yard, his big handlebar mustache twitching back and forth, energetically cuss them out. He'd do a world-class job of it, too—first in Italian, then in English, just to make sure they understood him.

Even though I had been raised in a Sicilian American household and spoke our local dialect, most of his diatribe against the Japanese was Greek to me. But when he yelled, "Figlio di puttana!" and in the next breath, "Sons of bitches!"—all of it punctuated by the internationally recognized sign language—that I understood.

The infuriated guards beat him over his shiny, bullet-shaped head, but he kept right on mouthing off, his belligerence firmly intact until the last day of the war.

But my favorite character of all was a loner from Montana, a guy named Hamilton. I remember the first time I really took note of Ham. It was the day he decided he had had enough of living jammed up with a bunch of men and lit out for home.

The harbor at Himeji was filthy. The ships docking there routinely dumped their waste and garbage overboard, and the busy, crowded port became so polluted, the Japanese warned us against even bathing our feet in it. It must have been all of twenty-eight degrees, with heavy snow clouds up above—but apparently neither the pollution in the bay nor the weather factored into Ham's decision.

Our unloading detail had just come off one of the ships when Ham suddenly jumped overboard. We stood on the dock watching him swim away while the Nips, all in an uproar, shook their fists and screamed at him to come back. "Baka! Idiot!" they hollered. "Get out of that water. Where do you think you are going, anyway?"

"Home," Ham yelled, over his shoulder. "It's only seven thousand miles thataway, and I think I can make it."

Cursing up a storm, the guards jumped into a small dinghy and rowed out into the harbor to capture the American suddenly gone berserk. After a short struggle that almost tipped over the craft, they hauled Ham into the boat. The haitai had to sit on him to hold him down. Ranting, flinging his arms and legs about, he threatened to plunge himself back into the ice-cold water, taking everyone with him.

With a great deal of fuss, they got back to shore and took him, shivering and shaking, into a little bento hut to dry out by the fire. In the shack, Ham really went to town. He screamed and yelled, rolled around on the floor and, in general, acted psychotic.

But other than trying to restrain him, the soldiers never laid a glove on him. I had heard that the Japanese believed the insane were possessed of evil spirits and should be given a wide berth, lest the spirits turn on those who mistreated them. The Japs handled the situation by making some of us take Ham back to camp. He went along without much trouble, but after we entered the gates he started up again. He threw himself on the ground, moaning and crying, then went to howling like a banshee. The guards wouldn't touch him; they made us pick him up and carry him to the guardhouse.

The building, next to the gate, had a tiny office up front, a small room with a couple of cots where men could sleep between shifts, and behind that, the jail. There were about four cells, measuring three feet square by four feet high, where the Japs put the serious offenders in camp. You couldn't stand up or lie down in the cells—that was part of the deal. We put Ham into one of these, and after taking his clothes away (standard procedure winter or summer for all prisoners, including their own), the Japs locked the door.

The guards on duty that evening didn't get much rest. Ham yelled all night long and all the next day. Nothing they said or did could stop him. Although he really rubbed them raw, the guards wouldn't touch him. The next evening, in desperation, they asked some of us to "please" find out what ailed him.

After we visited Ham in his cage, the guards questioned us. "What makes him scream continuously? He is not hurt."

"He told us he needs more room," I said.

The tired and aggravated guards agreed to take out the partition between two cells, and in no time Ham had stretched out and grown quiet. But that didn't last long; a few hours later he was back to sounding off at the top of his lungs. The guards summoned us again.

"Now, what?" they asked.

"He says he wants some cigarettes," we told them.

"Oh, all right. Anything to keep him quiet," they said, tossing us a pack to take back to the cell.

This went on for about a week. Ham would holler, and the guards would cave in to his demands to shut him up. Before long, they were catering to his every whim. Once things were definitely going his way, he became more agreeable, and the guards rewarded him by giving him back his clothes.

Soon they began to let him out to perform a few chores around the guardhouse, always returning him to his "double room" at night. Ham, who hated the crowded conditions in the barracks, didn't object. He emptied ashtrays, swept the floor in the office, and ran errands for the Japs.

The camp staff got used to having Ham around, and Ham took advantage of the fact. As they granted him more and more liberties and exacted no punishment for breaking the rules, his behavior became outrageous. If he saw a pack of cigarettes lying on someone's desk in the office, he'd help himself to the whole thing, say "thank you," and walk away. In self-defense, the Japs had to keep their smokes in their pockets or locked up in their desk drawers.

Ham drove them nuts by smoking in the courtyard or by deliberately not wearing his cap outside. He'd grin and apologize, but the minute the Nips turned their backs he'd go back to breaking the rules. The guards just shook their heads at the American fool and let him get away with it, probably afraid of the evil-spirit thing. You had to hand it to the guy. Either he was truly certifiable, or this was genius at work!

During the dark and dreary winter days, when so many prisoners were sick and starving, Ham took to pilfering from the officers' kitchen. The startled Nip cook had to keep his rage in check when Ham came strolling in, cheerily calling out, "Coming through!" and served himself soup, rice, and whatever else he wanted from the pots on the stove. Most of the time, he'd give it to the men who were on half-rations. Not only that—he'd stay and wash their clothes or help with small tasks they were too weak to do. He saved cigarette butts for pipe smokers like me, sharing his unlimited supply of smokes with the others.

After a while, Ham came back to the barracks. In June 1945, when about a third of the men were transferred out of Hirohata (destination unknown), they threw the rest of us into one building, possibly because that made it easier to guard us. Right about then, the authorities announced that they were testing camp security; Japanese soldiers dressed as Americans would try to gain entrance into camp. The Japs said that if we caught an imposter and turned him in, they'd give us extra cigarettes.

Of course, we reversed that to mean American paratroopers had either been sighted in the area or were expected to drop from the skies any day now and conduct rescue missions. We unanimously agreed that

HAMMING IT UP   271

we'd give anyone who came through the window all the help he could stand.

The suffocatingly close quarters we now endured from having three times more men in one building proved to be more than Ham could bear; he had to get out of there. Because he was "special," the Japs allowed him to build a little lean-to up against the fence to get away from it all.

The rules against prisoners having any metal or tools apparently didn't apply to Ham, for he managed to come up with a hammer, some nails, pliers, a screwdriver, chisels, and a pair of scissors. He stole most of the stuff from the Nips, but they simply looked the other way. In addition, the guys on the scrap pile kept him supplied with items they thought he could use. Pretty soon he was in business.

Ham always had some little project going, like making a cup from a tin can, fashioning a handle for it from this or that. Then the guards and the soldiers began to take him things to fix, usually paying him in cigarettes or candy. One fellow, though, a noncom who used his services often, never bothered to leave a tip. After a while, Ham had it in for him real bad.

New shoes were a big event in the Japanese army. The leather shortage was so acute, the only way to get a new pair, Ishida advised, was to visit the local geisha house early in the evening, then be the first one to leave, while everyone else was still inside having fun. "That way," he said, "you can have your pick of the shoes lined up outside the door."

The brand-new pair brought to Ham one Saturday afternoon for polishing were beauts—pigskin, I think, real soft and good-looking. The proud owner was the same stingy guy Ham hated. "Shine them up real good, Ham," he said. "I have a date in town and I want to look nice."

"You want me to shine them all over?" Ham asked.

"Of course, all over. I will be back for them in two hours. Be sure they are ready."

Ham took the shoes from the sergeant, placing them side by side on his workbench. The noncom left to bathe and dress for his date. Through the barracks window, a couple of us could see Ham pick up a shoe and proceed to take out the stitches holding it together. We stared in horror. "My God, the son of a bitch is gonna get killed!"

Several other guys heard the buzz of excitement and drifted over to see the show. We watched in utter amazement as Ham systematically pulled out all the hobnails, plucked off the shoelace eyes, separated the layers of leather in the sole one by one, and extracted the nails from the heel. "Look at that lunatic," someone said, laughing. "He's finished the first shoe, and now he's starting in on the other! I can't believe it! This is too nutty, even for him!"

For the next hour, half the men in the barracks stood crowded together at the window, watching Ham dismantle those shoes piece by piece and then carefully polish both sides of the pieces.

A door banged across the way. "Uh oh," I said. The noncom, dressed in his best uniform, was leaving his quarters on his way to Ham's place to pick up his shoes. Boy, this was gonna be something!

In almost devilish anticipation of the imminent fireworks, gleeful men elbowed and nudged each other, scrambling for a better vantage point and a glimpse of the sergeant's reaction the instant he got a load of his handsome footwear. And yet we hardly dared look! A joke was a joke, but Ham had gone too far. The Jap was bound to shoot him in a rage—or worse, chop off his arms!

The soldier demanded his shoes. We watched his cocky smile slowly freeze and the color drain from his freshly shaven face as Ham scooped up the pieces into a pile and shoved them over. The noncom looked at the little heap of shined-up leather scraps in front of him, then at Ham, then back at the "shoes" again. It seemed to me that minutes went by before he could speak. His jaw worked hard as he tried to form words; we leaned forward, straining to hear, but no sound came from his lips.

Then the sergeant jumped about two feet off the ground and screamed. I half expected him to murder Ham on the spot. Instead, he grabbed up some of the leather remnants and ran over to headquarters to show the camp commander what the little cobbler had done. Crazy or no, evil spirits notwithstanding, this time Ham would pay for his shenanigans.

We waited, tense and now worried about the fate of our friend. Several hours went by, but no one sent for Ham or came out to arrest him. They must be planning something spectacular for the ol' boy, we thought. They might even take this to the highest authorities in Osaka. In that case, it could mean the firing squad!

We could have saved ourselves the worry. As it turned out, we had underestimated the head man's grasp of the situation. José had been sweeping up at headquarters and witnessed the scene in the office. That evening he raced into the barracks, eager to report the lurid details to us.

"Oh man!" José said with great relish. "You should have been there! The soldier rushed into the building and demanded to see the CO! He was so angry he could hardly speak! His voice was very high and loud, and he talked so fast no one could understand him. He kept waving these scraps of leather in the air and pointing to his feet."

"I made myself very small and stood real still so no one would notice me," José went on. "When the lieutenant demanded that the sergeant get control of himself, he calmed down a little, and it became clear that Ham had done something to his new shoes. Finally, after many questions, the lieutenant learned what happened. Boy, I thought he was gonna send for Ham. I said to myself, Ay caramba, he's really in trouble now. But instead of being mad at Ham, the lieutenant began to curse the sergeant!"

José paused a minute to catch his breath. "Now," he continued, "all eyes in the office were on the CO. I could see him becoming more and more upset by the minute. He got up from his chair and paced up and down. The sergeant appeared to be worried. He no longer strutted around like el matador. The more the commander stomped around, the lower he hung his head. I can tell you he was not the same macho man. His voice became a whisper as he answered each question with a very respectful 'hai, hai.' Then, all of a sudden, the boss really got mad! He came around the desk, and whacked the soldier one over the head! Whammo! 'You are at fault!' the commander yelled and hit him again. Pow! 'Ham is baka, an idiot! Everybody knows he is not responsible!' Slap! Then the CO worked him over some more! Madre de dios! Aligeró mi corazón! Mother of God! It did my heart good to see that bastardo punished."

José fell on his bunk, breathless from his dramatic rendition of the event that left us lying in the aisles. With each retelling, the story got funnier and funnier to the men, who came to regard Ham as something of a hero.

As for the camp's Section-8 designate, Ham's nonchalant response to the whole thing was, "That'll teach the son of a bitch a lesson he won't forget! I'll bet he ain't never gonna ask me to do another thing without payin' me for it!"

P.S. The day the war ended, Ham made a quick recovery. He turned out to be as sane as the rest of us.

31 From Rags to Riches

The rev of the engines, up high, woke me out of a sound sleep. Something about it seemed different. Puzzled, I swung my legs over the side of the bunk and saw that I wasn't the only one who'd heard it.

After a while, most people working around planes can identify an aircraft flying overhead without looking. The ones you hear every day don't attract any undue attention. But let a strange one fly by, and all heads go up automatically. Two other airmen, awake in their bunks, heard it too.

We got out of bed and noiselessly climbed the rafters to the big skylight at one end of the gabled roof. It was a warm June night—the kind made for flying. A big full moon lit up the sky, giving unlimited visibility in every direction. Then we saw it! "My God, look at that son of a bitch!"

The plane must have been about thirty-five thousand feet up, but it was still the biggest damn thing we'd ever seen! As she flew across the face of the moon, her silhouette easily covered a quarter of it. I think we knew instinctively that it was ours, but I don't remember if anyone said so. Thrilled down to our toes, we just watched until it flew out of sight. Deep inside, I knew the war was over!

"All three of us sat there for a long time afterward, completely awed by the sheer size and power of the ship. To my knowledge, when I had joined the air corps nothing like it existed, even on paper. Where had it come from? Either the plane had quite a range or we had airfields close by. No carrier could launch such a bird! A million questions buzzed around in my brain, and I got no more sleep that night.

From day one, according to the rumor mill, the Japanese had achieved a string of victories, America couldn't fight her way out of a wet paper bag, and Japan definitely held the winning hand. If you wanted proof, just ask a Nip! In Japan, the ex-soldiers at the mill taunted us with the news that their army had just whipped us at Bougainville or decimated us in the Philippines, not to mention the Celebes.

"Wait a minute! Did they say the Philippines?" we'd later ask each other. "What, again? And the Celebes? Hell, that's only a couple of thousand miles away!" Maybe we were the ones gaining ground, not the other way around!

The guards and soldiers loved to ask each of us where we came from. Whether we said New York or New Orleans, their air force had bombed it. We discounted their talk as so much bull, of course. Aircraft simply did not have that kind of range. Besides, without the necessary raw materials, it would have been impossible for them to build such a bomber.

But now, with our own eyes, we had seen an American plane with enormous capability. Watching it fly overhead without being challenged, coupled with the bits and pieces of information we had picked up, convinced us we were close to winning.

The next morning, the place was electric with the barely contained excitement of the men. The Japs knew something was up, too, and we had to really watch our step; both civilian and military guards were meaner than ever. But no matter what they did, they couldn't kill the euphoria building up inside us. I felt like my heart and my head would explode. The silly grin on my face matched everyone else's. It wouldn't be long now. All we had to do was wait. At last—at long, long last—the Yanks were coming.

We didn't know it then, but what we had witnessed the night before was the first reconnaissance flight over our area. Before that, the Yanks had been real busy to the north and south of us.

We later learned that as early as April 18, 1942, sixteen B-25s, under the command of Lt. Col. James Doolittle, had taken off from the USS *Hornet* on a low-level daylight attack against Tokyo, Yokohama, Kobe, Nagoya, and Osaka. All the aircraft but one reached their targets and dropped their payloads. The plan was for them to continue across Japan and land at airstrips in China. Because of fuel shortages, none made it to the airstrips. Some were ditched at sea, some crash-landed, and some simply crashed after the crews bailed out. One plane landed safely but in Russian territory; the Russians interned crew and aircraft for the balance of the war. Three airmen were killed in bailing out or ditching, and eight were captured by Japanese forces; the Japs executed three of the captives. The rest of the raiders were rescued by Chinese guerrillas and smuggled out later. The bombing did relatively little physical damage, but the psychological effects were great. Not only did the raid shake up the Japanese and result in loss of face for them, it gave the Allies a much-needed boost in morale. It also pinned down at least some Japanese fighter planes at home, keeping them out of the fray in the Pacific.

But it would be a long time before we had enough bases in the Pacific to attack the mainland unopposed. Not until June 15, 1944, did the first long-range bombers, the B-29s developed for specific use against the Japanese Islands, fly from airfields in China and bomb important industrial sites in northern Kyushu. With the invasion and ultimate capture of the Mariana Islands, one hundred B-29s flew from Saipan to hit Tokyo again in November 1944. The attacks on Japan's home islands grew in size and intensity as the 20th Air Force received more units.

In March 1945, General Curtis LeMay decided to use B-29s in low-level night-bombing raids to drop incendiaries on the highly vulnerable Japanese cities. On March 9, 279 Superfortresses flying at altitudes of four thousand and nine thousand feet burned fifteen and a half square miles out of the heart of Tokyo. By the middle of March, Iwo Jima was declared secure after heavy casualties on both sides, and air bases on the island became operational in early April.

With the capture of Okinawa in July, providing invasion forces with direct land-based air support and supply bases, the bombers began carrying out continuous raids against key industrial targets and the cities of Nagoya, Kobe, and Osaka. A pilot from my hometown later told me

On May 29, 1945, more than 450 B-29s of the 21st Bomber Command dropped incendiary bombs on Yokohama. The resulting fire destroyed more than seven square miles of the city.

National Archives

that his unit opened their bomb-bay doors over the steel mill at Himeji on their run to Osaka and points north.

Set to detonate one hundred feet above ground, the bombs scattered their deadly payload for miles in every direction, showering the towns and villages below with white-hot metal and napalm. The intense heat from the myriad fires reached more than two thousand degrees centigrade—capable of melting iron.

Cyclonic winds produced by the bombing created a chimneylike effect, sucking up buildings and people for hundreds of feet. Within minutes, everything turned to ashes. No amount of water could extinguish the mile-high firestorms unleashed by the jellylike fuel, calculated to cause optimum damage to the largely bamboo and wood structures in Japan.

The combination of air attacks and a blockade of the home islands imposed a heavy toll on Japanese industry, urban areas, and people. The softening up by the Allies prepared the way for the invasion of Japan. But the decision to use the atom bomb to end the war made an actual landing by U.S. forces unnecessary.

Following that first reconnaissance run over Hirohata, about eight or ten flights heading north came over two nights later. Even more flew over a couple of nights after that. The rafters of our barracks vibrated from the pulsating throb of the giant four-engine planes.

We should have been dancing in the aisles, but we couldn't—not with the ubiquitous guards always within spitting distance. To all outward appearances, we seemed quiet and strictly low-key. But inside of us, flags waved, bells rang, rockets went off, and bands played in the biggest damn Fourth of July celebration ever conceived in the minds of men!

A view of destruction by U.S. incendiaries in Sendai, Japan.
U.S. Army Signal Corps

And that was just the beginning. In the days and nights to come, during the months of June and July, our planes filled the skies, making it impossible to keep track of the increasing numbers roaring overhead. But the excitement of seeing hundreds of our bombers day after day had an unexpected downside. Our elation and joy soon turned to fear and exhaustion. As the bombing got closer to the camp and the small village of Hirohata, angry guards imposed even harsher penalties for the slightest infraction of the rules. They forced those of us suffering from beriberi to work even though we could hardly manage the trek to the mill or the port.

Routine air-raid practices became the real McCoy. Just about the time we'd reach the mill or the docks in the morning, the siren would wail and everyone in the mill would take off for the shelters—everyone but the POWs, that is! We'd have to run two miles back to camp. This might happen two or three times a day. Sick, little more than walking skeletons, we couldn't stand all this prosperity and began to plead, "Please, go bomb somewhere else!" When the Japs locked us away in unmarked barracks, they added terror to the equation. The deafening sound of the planes flying overhead filled us with a terrible fear that we'd be killed by our own bombs.

But when the flights ceased altogether, we became even more frightened. After two months of nonstop missions, suddenly the skies were empty. For almost a week, nothing happened. The rumor mill had been pumping out appalling figures faster than we could digest them—terrible statistics about the death toll of civilians in burning Japanese cities. (We didn't doubt that; from a distance of four miles we had seen Himeji go up in smoke.)

Then August 6 rolled around. "Pika don, pika don," the guard at the mill kept yelling at me. "Sixty thousand Nipponjin killed today in Hiroshima by lightning bomb!"

"Wakarimasen. I don't understand you," I said. "There's no such thing!"

After all, as a bombardier, armament had been my business, and I'd been damn good at it. But a single bomb that could kill more than sixty thousand people? "Fukano! Impossible! Kichigai! No way! Baka! It's totally crazy," I said, laughing. The guard misunderstood my laughter. He struck me across the face, splitting my lip. My cheek stung like fire from the blow.

Three days went by. We heard about a second *pika don* that the United States had dropped on Nagasaki, a smaller city on the southwestern tip of Kyushu Island. This time the reports declared that more than thirty thousand had been killed and more than twenty-five thousand wounded.

The following day the Japs locked us up in camp. "No work," they said. We didn't know what to think. But the shock of seeing all those badly burned civilians streaming past the fence a short time later convinced me the rumors were all true—and our lives probably weren't worth two cents!

On August 15, after five tense days with nothing to do but sit around and worry a lot, we suddenly realized the compound was deserted. Curious, we went looking and found all the guards and soldiers in the office, huddled around the radio with their heads bowed, listening to Emperor Hirohito's speech of surrender. After that, events just snowballed.

The next day the camp commander paid us a visit. "Japan has surrendered," he said to Dr. Seid. "The war is officially over. The soldiers will soon be sent to Himeji for repatriation."

That night, while we slept, the soldiers gathered up their equipment. By morning, they were gone. A week or so later, the hated civilian guards simply melted away, leaving the officer as the only Japanese official in camp.

"You are to wait in the vicinity for a train to come and take you to Yokohama," the former CO explained. "It should be here in sixteen to eighteen days. The mill whistle will alert you when it arrives at the siding in Hirohata, so do not stray very far from the camp. I will remain here strictly in the role of protector, to guarantee your safety."

As it turned out, the CO didn't stick around for very long, so we lost no time reorganizing the running of the camp and making plans to protect ourselves. We found a few rifles and some ammunition in a small armory back of headquarters. The reaction of the locals to the devastation of the area was still unknown, so we posted armed GIs in the guard towers, at the gate, and around the perimeter of the camp.

While others took care of security, a couple of us attended to more important business and broke into the storehouse. Cookie led the raid on the rice, with an added incursion into the former staff's supplies. We were disappointed to find the Red Cross boxes had been robbed of jam, sugar, chocolate, and cigarettes by the Japs as they left camp. A little coffee and milk remained, but that was all. Even so, what a feast we had that night! We doubled our rice ration, and the soup was fairly brimming with vegetables.

Life at camp resumed with some normalcy. With an unlimited amount of coal now available to heat the water, we set up a schedule to bathe every day. The local Japanese people were still keeping a low profile. Except for the refugees from Hiroshima, no one ventured outside their houses. After a few days, when the threat of retaliation didn't materialize, we opened the gates. But we stayed close by; no use tempting fate!

Not long after the surrender, our navy and air force pilots began to scour the country, bird-dogging the POW camps. Three navy shipboard fighter pilots working our area flew over and spotted us. We waved to them, and tipping their wings, they proceeded to give us one hell of an air show.

Climbing above the clouds, the skillful daredevils dove straight down, screaming below the level of our kitchen smokestack and the guard towers, only to pull out at the last minute, barely skimming the rooftops. Then, to the cheers of the jubilant men on the ground, they made another pass, soared up into the air once more, and in a series of power moves, slid into a tight bank, executed a few rolls, leveled off, and zoomed into camp again, nearly knocking the caps off our heads.

Before they flew off, they signaled that supplies would arrive the next day. The message said, "Paint P-W in big white letters on the roof of your building and await further instructions."

Well, we were just like a bunch of kids on Christmas Eve waiting for Santa to come. No one could sleep. The Italians had joined us right after the surrender, so we spread out, occupying both barracks. The lights burned bright and late while the men luxuriated in being free—talking and dreaming of little else except going home.

About eight or nine o'clock the next morning, three B-29s roared over the camp at about five hundred feet. I thought they looked big up high, but at that altitude, those babies were enormous! And the noise— it assaulted our ears and shook the ground. They flew so low we could see the grins on the faces of the crew; I think one of the pilots had a mustache. They signaled to us to get out of the way, then made one more pass to gauge the wind before beginning their drops.

They made their approach over the rice field across from the camp. I saw the bomb-bay doors in the belly of the planes fall open, giving birth to hundreds of brightly colored nylon parachutes. But instead of the firebombs that had brought so much terror and destruction to Japan, bundles of crates, boxes, and 55-gallon drums lashed to pallets came hurtling down from heaven, bringing life to the American and Allied prisoners of war.

The intense colors of the chutes against the backdrop of the brilliantly blue summer sky hurt my eyes. Red ones, blue ones, gold ones, green, black, and white ones—so many—I tried counting them and gave up at fifty.

Emotions that I had tamped down for so long flooded over me and threatened to overwhelm me. Years of pent-up anger, frustration, fear, and despair collided with relief at being free. All of it boiled up together into one big knot in my gut. But it was all right; it was safe to feel again. Tears kept filling my eyes. I sobbed and laughed at the same time; my body shook from the sheer joy of being alive. I praised God over and over for having spared me, for having let me and the men around me live to see this day. At the same time, I grieved for the ones who didn't make it—friends, comrades, buddies, men and women whose bodies lay in unmarked graves on foreign soil. There were so many, and so young. I thanked God for my country, for the thousands of courageous Americans who came after us, sacrificing so much for freedom's ideals. I felt blessed.

Almost before the last bundle hit the ground, we ran out the gate, screaming like wild savages, each man intent on his prize. We spread out across the field, wading in mud up to our waists, and fell on the first thing we came to.

Some of the drums had broken away from their chutes and hit the

Air drop to American POWs after the Japanese surrender.
Illustration by Lauren Y. Pursley

rice paddy like bombs, leaving large craters and covering everything around them with mud. The contents of many of the boxes and crates, busted up on impact, were broadcast like seed.

We ate any foodstuffs we found, regardless of what it was. I was lucky. A box of Hershey bars had broken open and chocolate lay everywhere. I grabbed one, tore off the wrapper, and crammed the whole thing into my mouth. By the time I swallowed the last bite, I was full!

That one slender bar hit my stomach, shot past my pancreas, and sailed right into my bloodstream. I felt like someone must feel who's hopped up on dope!

Others were not so fortunate. The man next to me found a busted can of corned beef. Like me, he foolishly ate the whole thing right there. A few minutes later, he was in such agony he nearly died.

The guys who flew these missions later said that they had anticipated a 20-percent drop loss. If by loss they meant broken boxes, drums, and crates, they were right. That's approximately what we had. But we weren't about to leave that stuff out in the field! We hauled every bit of it back to camp.

"Cookie," we yelled, as we carted the damaged goods into the yard. "Get out the biggest pots you've got! We can't let this stuff go to waste. We're gonna have us a big gumbo."

"Okay, but I ain't responsible for how it tastes."

"It can't be any worse than the slop we've had to eat these last four years."

"True," he said, and helped us pour all the busted cans into the boilers. Meat, soup, candy, vegetables, beans, pudding, fruit cocktail, peaches, potatoes—you name it. It was the worst concoction you ever saw, and it was beautiful!

"Get out your rice bowls and get in line," Dr. Seid instructed us. "After your bowl has been filled to the brim, you can sip it, gulp it, or save it, but if you want seconds, you'll have to go around to the end of the line and work your way back up. This will give your stomachs time to recover and keep the food from killing you."

It was as though my taste buds had had amnesia! I had actually forgotten what regular food was like, making everything I put into my mouth a totally new experience. With each bowlful of "air-drop soup," I discovered a new taste sensation. Sometimes cherries floated to the top, sometimes it was chocolate, asparagus, or anchovies. It didn't matter. We were all a little crazy at that point, and it was all delicious!

We used everything the planes had dropped, wasting nothing—especially those silky nylon parachutes. I copped a Chinese-red one and a bright gold one and wrapped them around my little straw mat. Man were they soft!

DDT, something unknown to us when we left home, "killed fleas," according to the label on the box. Unlike the Japanese flea powder, the directions called for applying it directly to the areas of infestation. We sprinkled it around the bunks and between the chutes, and settled down for the best sleep we'd had in years—and couldn't!

Even with a carton of my favorite brand of smokes, a box of Hershey bars by my side, and minus the fleas, it was no use. Everyone was too excited and happy, too supercharged from all the high-quality food and sweets. There would be no such thing as sleep for the next few nights.

The supplies from that initial drop would have been enough to sustain us until we left Japan. One meal a day of the rich American food was equivalent to several days' meager rations as prisoners. It would take a while for our systems to adjust. But that didn't faze Uncle Sam! He'd heard that we were hungry, and he was determined to feed us!

We had barely stumbled out of the barracks the following morning when six Superfortresses came screaming in loaded with supplies. The guys from Saipan were back! This time they dropped medicines, clothes, shoes, razors, shaving cream, toothpaste, toothbrushes, soap, khaki-colored towels and wash rags, matches, more cigarettes—and more food! There was coffee, sugar, milk, candy, gum, vitamins, and everything they had ever put in a can, including orange juice.

Yesterday we were starving. Today we were millionaires! Although the planes dropped the second load across the road as before, we didn't bother with the stuff ourselves. Some of the local people had begun to leave their homes in search of food and fuel. We hired them and, for a piece of the pie, they gladly hauled it in for us.

The whole time in Japan, we had been denied matches. Now grown men sat around striking matches to their hearts' content, just watching them burn for the sheer pleasure of it, only to light another and another. We must have gone through a ton of matches that way.

Same thing with cigarettes. For the first time in almost four years, we had cartons and cases of every brand made in the U.S.—Lucky Strikes, Kools, Camels, Chesterfields—name your favorite and it was there. We'd light a cigarette, take a puff, and flick it away. Then we'd immediately light up another one and do the same thing. We reveled in the knowledge that we had more than we could use. Fortunately, these odd little cravings were satisfied rather quickly.

With a couple of good American meals under our belts, we suddenly had no need for pilfering, hoarding, or—best of all—stealing from each other, too often the case in the past. We were on the road to recovery— mentally adjusting to the drastic change in our circumstances, and doing okay physically.

With a total of nine B-29s making deliveries, when three would have been plenty, we now had food and supplies stacked on shelves over and under our bunks; we stumbled over it in the aisles, and it spilled out into the courtyard. We could have stayed there for months without making a dent in the stuff. But the men from the Marianas insisted that we had three more planeloads coming.

It was impossible to wave them off; we tried. Our navy guys got up on the roof and signaled to the pilot that we already had more than we'd ever use. "Nothin' doin'," they said. "Orders are orders. We've come nearly two thousand miles, and you're gonna get every last box, barrel, and crate whether you want it or not. So just clear the decks down there!"

After witnessing the air drops, the local people began showing up at the back gate. Many of them were the same men and women who had been helpful to us in the past. Now that the shoe was on the other foot, some of the former guards in camp and honchos at the mill begged handouts or tried to buy a little of the food they knew we had. Usually, they sought out the GIs they had been friendly with.

One of them, the boss from the scrap-sorting warehouse, asked for me. "Food is scarce and becoming more and more difficult to get," he said. "Would you be willing to sell me a little rice or tinned meat for my family?"

The man had never given me a rough time. He had always been fair and decent in his handling of the prisoners under his control. His sense of pride, which compelled him to buy rather than beg, moved me. Since we had no restrictions regarding the distribution of the goods, I gave him canned goods, rice, cigarettes—and candy for his kids.

The air drops damaged several houses close by. Some had holes in their roofs from the misguided missiles. A 55-gallon drum, parting company with its pallet, hit the corner of a building and knocked it down. We waited for repercussions from the locals, but none occurred. We decided it was safe to go farther afield.

It felt good to get into new American-made clothes. Somehow the military shirts, pants, coveralls, and shoes restored our identities. I hadn't had a real pair of shoes in a long time. I found a pair in my size and took a walk down the road to try them out. I went about a mile, and by the time I got back, my feet were ruined!

Every day we'd wander around, usually in groups of twenty, exploring the countryside and the two little villages nearby, mindful of our departure date and alert to the first sound of the steel mill's whistle that would signal our train's arrival. At first we traveled on foot. But before long, everyone found something to ride. While bicycles were the most common, one fellow showed up on a little horse and several guys were driving old trucks.

God knows where the Italians found the little red fire engine, but about forty guys sat on top raising hell as they came down the road, sirens blaring away! That looked like the way to go, so I ditched my bike and joined them.

The Italian sailors had been in port several times before and knew their way around. Most of the Americans were denied alcohol for almost four years, and it had been a year and a half since the Italians had their last drink, so they said it was imperative we make a stop at the local saké mill to get a few bottles. After that, we rode up and down the lanes killing time, looking for fires. Surprisingly, no one offered to start one so we could put it out!

On one of these wild excursions, the Italians invited us to go with them to a geisha house in one of the villages. I had to laugh when it turned out to be one of Whiskey's favorite haunts, which he had so often supplied with our rice. But I should have paid more attention to Ishida's advice, because the old guy knew what he was talking about. When I finally came out, my new shoes were gone! To make matters worse, the "tall" gal Mamasan promised me stood all of five feet in her tabi.

Now that I was "rich," I decided to repay the young girl from the scrap-sorting detail who had helped me when I needed it. I filled a barracks bag with rice, canned food, cigarettes, candy, and other supplies and set out to find her.

Curiously, the Seitetsu Steel Mill was not bombed during the raids. Later, when I asked my friend who'd flown so many missions over the factory why, he said intelligence had shown that the mill's production was negligible; it didn't warrant destroying. The company had been shut down since the first atom bomb was dropped, but I called in at the barracks on the chance that Mariko and her family were still in the area. I was in luck.

Mariko's eyes lit up at the sight of the food and goodies, but her face resembled a sunbeam when she bit into a Hershey bar. I don't believe the young girl had ever tasted chocolate before. She just closed her eyes and smiled as she savored the rich creaminess of the candy.

Her girlish reaction to her first whiff of Camay soap was equally heartwarming. Cupping both hands around the sweet-smelling bar, she held it up to her nose for a long time, breathing in the delicate perfume. From her expression, I couldn't tell if she wanted to eat it or what!

Mariko and I had a long visit. I thanked her and her little brother again for their friendship. I tried to tell her how much she had meant to me in the midst of so much cruelty and despair. I think she understood.

There were others like me—POWs who had been lucky enough to receive help from compassionate Japanese people. They, too, sought out their benefactors with gifts of food and a few luxuries to show their appreciation. No one with any sense wants war. We realized that these folks were no different from us. They had been caught up in something not of their choosing. They had given it their best shot, but they too were glad when it ended.

I did normal things, like getting a haircut. Not that I needed one— the length of my hair was little more than the Japanese army regulation *ni cinchi* (two centimeters). It was just the idea of the thing.

A few of the men began coming back to camp at night with souvenirs. When two of the guys showed up with a Japanese sword, everyone else decided that they wanted one, too. We knew that some of the swords had been in the families of these men for hundreds of years; that made them all the more desirable. We crowded around to hear the gory details of how the men had come by their prize. "Boy, I bet you had to wrestle the taii [captain] to the ground, right?" someone said.

"Yeah. He was a real dangerous-looking character on a bike. I think he was on his way to be demobbed in Himeji. We could see his sword dangling from his belt."

His partner spoke up. "Man, we had to have that!"

"It must have taken a lot of guts to stop him."

"You bet it did! I mean, anything could have happened. He could've even pulled a gun on us."

"Wow! What happened next?"

"Well, we just walked up to him and simply took the damn thing away from him."

"You're kiddin'!"

"No, I'm not."

"Then what happened?"

"Nothing."

"You mean he didn't do anything to you?"

"Nope."

That's all we needed to hear! For the next few days, we lay in wait for other officers coming down the road in front of the camp.

We netted a few swords, but not enough to go around. Word of the treasure-seekers must have gotten around, because the officers began to avoid the area altogether.

The trains ferrying the soldiers home would be a better source, we decided, so we took off for the station at Hirohata. Boarding singly or in groups of two or three, we'd wander through the packed cars looking for booty. Talk about the biggest damn fools ever born! Here we were in enemy country, pushing, shoving, and elbowing our way through cars jammed with army troops who had just been defeated, who were madder than hell at having lost face, and who for all we knew were armed to the teeth. I shudder when I remember how we'd stop in front of an officer and reach over to relieve him of his sword. We didn't have the sense God gave a goat. It's a wonder no one got his throat cut, but it didn't occur to us to be afraid.

Perhaps the sword represented a symbol of our past humiliation. But whatever it meant, I still didn't have one. I was determined not to go home without one. All alone, I jumped on a train to begin my search. As I started down the aisle, I saw two or three officers in the car but no swords. *Not bloody likely,* I thought. *They all have one. They must have heard about us and squirreled them away somewhere.*

The first officer I came to was young; couldn't have been more than twenty-two. I checked him out but didn't see any sign of a weapon— that is, until I glanced down at his feet. I spotted the dull gleam of the hilt sticking out from under his seat. Without a word, I reached past his jackboots and grabbed the sword. I looked at him for a second. He returned my stare with eyes that expressed his loss, but he said nothing. Turning away, I made my way back through the crowded, swaying coach to the vestibule, getting off at the first stop with my badge of courage, my symbol of liberation.

While on one of these stakeouts at the train station, I heard about a couple of guys who caught Donald Duck on the platform there—no doubt, on his way home. Mugged at the hands of his former victims, he probably arrived without his clothes. The GIs grabbed him, hauled him behind one of the buildings in the train yard, slapped him around a little, then made him strip. The avenged ex-prisoners then walked away with his uniform, his underwear, his boots, and his cap.

It was almost time to leave. Just before the train arrived, I went back to see Mariko. I gave her more food, some rice, my blankets, and about 150 yen—money I conned out of some of our "entrepreneurs," from deals they had struck at the back gate with the locals.

Japan's *haikyu* rationing system was already beginning to break down. Even if someone was still in charge of the system, there was nothing much to distribute. Things were growing worse day by day. Between the terrible food shortages, which would escalate in the months to come, and spiraling inflation that threatened to destroy what was left of their country, the Japanese people would suffer immensely.

32 All Ahead, Slow

At the first blast of the mill's whistle, we hightailed it back to camp. The promised train pulled into the station at Hirohata one evening, on or around September 5—about eighteen days after the initial air drop. Next stop, Yokohama—and the ships that would ultimately take us home. We were ready!

Ten cars made up the train. We loaded three of them with the food and supplies we hauled from camp, and by 10 A.M. the next day everyone had boarded for the trip north.

Pulling out of the depot, I experienced the tangle of emotions I felt the first time I saw the B-29s coming in. It hit me all over again. The war was over. We were really going home! As we left the village and sped through the countryside, the atmosphere among the men seemed lighthearted and happy. The guys in my coach were a rowdy bunch. I expect they were covering up their raw feelings with nonstop talk and laughter that was a little too loud.

Coming into the city of Himeji a short time later, our buoyant mood turned sober. The horrific firestorm we saw from the camp's courtyard hardly prepared us. Everywhere we looked, total destruction lined both sides of the tracks. Only two buildings—a bank and a temple whose masonry shells didn't burn—were left standing in the once thriving, bustling city. Everything else was flattened. The whole area looked like a vast wasteland. The scene was unbelievable.

Roads and intersections led nowhere. Remnants of fence timbers poked out of the charred earth at crazy angles. The stone walls of water wells marked the locations of once lush and carefully tended gardens that were now denuded and black, devoid of any sign of life. Behind patterns of artfully raked gravel still evident in places, concrete or stone steps climbed to dwellings that were no longer there.

At the edges of the city, fields scorched by errant firebombs resembled giant cigarette burns in a huge, green carpet. We saw few people except for a handful of civilians who pawed through the ashes in search of lost relatives—or for something, anything, they could salvage.

The same picture of complete and utter desolation repeated itself over and over again, as we traveled all that day and night on a rail line that had either escaped the bombings or had been hastily repaired. Whole villages and small towns were reduced to nothing but rubble. The more sizable industrial cities of Osaka and Nagoya had sustained heavy damage. All along the way, the pitiful survivors camped out in ditches under makeshift shelters and lean-tos erected from scraps of tin they managed to find.

We expected to see bomb craters, but incendiaries leave no holes in the ground. We couldn't understand the collateral damage. Surveying the ruins of Japan's industrial sites from a strictly military point of view, we thought our bombers had done a good job of it. "But why sanitize civilian areas in the cities and level the villages?" we asked.

At first, it didn't make any sense. But when we noticed the drill presses, punch presses, lathes, and other small machinery in the ashes of the houses, we began to understand the reason for such devastation to the general population. In addition to the factories and mills pumping out war matériel, it looked as though nearly everyone in Japan had some kind of little plant going in his home. The economy was on such a footing that after putting in a full day at the mill, Mr. Sasaki might be making half-inch bolts at his house in the evenings, while Mr. and Mrs. Yamamoto across the street made the nuts and washers to fit them. No one was exempt; everyone labored night and day to bring about victory. Burning the wood-and-paper houses was the most effective way to end the Japanese war effort.

What seemed cruel had been, in fact, the only way to ensure peace. The Japanese were committed to their emperor. He was a god to them, and as long as he said fight, no one dared buck the system, much less give up. Although I met Japanese people who were genuinely kind and gentle, I believe the Japanese as a whole were prepared to give their lives down to the last man, woman, and child, possibly killing a million more Americans in the process. Faced with this knowledge and committed to ending this damnable war that had dragged on for nearly four long years as quickly as possible, all-out destruction of the country, or the atom bomb, was the only answer for America and her allies. This was the reality of total war waged against an implacable enemy.

As we reached Yokohama the next morning, the train slowed down for the ride through parts of the city, and while much of it had been bombed, for the first time we saw American MPs, stationed on every corner and directing traffic in the streets. We had taken some foolish chances and (fortunately for us) suffered no ill effects, but up until then we had been alone and unprotected. The sight of the GIs in jeeps and army trucks, clogging the roads and intersections, intent on the business of occupation, was very reassuring.

A large warehouse in the port area had been taken over as a reception depot for the thousands of ex-POWs who were arriving daily by train from camps throughout Japan. Besides Americans (the majority), there were Canadians, British, Australians, Dutch, and Chinese. Inside the warehouse, army blankets strung up on clotheslines cordoned off areas where each man would receive a medical exam before leaving for the Philippines. There we would be sorted out by nationality and branch of service prior to completing the last leg of our journey home.

The scene was organized chaos. So many sights and sounds vied for my attention all at once: being surrounded by our own troops for a change; hearing English spoken almost exclusively, especially the irreverent slang and salty language used by the Americans in charge; feeling safe when I saw all the navy and Coast Guard ships lined up in the harbor; a feeling of being "home" even though I was seven thousand miles away. Hey, I was back in the fold again!

I remember seeing a black infantryman standing guard near the warehouse, the first black man I'd seen in almost four years. He was magnificent—nearly seven feet and weighing about three hundred pounds. Reaching up, I felt his biceps, visible through his form-fitting, pressed-to-perfection uniform. "Boy, am I glad to see you!" I said, grinning from ear to ear. He just smiled.

Then there were the nurses. Despite their baggy, olive-drab coveralls, they looked sensational! American and female—what more could a guy ask for? Professional to the core, they cared for the endless lines of emaciated men who looked like the living dead, without turning a hair. But they couldn't hide their reactions to our upbeat morale. Even some of the stretcher cases were able to manage a few wolf whistles and appreciative noises.

"Say, baby, are you busy tonight?" asked an emaciated boy as an attractive nurse took his vital signs.

"Never mind him, darlin', what about me?" said the soldier lying next to him.

"Honey, those two are losers. But you and I could make beautiful

Allied prisoners of war collect their meager possessions as they prepare to leave a POW camp near Yokohama on September 6, 1945.

U.S. Navy photo from Corbis-Bettman, New York

music together," said a third, who had tubes in his arms and bottles strung overhead.

I noticed that the nurse's eyes were a little too bright, but she managed to give each man a brilliant smile. "Whoa, you really make it hard on a girl! You're all such great guys, how can I possibly choose?"

Maybe it was pity on the part of the nurses, but it seemed like the old, tired, corny lines, used in the past by America's finest, still had the desired effect. Just playing the game did wonders for our egos, which were in worse shape than our bodies.

First, all our new clothes were taken away. Then we were treated to leisurely showers with plenty of hot water and soap, followed by a thorough delousing. After we received more clothes (navy dungarees and white skivvy shirts, about eight sizes too big), the nurses and doctors began checking us over. I watched as the men in the long, snaking lines were slowly swallowed up one by one into the inner sanctums behind the makeshift partitions.

Finally my turn came. Two hands, reaching out from the other side of the blankets, pulled me in and popped me with shots in both arms and, after dropping my pants, one in each cheek. "Hey, you guys have come a long way since we've been gone!" I joked, pleasantly surprised by the imperceptible sting of the tiny hypodermics. "This beats the horse-sized needles you used on me four years ago. The mosquito bites on Bataan hurt worse than this."

"Yeah? Well, that's not all that's new, Bub. Just wait'll you get home. You ain't seen nothin' yet!" was the orderly's snappy reply.

The rest of the exam progressed with the military's usual degree of finesse; some things never change. If you were breathing and could walk at all, they pronounced you okay. We were the lucky ones; we could shift for ourselves, while a large number of the guys in really bad shape (whose rescue had almost come too late) got first priority and immediately went aboard the hospital ships in the harbor.

The speed with which they processed all the men that day was nothing short of fantastic! They put me on a Coast Guard ship with sixty other ex-POWs, and we got under way before dark. "The shaft on one of the ship's propellers is bent, and it will be all ahead, slow," the captain announced. So? Who cared? After being issued more navy gear, in-

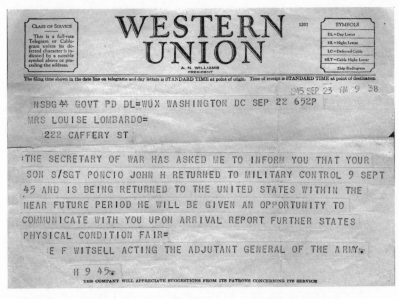

Liberated: telegram from the U.S. War Department dated September 23, 1945.

cluding a sailor's white hat, a carton of cigarettes, and box of candy, no one was complaining.

How can I describe my thoughts and feelings as I stepped aboard one of our vessels to leave the country whose people had held me prisoner for almost four years? Through it all, I never doubted I'd go home, but it had been a long, hard journey. This chapter in my life was finally over.

What a difference just a few days could make. The transformation from prisoner and slave to liberated and free was instantaneous. Like a molting snake shedding his old skin, I felt like a new man!

The recurring diarrhea that kept us wrung out was gone. I walked better. The nutritious diet and vitamins were helping to ease the pains in my hips and legs. The all-pervading mist of fear that had constantly enveloped us every waking moment, making us paranoid and edgy, had evaporated.

I felt completely relaxed, surrounded by everything American— plenty of good chow, clean sheets, comfortable beds (even though stacked six bunks high and smack up against a bulkhead, with mine positioned right below the waterline), and the companionship of men who wished me well, instead of dead.

First off, I made friends with the ship's cook, and he made sure I got my coffee pretty regular. Over the next six days, we slipped into a pleasant routine of rest and light exercise in the sea air out on deck. Thanks to Cookie's hearty meals and the fresh doughnuts down in the coffee room, we began to pick up weight.

Sitting around and shooting the breeze in their lingo, the off-duty sailors got the idea all of us were navy men—until some of us would switch to air force jargon, then back again. "What the hell branch of the service were you guys in anyway?" they asked. We explained that the marines and navy personnel had charge of organizing the prisoners in many of the camps, and we'd sort of adopted their slang.

Some of the ship's crew questioned us a little about our experiences as prisoners. A few of the men couldn't or wouldn't say much. But for most of us, it wasn't a problem. Without knowing it at the time, we did the right thing by talking it out, even comparing notes. That helped to put the whole thing into perspective.

Something else I didn't know at the time—I would have the good sense to marry a girl who listened. Being able to laugh with her about all the nutty things that happened, to get angry at times, and even to cry unashamedly, remembering the many hardships, has made it easier to lay the ghosts.

My wife, Inez, helped me deal with the question that still haunts me to some extent: "Why did I make it while others perished?" The experts tell me that this is a form of guilt common to ex-POWs. Maybe God wasn't finished with me yet; unfinished business—an intriguing notion that makes me want to get up every morning.

Docking in Manila was like returning to the scene of the crime. The first time we came in, Thanksgiving 1941, two ships from the Spanish-American war still lay half-submerged in the harbor. No one had ever bothered to remove these relics from another era. This time, hundreds of sunken ships—all Japanese—littered the bay. The wharves were repaired by the time we arrived, but it was plain that when MacArthur returned, he had given the enemy one hell of a fight!

Eighteen-wheelers waited at the dock to take us to an area southeast

of Manila where a tent city had been set up until we could be repatri-
ated. We piled into the trailers, outfitted with wooden benches that easily held a hundred men. Our driver was a WAC, our first glimpse of a
member of the Women's Army Corps, unknown to us until then. She
was tiny—maybe five feet and ninety-eight pounds dripping wet—and
no beauty. Beneath her tan her skin showed the yellowing effects of the
malaria prophylactic Atabrine, but she got her share of whistles and
"hubba-hubbas" just the same! Despite her size, this gal was no lightweight; she could haul! When she took off in the truck, she dumped
most of us on the floor.

On the outskirts of the city, long tents served as reception centers.
Once again they took our clothes, deloused us, and issued us more navy
blues. These fit much better. We each got a smallpox vaccination and
six more shots: five injections, plus a shot of whiskey. "Can we get another if we go around again?" we joked.

They paid us about five hundred dollars apiece, but we couldn't buy
anything; everything was free. Every day at the PX, they gave us tickets good for five cans of beer, five cigars, three packs of cigarettes, five
candy bars, and all the Coca-Cola we could drink. Oh yeah, come to
think of it, I did spend a dollar; I bought a wallet to put the scratch in!

The mess hall was open twenty-four hours a day for the ex-POWs.
Twenty or so cooks manned the galley, and you could order whatever
struck your fancy any time of the day or night. It was like a miracle!
Everything imaginable was available—fresh fruit and vegetables, rolls
and pastries, ice cream by the ton, food like Mom used to cook, and all
the meat you could eat. When you said "Steak"—well, brother, all they
said was, "How big?"

Every day thousands of American and Allied troops came through
that camp from Manchuria, Formosa, and the Dutch East Indies, as well
as from Japan. I met up with several of the men from Hirohata and
some from Cabanatuan who made it back. It was like old home week
around there. But one day I happened to look up, and there stood my
old friend Laurence, better known as Omasa. "Hey, you son of a bitch!"
I yelled from halfway across the mess tent. "Where have you been? You
sure look bad!"

The big guy was grinning so wide I thought his face was going to split in two. His once barrel chest was sunken like his cheeks, his clothes fit like mine, and his skin was waxy. "Man," he said, "I've been to hell and back, but you must've been on the same trip, 'cause you don't look so hot yourself!"

I grabbed his hand, and he gave me a big bear-hug. We just stood there for a minute or so, holding on, trying to compose ourselves. "What happened to you? One minute you were there on the deck of the ship, and the next minute you were gone," I chided him gently, trying to blink away the tears that threatened to fall.

"We got separated in the confusion," he said. "All I know is when they divided what was left of the guys in the hold, I ended up on the northwest side of Honshu, across from Korea. A little place called Niigata."

"How was it?"

"Terrible, just terrible. I was either freezing cold or soaking wet. I worked the night shift in a coalyard, much of the time on an elevated trestle, fifteen feet in the air."

"It must have been tough!"

"Well, the whole time I was freezing my rear end off up there, I thought about you and our merry little band of rogues running up and down Luzon, dodging guerrilla attacks in a pair of thongs and a G-string. It helped a little. That was paradise compared to Niigata. So how was *your* tour?"

"Me? Oh, hey, it was just swell! I had it made! After our wonderful ocean voyage, I landed in a great place not far from the beach. I mean, sea breezes, cuisine out of this world, and not much to do. You know, just laze around and relax. I even got to take me a harbor cruise now and then. Man, it was quite a vacation, and all for free. Oh, yeah, and the women! Hell, would you believe the Japs took me to the skivvy houses pretty regular?"

"John, you haven't changed a bit," Laurence said, shaking his head and laughing. "Still the same old bullshooter."

Laurence said conditions were very bad in Niigata. "At first, we slept on grass mats on a concrete floor, usually in our clothes to keep warm. The food was skimpy, mostly rice and daikon soup; a rare treat when they threw in some dried fish.

"The work was brutal and dangerous. Up in the air in all kinds of weather, pushing and guiding coal cars along the tracks like we did, we suffered many sprains and bruises on our legs. Once, a medical corpsman had to lance my swollen and inflamed knee—without any drugs to deaden the pain.

"I didn't work for two days, but as I lay there, my knee throbbing, with nothing to eat, feeling the body lice on me and watching them crawl around on my blankets, I guess I came close to not caring if I made it or not. I wondered if dying wouldn't be easier than existing as we were. Fortunately, the feeling of despair soon wore off."

Laurence looked painfully thin, his big wrist bones stuck out a mile. *We'll have to fatten this boy up*, I thought. "Hey, let's see what's on the menu before we turn in," I said.

Our talk went on for hours. It must have been three in the morning before we hit the sack. His year and a half had been a living nightmare. I think he had even less to eat than I did. At least I could eat what we stole off the ships.

While in Manila, I also talked with a man who had been sent to Manchuria. He told me about being forced to labor from dawn to dusk, day after day, in an unsafe, poorly ventilated mineshaft.

"As the men cut deeper into the rock, pillars of coal were left at intervals to support the ceiling of the shafts," he said. "Later, they used us as 'thieves' to chip away at these supports and extract even more of the mineral. Most of us, untrained in mining, were expected to know how to break the columns without having them collapse. 'Thieves' in the U.S. are paid extra for this hazardous job. In Manchuria, when accidents occurred, we were just expendable."

The prisoners were subjected to cruel, sadistic guards who punished and beat them when they became sick and couldn't keep up the pace. They had no medical care in the camp, and many had come back with bad coughs. Their diet was criminal—moldy rice full of weevils; hardly any meat, but what meat they got was usually rotten and full of maggots.

"And the weather! When the men died in winter, the ground was so hard, you couldn't get a shovel in it. We had to stack the bodies like cordwood until it thawed in the spring. God, John, at times I thought I'd die from the cold."

For the remainder of the next two weeks, we waited for the ship that would take us home. The requirements were simple: rest, eat as much as we could hold, try to recuperate from the past, and adjust to the idea of being free. (For most, not a problem!) Those of us responding nicely to the vitamin therapy, and now mostly just hungry, picked up about a pound a day. Every time we got a new batch of clothes, they had to be a size bigger.

Some of us got to go into Manila a couple of times. A lot had changed. For one thing, traffic now moved on the right. Much of the city was destroyed in wresting it from the Japanese. At an intersection in the San Miguel district, I saw a large chunk of the fifth-floor corner of a bank building, suspended by its rebar, dangling in midair.

Antsy, unable to keep still, we roamed around the tent city, getting acquainted and catching up on past events with those involved in the action. I learned that the first carrier strikes against Manila and Luzon Island had come in the last days of September 1944.

On October 20, General MacArthur made good on his promise to return to the Philippines, coming ashore with the central Philippine attack force on the east coast of Leyte Island. Challenged by a full-scale Japanese naval operation designed to drive them from the Philippines, the Americans fought the biggest sea battle of the war, the Battle of Leyte Gulf. Between October 23 and 26, the U.S. succeeded in destroying or disabling twenty-six combatant ships, effectively crippling the Japanese navy.

In December, landings were made south of Luzon, on Mindoro, and after repeatedly shelling Manila and Luzon Island, the Yanks came ashore in Lingayen Gulf on January 9, 1945. By the end of January, further landings had been made near Subic Bay and at Nasugbu, south of Manila Bay.

Word of the planned execution of all POWs by the fleeing Japanese had reached MacArthur, and a mad dash to rescue the inmates of the prisons in the Philippines was made. In the early morning hours of January 30, one hundred 6th Army Rangers, accompanied by several hundred Filipino guerrillas, surrounded Camp Cabanatuan and waited.

Seventeen days earlier, the Nip guards and soldiers had left the camp to fight the Americans who were making inroads into Luzon. The Japs had provided a ten-day supply of food for the prisoners and warned them not to leave the compound. When they didn't return after the tenth day, the always-hungry Americans broke open the stores and helped themselves to the provisions left in haste by the Japs. Hoping they had been permanently abandoned, they panicked a few days later when they thought their guards had returned.

It turned out to be a Japanese infantry unit. Tired and hungry, they simply marched into camp and asked for food. Except for posting guards in the towers, they left the POWs alone; they were still there when the U.S. forces came.

Around 8 P.M. on the night of January 30, the Rangers attacked the camp, killing the 500 Japs and liberating the remaining 513 prisoners in Camp Cabanatuan within thirty minutes.

On February 4, after months of pounding the city of Manila, Yanks in tanks rumbled up to the walls of Bilibid Prison in the heart of the city, where Allied civilians and eight hundred starving American men, too sick and weak to be transported to Japan on the "hell ships," were still interned.

One of the civilians, fearful the tanks might be Japanese, watched from his third-floor position and observed two of the tanks, obviously lost in the middle of Lope de Vega Street. The prisoner described it this way: "The turrets opened and two heads emerged, each smoking a cigarette. 'Hey, Casey,' one exasperated driver said to the other, 'Haven't we been up this friggin' street before?'"

Santo Tomas University, located near Bilibid, had been turned into a civilian prison by the Japs in the early days of the war. I recently learned that my cousin's aunt, Della Aucoin, was held there. Her husband was a sugar engineer, and after the grinding season ended in Louisiana, it had been his practice to travel to other countries, harvesting two crops a year, and help run the factories.

The Aucoins, like so many civilians who failed to get out in time, were caught in Manila when the Japanese came to town. Della and her husband and children were rounded up and imprisoned in Santo Tomas. For more than three years, they lived in fear of their Japanese guards and starved along with their fellow inmates, including the one hundred American army and navy nurses captured on Corregidor in May 1942.

Della said she prayed for the day when the Americans would return. She told me of the rapes and torture, the sickness they endured without much in the way of medicines, and the daily grind of prison life. She said two of the guards took one of the women in her section to another cell and slapped her around nearly every day. It broke her heart to hear the screams echoing all over the building.

Many died during those years, and Della had no illusions about the fate of her family. She was thirty years old at the time of her capture, and thirty-three at the time of her release, but she said she aged at least fifty years. Not until sometime in 1944, when the prisoners began to get word of the war's progress, did hope return.

"The little Filipino children playing in the streets nearby began to sing the news to us in Tagalog," Della told me. "They'd take some popular American tune or a nursery rhyme, and singing at the top of their little voices, they would exchange the normal lyrics for the latest accounts of our naval victories in the Pacific. We also knew when MacArthur landed. What a day that was! The Japs could hardly contain us.

"These same kids also knew the location of the mines the Japanese buried in the streets of Manila after the war began to go sour for them. When the Yanks drove into the city, they quickly took advantage of the children's special knowledge, and it was not unusual to see a tot perched on the fender of a tank giving hand signals to the drivers inside.

"In fact, on the morning of February 4, 1944, we could hear the powerful engines of our rescuers, and I saw a small boy on one of these huge machines saying, 'Go left here, Joe, and go right there, Joe.' Then, as they stopped in front of the university, I heard an American male voice call out to another tank driver, 'Where the hell is the damn gate?' His young comrade shot back without any hesitation, 'Make your own damn gate!' And with that, they came right through the wall!"

Della had an interesting postscript to her story. She said that later, while the inmates of Santo Tomas waited to be processed to go home, two uniformed American servicemen went up to the woman whose cries could be heard all over Bilibid when they hauled her in for questioning every day, and apologized over and over, saying, "We are so sorry to have frightened you the way we did. It's just that your screams were so convincing to the Japanese prison authorities, you provided a perfect cover for our covert activities." These American-born Japanese turned out to be spies for our side!

Our cruisers and destroyers continued to bombard the entrances to Manila Bay, and U.S. troops landed on the Bataan Peninsula and Corregidor on February 15 and 16. In the meantime, the capital was bitterly defended by the Japanese with steady house-to-house fighting. Daily bombings and heavy shelling were necessary to flush them out.

The Nips also booby-trapped and leveled much of the city out of revenge and spite. The once-beautiful sections of the town, Intramuros, the old walled city of Spanish times, as well as many of the historical churches and buildings lay in ruins. One hundred thousand dead Japanese and Filipinos littered the streets; their bodies had to be bulldozed into piles and burned by flamethrowers. It took until March 3, 1945, one month after it had entered the city, for the army to declare Manila secure.

We left the once-proud city almost two weeks to the day after arriving from Japan. A Liberty ship carrying two thousand troops was headed for San Francisco and had room for three thousand more, the captain said. "There is one thing you should know. You'll only be fed twice a day. If you'd rather wait for another ship, that's fine. It's your decision."

Only twice a day—imagine that! I think all of the ex-POWs assembled there sort of looked at each other and laughed. I don't believe anyone stayed behind because of one meal, and a roster was made up for all three thousand.

As we entered the final leg of our journey, the ponderous thoughts of the returning GIs matched the ship's slow, sluggish speed of eleven knots and made the trip across the Pacific a long one. Worn out from all the euphoria and the roller-coaster pace of events in the last few weeks, we now had a chance to focus on resuming our lives. The war had turned everything upside down. There were bound to be changes, not only in ourselves but in the way people now looked at life. Could we adjust? Could we pick up where we'd left off? We wondered whether to reenlist or find a job. Were we too old, had we seen too much, to return to school? What did the future hold for men and women who might be emotionally scarred? Were we tough enough to go on? Would there be anyone there to help? Did she wait?

At night, aware of the possibility that some Jap submarine commander might still be fighting his own private war, we sailed under blackout conditions. We didn't dock in Hawaii but passed north of the islands, stopping at a place called Ulithi to pick up a few GIs on the tiny atoll.

Compared to my first trip going over on the *President Coolidge* (which, unfortunately, sank in October 1942 when she struck a U.S. mine on her seventh military mission), this trip was slightly less luxurious. No dance bands and singers entertained us, no charming hostesses engaged us in conversation to keep our minds off the fighting. There was no gambling, no gourmet dinners; hell, there were not even any staterooms. We slept out on deck, in the passageways, everywhere. But that was okay. We were going home!

33 Freedom Train

The morning we arrived, San Francisco was socked in, enveloped in a chilly mist that muffled the lonesome sounds of the buoys and foghorns. Ahead, the Golden Gate Bridge loomed like a giant necklace strung with dewdrops. Standing on deck, hardly able to see my hand in front of my face, I recalled the day, ages ago, when I left the beautiful Bay with its sharp, crystal-clear air. Now I found myself a little disappointed at the prospect of a damp and dismal homecoming. This looked more like the harbor at Himeji.

The big ship glided slowly through the water, passing almost soundlessly beneath the shrouded bridge. But no sooner had we cleared it than the layers of cotton wool blanketing everything separated as if in apology, revealing patches of the deep-blue sky I remembered so well. In a matter of seconds the fog lifted like magic, laying the City by the Bay before us like a sparkling jewel in a perfect setting.

Two or three excursion boats plying the harbor came out to meet us on our starboard side with jazz bands blaring the latest tunes and, of all things, women dancing on the decks! Enjoying their spirited imitation of the Rockettes, I noticed that skirts had gotten shorter since we'd been gone.

Ships' bells rang and whistles blew to signal our arrival, and we noticed that the message "Welcome Home!" had been spelled out with large white rocks over on Angel Island. We all rushed to the railing waving, cheering, laughing, and blowing kisses to the women on the boats

below. What a homecoming! The happiness and excitement were almost too much, producing such a high that I thought I would burst.
Could there ever be another day to equal this?

A voice came over the ship's horn. We were making so much noise
we almost drowned it out, but somehow we piped down long enough
to hear that the ship was about to sink! With all five thousand men
hanging off one side, the ship was listing, the captain warned. Whether
he was on the level or just having some fun with us, we took him at his
word and spread out quickly.

Once we docked, the ex-POWs piled off the ship first. I might as well
confess it—yes, I kissed the ground after stepping off the gangplank. So
did a lot of men. Words cannot possibly express how it felt to come
home at last.

Friendly Red Cross workers greeted us warmly and served everyone
coffee and doughnuts there on the dock. No one rushed us. We took
time to enjoy the food while basking in all the attention they lavished
on us. When we were ready, buses took us to Letterman General Hospital in the Presidio. By now we knew the routine by heart. We exchanged our dungarees for corduroy hospital pajamas; they deloused
us yet again; and we got more shots, more whiskey, and more money. I
had accumulated almost a thousand dollars at this point. It still didn't
mean very much.

They assigned us beds in the different wards to await the thorough
physicals we would undergo. Better figure on being there for ten days,
they said. In the meantime, the CIC (Counter Intelligence Corps) and
the FBI debriefed each one of us regarding the brutalities, atrocities,
and war crimes committed by the Japanese in the camps. The fellow
who interviewed me turned out to be a friend and former classmate
from LSU. After congratulating each other on making it through the
war, Tom and I got down to business.

Red Cross volunteers placed calls for us to loved ones back home.
They allowed us one call per customer, and when it went through, we'd
be notified. I gave them Mom's name and went back to my ward.

That first day, I made contact with an attractive nurse as she got me
settled in my ward. Looking up at her with a smile when she attempted

to take my temperature the next day, I said, "I'd really like to break out of here tonight and take you with me. Whaddaya say?"

She just laughed. Not exactly the response I wanted. I must be rusty. I tried the direct approach. Taking the thermometer out of my mouth, I said, "The last time I came through here, I didn't get a chance to see Chinatown. After four years, it would be a shame to miss it again. The air force has been throwing money at me ever since they rescued me, so we could really do this thing right. We could even go dancing."

Still laughing, she replaced the thermometer between my lips. "Slow down soldier! You're in no shape to go dancing."

Did I see the door opening, just a crack? Taking the thermometer out of my mouth again, I shoved my argument home. "I'll see the sights somehow before I leave, but it would be a lot more fun with you."

Putting the thermometer back firmly, she moved to the next patient, saying over her shoulder, "You can't get out of here without clothes, and you can't walk around Chinatown in your pajamas, so there's no point in discussing it!"

I took the thermometer out again and called out in my best southern drawl, "I'd never take a lady out in my pajamas! If I can get clothes, will you go?"

Laughing at my persistence, but not really believing I could be that resourceful, she humored me. "If you can get some clothes, I'll go."

I made my plans. Seizing the first hospital corpsman I saw, I bribed him with a few of Uncle Sam's crisp new bills. "How's about helping a guy out?" I asked.

He eyed the greenbacks I held out temptingly and smiled. "What'll I have to do for it? Murder somebody?"

"Nothing so drastic. All I need is an air force sergeant's uniform that'll halfway fit and size-ten shoes."

"Man, murder would be a whole lot easier! We're not allowed to let you guys out. Keeping everyone in pajamas is the only way we can tie you down long enough to process you."

It was my turn to laugh. "If you think that'll keep us inside, think again. Compared to a G-string and wooden shoes, these pajamas look like full-dress uniforms!"

Reinforcing my argument with another bill or two and looking him straight in the eye, I went on quietly, "It's been a long time, buddy, and this would mean a lot to me."

He hesitated, then came closer. Pocketing the money smoothly, he said, "I'll see what I can do."

Later, lying back and thinking of the swell evening ahead, I heard my name being paged over the loudspeaker; Mom was on the phone. Although very happy to hear my voice at last, she still had questions about my health. I didn't have time to go into all that, so I made her laugh instead. "Don't worry, Ma," I said. "I'm okay. They're feeding us every five minutes, I'm gaining weight like crazy, and I've even got a date tonight!"

"I might have known it would take more than a war to get the best of you!" she said.

I asked about all the gang back home. She told me my Grandmother Caro (her mother) had died while I was in Cabanatuan, and my Grandmother Poncio had passed away in 1944. She said my grandfathers looked forward to seeing me; everyone was all excited about my return. I told her I'd call her back when I had a schedule. "For now," she said, "just knowing you're okay will have to do."

I went back to the ward to wait for the orderly and my clothes, but a few minutes later I heard my name called over the loudspeaker again. Puzzled, since I'd had my one allotted call, I went back and picked up the phone. Aunt Geneva, my father's sister, was on the other end of the line. Mom had immediately called to tell her about our conversation. But Geneva had questions of her own, and she wasn't one to wait for answers, so she picked up the phone and placed her own call. By some miracle, she had gotten through!

"John Henry!" she yelled into the mouthpiece. "Have you still got all your teeth and hair?"

"Well, yeah," I said. "Why do you ask?"

"I've been reading about the ex-POWs returning home. Many of them are said to be in pitiful shape. No hair, no teeth, real weak, and unable to walk. I was worried about you, and I wanted to be sure you were really all right."

"Aunt Gee, I have all my teeth, although I need to see my dentist. My hair is real short, but it's growing fast, and I'm standing here talking to you, so stop worrying."

"Oh, I'm so glad. I'll see you when you get home, darlin'," she said, and rang off.

Walking back to my ward, chuckling about my old sweetheart's questions, I almost failed to notice the uniform with the requisite sergeant's stripes draped over my bed or the shoes on the floor. Hot damn! The corpsman came through after all. He had a good eye for size, I had to say that for him; the uniform didn't fit too badly, considering. The cap, set at a rakish angle, helped the overall effect. At any rate, feeling my oats, I thought I looked pretty dashing.

That evening, before going off duty, my nurse came by the ward. Her dark eyes widened when she saw me dressed in uniform and waiting. She didn't argue. We left, only stopping at the nurses' quarters long enough for her to change.

After dinner in a nice restaurant in Chinatown, we hit the hot spots where the music was snappy—or slow and romantic. The music spilling out of what looked like a movie theater made us curious. Going inside, we watched the older couples in the big ballroom dancing in a wide circle. I'd seen a conga line or two in my day, but this was something new!

Under a large mirrored ball that threw iridescent diamonds of light over the dancers, men and women dressed in evening clothes glided over the floor, doing the same steps together in time to the music. Spread out around the huge hall, they would cover the perimeter of the room several times before the music stopped.

We had stumbled into some sort of dance club. We felt clearly out of place and a little embarrassed. But that didn't make any difference to the gracious people there. Two couples hurried over and invited us to join them. After a few false starts, we were keeping up with the best of them. I'm not a great dancer, but the wings on my feet helped a lot!

The rest of the evening went by in a blur—a crazy, fun night—one of the best. I think before it was over we even found a bowling alley and managed to bowl a few lines. I wasn't tired a bit; I felt reborn. Everything seemed new, fresh, exciting. I fell in love with life all over again. I wanted to hold onto that night, never letting it go.

But it slipped away in spite of my best efforts. The sky grew lighter behind Telegraph Hill; my date worked the morning shift, and I had to find a way back into the hospital. After seeing her home and lingering for a while, I entered by a side door she recommended and made my way down the corridor—only to find the place still jumping. The word was out! MacArthur let it be known that unless his boys committed cold-blooded murder, no one could jail us. When the guys got wind of that, they took off, hospital rules and pajamas notwithstanding! MPs had rounded up the guys downtown and brought them in by the truckload, all in various stages of complete happiness.

I was asleep when my favorite nurse woke me and informed me that I had lost something. "The maid found your wallet. Apparently it fell behind the cushions on the couch in the living room." She handed it over, still stuffed with dollar bills. I thanked her, but she could have kept it for all I cared. I hadn't missed it. My mind must have been on other things, I guess.

All this time, they fed us continuously. I began to put on weight so fast my illicit uniform strained at the seams when it was buttoned. I managed to hang onto it, breaking out several more times with the gang in my ward before the hospital authorities caught us one night, took the uniform away, and slapped us in the psycho ward. They were getting nowhere trying to process the wild and woolly men, so in desperation they locked us up. It did the trick. Finally they established an orderly routine, and in between visits to various labs and specialists, we renewed old friendships, made new ones, and learned the fate of a lot of buddies who didn't make it.

Only 15 of the 250 men in my squadron survived. Freddie Barr didn't come back. My last recollection of him was of the two of us sitting on the huge pile of shoes in Cabanatuan, sorting them into pairs. Laurence told me that Freddie had died in October 1944 on the hell ship *Arisan Maru* when an American submarine fired torpedoes into the hull of the unmarked vessel. The Japs cut the ladder lines into the hold, shut the hatches, and left the ship. Many of the men swam out of the listing freighter toward nearby Japanese destroyers, but the sailors pushed most of them off, using long poles to drown them. Some of the survivors said they heard the men still trapped in the *Arisan Maru* singing "God Bless America" as the ship filled with water.

We weren't the first ex-POWs to return to the States. Some of the others, captured by the Japanese on New Guinea, Guam, or Wake Island and later liberated by American forces, returned before my group did. The plan, carried out in the best military tradition, usually called for flying the sailors and marines home, with the air force (natch) going back by ship.

In the days that followed, we spent long hours talking to each other about the war, the camps, and the survival tactics we employed. Sometimes the laughter spilled out into the hall, causing the nurses to run in and fuss at us for disturbing the other patients. But they usually stayed to laugh with us and listen to stories that defied all logic. Sometimes they had to leave, fighting back tears. The psychologists and psychiatrists who talked to us were amazed at the resiliency of the men. Overall, they said, very few had cracked under the strain.

In addition to giving me a medical exam (basic diagnosis: hungry!), the military attempted to rebuild our service records from scratch. All of the men were in the same boat; everyone had lost everything he possessed. At that point, I couldn't even prove I was me! Working out of barracks converted into temporary processing centers, WACs and WAVEs handled the routine paperwork.

Women in the armed forces was still a novel idea—but in our opinion a very good one—and we enjoyed the "scenery" tremendously. Back where I came from, the grownups talked either Sicilian or French when they didn't want the children to know what was being said. Standing in line one day, and thinking we were being cagey, several of us began discussing in Japanese the looks of an exceptionally good-looking woman. I'm afraid our comments, followed by a lot of raucous laughter, weren't very nice. As we rounded the corner, a Japanese American girl working within earshot of our crude remarks gave us a withering look that stopped us dead in our tracks. She knew exactly what we'd been saying, and she let us know she didn't appreciate that kind of talk one bit! We learned two valuable lessons that day. First, women had more than proven themselves, taking their rightful place in the workforce and in society. Second, the world to which we had returned was becoming an international community; foreign languages would become commonplace, even in Small Town, USA.

Hospital trains were being readied to take each of us to the medical facility nearest his home. For the boys from the southern part of the United States, that meant Brooke Army General in San Antonio. The day I left, I went down and said goodbye to my favorite nurse. I kissed her on the cheek and gave her a big hug, telling her how much our night on the town meant to me. She wished me the best of luck and kissed me back—but not on the cheek! Finally, dressed in our red or navy corduroy pajamas, we boarded the first-class accommodations, leaving the Presidio and San Francisco for the trip across the country.

This train had the right of way. Whenever we came through, the other trains en route—freight or passenger, it didn't matter—got pushed off onto a siding to let us pass. Talk about traveling in style. The food was out of this world—and the service! Swordfish, steak, and strawberries, all impeccably served by white-jacketed stewards.

The contrast with our living conditions just six weeks before was so great, it was like being on another planet. Ensconced in plush seats designed for maximum comfort, in a perfectly controlled atmosphere, and pampered royally by two nurses and two corpsmen in each car, we headed for home. We traveled the length of California, paralleling the Coast Range, through the valley to Los Angeles.

The train carried us along the southern route through Arizona, New Mexico, and Texas, and the endless deserts of those western states with their ever-changing colors of gold, red, and purple. Although the route and scenery differed from the coast-to-coast trek I'd taken four years before, the beauty of this vast country still impressed me. Before my journey ended, I'd go home to the land of lush green swamps, cross the great muddy rivers, and see the mighty oaks with their sweeping limbs that touched the ground.

We slept on mattresses specially built to cushion every bump. Kidding around with one of the nurses that first evening as I climbed in between the freshly laundered sheets, I remarked with all sincerity, "Y'all have really treated everybody like kings, doing everything you could think of to make us happy. Y'know, about the only thing you haven't done is tuck us in and kiss us goodnight."

"Well, if that's all it takes to make you happy," she said and, tucking me in, she leaned over and gave me a sweet goodnight kiss. Now, man, that's livin'!

The trip took about forty-eight hours. On the afternoon of the second day, we stopped somewhere in Texas to wait for a train up ahead to switch off onto a siding. "Well, whaddaya know?" drawled one of my fellow passengers, looking out the window. "If this don't beat all!"

"What's the matter?" I asked.

"Man, my house is only a quarter-mile over that hill!"

"No kiddin'."

"Yeah. And for two cents, I'd hightail it outta here and be home in time for supper."

"What's stopping you, buddy?"

"Come to think of it, not a damn thing!" he said. Grabbing up his meager bag of possessions, he calmly walked down the aisle to the vestibule, opened the door, and took off.

John Henry Poncio out on the town in San Antonio, Texas, with a friend.

"Hey, come back," yelled one of the corpsmen. "You can't leave now!"

"Don't worry," the boy called out over his shoulder as he crossed the tracks and climbed over the barbed-wire fence that bordered a field. "I'll see you guys in San Antone in a few days. Right now, I'm gonna give my mama one helluva surprise! Hooowee!"

The medical examiners at Brooke General in San Antonio took about a week to determine if I was fit for home leave. Only those with severe physical or mental problems, weak hearts, or communicable diseases had to stay for any length of time. The effects of my beriberi were clearing up, I was getting stronger every day, and I no longer looked like a walking skeleton—although I was still hungry!

The boy who had left the train outside of San Antonio made it back by the third day. "Boy!" he said. "I nearly gave my mama and daddy a heart attack. But, hell, I was just too close not to drop in and say hello!"

I met up with Laurence before I left San Antonio. He said he was going back to Fort Worth and the florist business. We shook hands and promised to stay in touch.

When they released me, the doctors told me, "Take off soldier. We don't want to see you for 180 days. Get reacquainted with your family, friends, and life in the U.S. before you make up your mind about the future. General MacArthur has ordered that all ex-POWs can reenlist regardless of their conditions. If you decide to stay in, you have first choice of duty. But right now you need time to assess your situation. When the 180 days are up, come back. We'll put you through the paces again to determine if you're fit for duty or need another ninety-day leave." Along with my orders, they handed me a fistful of ration books and a train ticket home.

I was alone for the first time in four years and, for the next 360 miles, free of restraints, rules, and the people who made them. No need to talk, respond, or even think if I didn't want to. While it felt great to blank everything out, it felt odd, too. I had a vague feeling of being disconnected, out of sync, out of touch. *The docs warned us about this, ol' buddy,* I said to myself. *It's only natural. Take it one day at a time! Hell, five minutes at a time, if need be! Coming down from a high sustained by everything that has happened in the last two months, there was bound to be a "thud" at the end of it. You made it through some rough times. Can't come apart at the seams when things are finally getting back to normal.*

I forced my mind into more familiar patterns of thinking, deciding right then and there never to dwell on the horrors in the camps, feel sorry for myself, or try to find someone to blame for the last four years—not even the Japanese. That had never been my style anyway, so why start now? To concentrate on the future, to pick up where I had left off after giving myself time to rest—that was the ticket!

Taking a deep breath, and feeling better, I lit a cigarette and sat looking out the window, just letting the familiar scenes roll by, soaking up the quiet time, preparing for the homecoming I'd dreamed about for so long.

My first stop was Lake Charles, where I visited Aunt Lena, Mother's sister, and her husband and son. I spent a day and a night with them in their big old house near Prien Lake. What a cook! The homecoming meal we'd planned and eaten so many times in the camps didn't compare to the one Aunt Lena fed me.

After a supper that left us all groaning, we went into the unique living room, which had always fascinated me. It had been designed for entertaining, with floor-to-ceiling doors to partition off the formal areas. When the doors were folded back, the room could accommodate a large gathering.

Over coffee, as we settled down on the deep sofas flanking the fireplace, Aunt Lena said, "John, I'm not going to grill you. You'll get plenty of that when you get home. But if you want to talk, we'll be glad to listen."

"I appreciate that," I said. "It's not that I don't want to tell you about it. I will, of course. But for now, let me just enjoy the good company, the peace and quiet, and the feeling of being my own man again."

"I understand perfectly. Tell you what, the whole time you were gone, I saved all the *Look, Life, Time,* and *Collier's* magazines, and I also clipped newspaper articles marking the progress of the war in Europe and the Pacific. I knew you'd come back, Johnnie-boy, and I figured you'd be curious about the things that went on while you were out of circulation.

"I know you want to see your mama as soon as you can, but when you're through galivantin' and making the rounds, come on back here and just get caught up. We have the latest records, a phonograph, and the refrigerator will be stocked with your favorite beer and plenty of snacks. You can sleep as late as you wish. No one will disturb you."

Reaching over, I planted a big kiss on her cheek. "You always knew me better than I knew myself," I said. "Thanks. I'll be back soon to take you up on your generous offer."

I left the next morning, stopping in New Iberia for a day to see my late father's brother John before heading for Franklin and home. We had always had a good relationship, and he was overjoyed to see me. He told me about Grandma's death and how she longed to see me before she died. Both of us were quiet, remembering her, grieving for her in our own way.

That night I went with Uncle John to an American Legion meeting. The Legion had been founded in Paris in March 1919, headed by Lt. Col. Theodore Roosevelt Jr. As a member of the American Expeditionary Force, Uncle John had been chosen as a delegate to the meeting in Paris and signed the charter.

In 1942 the charter was amended to include veterans of World War II. The Legion's requirements were honorable service and an honorable discharge. Their major interest and concern has always been the care of disabled and sick veterans, the establishing of hospitals for veterans, and the championing of bonuses, compensations, and pensions for disabled vets, their widows, and their orphans.

I think he was proud to sign me up as a member and to introduce me to his friends. I was proud to be there.

No one knew exactly when I'd be arriving in Franklin, so I took a taxi from the station, stopping at a florist's to buy Mom the biggest bouquet of flowers I could find. (I thought of Omasa and smiled.) Pulling up in front of the old place, I paid the driver, dashed up the steps, and opened the door.

My sisters Maebelle and Rita sat in the living room, and Mom was in the kitchen. As I walked in Maebelle looked up and screamed, I think. Then she and Rita jumped up and threw their arms around me. Mom, hearing all the commotion and squealing that only teenaged girls can do, hurried in still holding her cooking spoon. We had a four-way hug—and a joyous one!

"Oh, John, my boy," Mom said, "you're home at last! Let me look at you." She loved the flowers, but the ration books were also a big hit!

I had been so well fed up to that point, I don't remember exactly what she served that night. One of the dishes may have been corn on the cob. After I finished the meal, I excused myself to wash my hands. I knew we were having fruit salad for dessert, but a few minutes later when I sat down and reached for the plate that had been at my place when I left, it wasn't there!

"Where's my fruit?" I asked.

"Maebelle ate it," said Mom. "She thought you were through."

"Damn," I said, tweaking my sister's ear. "I didn't think I had to worry about things like that anymore," I teased her. "If I figured you had designs on my food, I would have put my arm around it to keep it from walking off!"

A very embarrassed Maebelle apologized over and over while Mom spooned up another helping. We had a good laugh when I explained about the way food would suddenly disappear in the camps if you didn't watch it like a hawk!

We sat up half the night talking about the last four years. Everyone had questions. What were the Japanese like? How did they treat us? Were they as bad as the propaganda said? Did they torture us? Did we have enough to eat? What did we do with our time? Did we have doctors when we got sick? Did I know when the first atom bomb was dropped? How did the Japanese people react?

Later, the talk switched to my brother Frank, who joined the air force in 1943. He became a pilot, flying the B-29s built to make war on Japan. He was still stationed on Guam three or four months after peace was signed.

When he got back, Frank said he was living proof that the average Japanese soldier was a tough cookie. "I had just walked up the steps to the officers' club one night when I heard the crack of rifle fire," he said. "I ducked just in time. A sniper's bullet went whizzing by, splintering the door frame about two inches above my head. Apparently, a haitai had failed to get the word and fought on despite the odds. A few of our boys got it before we finished sweeping the islands."

Maebelle had gone to work for the draft board when she finished high school the year before. Lazing around the house one day, she asked me, "Have you registered for the draft?"

"Who? Me? Register for the draft? Are you nuts?"

"Well, it's the law, you know."

"No, I didn't know, but to hell with the law. It can't apply in my case!" I argued hotly.

"It applies to everyone, regardless of status, even those on active duty," she said—somewhat smugly, it seemed to me.

"Forget it kid. The answer's no! I'm not registering for the draft, and that's final!"

"John, listen to me," she pleaded. "You always were a rebel at heart, but this time you're just not thinking. You could get into a lot of trouble if you don't."

"Ha! And what can they do to me? Haul me off to jail?" I said with a laugh. "Do you really think I'm afraid of being put in a place where they feed the inmates three squares a day?"

She grew silent. I could see the wheels turning, but she didn't give me any more static. She was old enough to remember that when I dug my heels in, there was no point in pursuing the subject.

It was the principle of the thing. I didn't give a damn about some stupid law on the books. Besides, all ex-POWs should be exempt from a thing like that. I put it out of my mind, but Maebelle didn't.

Not wanting me to become a victim of the system, she registered for me the next day. She wisely kept it to herself for a long time afterward. Then, when I had time to cool off, she confessed, and we had a good laugh over the whole thing. I remember with love and respect her wisdom, even at the tender age of eighteen—my sister who would later die of a brain tumor while still so young.

After spending a few days with my family, I continued east to Morgan City to see Grandpa Poncio. He had aged somewhat, and he was getting frail, but he still had that proud, ramrod carriage that I remembered. When I walked into the house, we fell into each other's arms and he wept. "Grandma, she worried so much about you," he said. "She wanted more than anything to see you before she died."

Embarrassed by his emotional display, he pulled himself together, and we talked and laughed about old times. He reminded me of the time the notice from the draft board had come to the house during the "Big One," World War I.

Uncle John had already left for the front and was fighting somewhere in France. Obviously, the notice was meant for him. But Grandpa, who had infantry training in Italy before coming to live in America, thought that Uncle Sam wanted him. "I tooka the old gun down from the mantel, saida goodbye to your Grandma, anda went down to report to the authorities," he said in his Sicilian accent.

"I stood in a longa line, and when they got to me, they tooka one look, and said, 'What are you doing here old man? There musta be some mistake!'"

His body shook with laughter at the memory. Then he continued with the story, pointing his finger at the imaginary bureaucrat. "'Hot dammie,' I said. 'There isa no mistake! I ama good soldier and I ama here to do my duty anda proud to serve my new country witha honor!'

"'Are you John Poncio?' he asked, scratching his head.

"'Yes, I ama he,' I said.

"'Do you live at this address on the card?'

"'Yes sir,' I answered.

"'Are you twenty-four years old?'

"'Are you a crazy man? Do I looka like I'ma twenty-four years old?'

"'Mr. Poncio, do you have a son by the same name?'

"'Yes, your honor, I do,' I said. 'Buta he joined the army lasta year, and isa already somewhere in France.'

"'Well, I think we can clear this up right now,' he said, and I could tell he wasa trying not to laugh. 'Obviously, the notice was meant for your son. I am terribly sorry you came down here for nothing, and we'll get the matter straightened out right away. Go home, Mr. Poncio. But rest assured America appreciates your loyalty and willingness to serve.' Anda he grabbed my hand anda gave it a good shake."

After visiting Grandpa, I made the rounds and saw my father's sisters, Aunt Gee and Aunt Rose, as well as Mom's kin in New Orleans. Everywhere I went, people were wonderful; they all wanted to touch me, feed me, and cry over my narrow escapes. The long hours of getting it off my chest to appreciative audiences were exhausting—but cleansing, too. I didn't want pity, so I glossed over the more gory aspects of prison life and concentrated on getting them to laugh at the survival tactics we had used and at how human nature, even in dire straits, could appreciate the irony of the situation. Each day the pain receded a little more, with only the bizarre and sometimes hilarious episodes remaining uppermost in my mind.

When I got back to Mom's, a two-hundred-dollar check from Uncle Sam waited for me on the hall table. A letter enclosed with the money explained that it was compensation for the claim of October 1941, entered on my behalf, and covered the cost of replacing my civilian clothes that had been dumped into San Francisco Bay. "Well, I'll be damned!" was all I could think to say.

I called Aunt Lena and told her I was ready to do some reading. "Come on down," she said. "We're expecting you!"

She met me at the train station, took me home, and showed me everything she'd saved for me. Magazines, newspapers, and other periodicals were stacked in the corners, on side tables, and on the floor next to the easy chair and ottoman. She had stocked the fridge with Cokes, Jax beer, fruit, ham, and cheese, and filled the cookie jar with my favorite coconut macaroons. Beside the comfortable double bed piled high with down pillows, a bedside table held a lamp, a phonograph, and the latest Hit Parade records.

My apartment was at the top of the house, secluded, quiet, and peaceful. Over the next seven days, this retreat provided the perfect place for me to hibernate, regroup, and learn about the world to which I had returned.

I found the information Aunt Lena had collected fascinating and riveting! As I studied the war in the Pacific, I was amazed at how our sailors in camp, piecing together bits of information and scuttlebutt from the Japs, had often come up with a fairly accurate picture of events soon after they happened.

I read about FDR's death and about his little-known vice president,

Harry S. Truman, who had courageously made the awesome decision to drop the atom bomb. I saw photographs of the deadly effects on Hiroshima and Nagasaki; the accounts confirmed what I had seen with my own eyes. The number of dead was even more chilling when all the facts were in. Still, I remained convinced there was no other choice; I believe the bomb saved more lives than it took.

North Africa, where the 13th was sent, had been a tough campaign. Later, I would meet up with Red, a member of my old squad in Denver. "John, you son of a bitch," he said. "I've been waiting all this time to tell you that if you hadn't fallen off the wing of your airplane while refueling it that day, landing in the hospital, there would've been no need to replace you. I ended up chasing Rommel all over the goddamn desert, buddy, and it's all your fault!"

When I got through telling him where I had spent the entire war, he didn't have much to say.

The bombardiers sent to Europe, where I had been chomping at the bit to go, also had a lousy track record in the beginning. Someone told me 110 percent of the planes were either shot down or crippled over Germany, crash-landing in enemy territory or on their return to England.

"How the hell can you lose 110 percent?" I asked.

"When you lose just about everyone, plus the 10 percent in reserve—that's how!"

As I read, my mind, like a dried-up sponge, absorbed everything it could about the modern technology brought about by the war. But the most exciting thing of all to me, was that in gearing up for the war effort, industry had taken a giant leap into the world of mass production. At the same time we built a massive army and navy, we had to produce the war machinery, and we had to do it in a hurry!

This called for a new approach to manufacturing. The retooling of America's factories and mills took place almost overnight. Raw materials, including families' donated aluminum pots and pans, were diverted from domestic use to military use so the ships and planes, tanks and trucks could roll off the assembly line in record numbers.

Although the effort meant sacrifice and shortages for Americans, we would experience a postwar boom the likes of which the world had

Master Sergeant Poncio, ROTC instructor, Louisiana Polytechnic Institute, Ruston, 1953.

never known. The Champion Company, which made sparkplugs before the war, made the 50-caliber machine guns I'd manned on Bataan. But as soon as the war was over, they went back to making sparkplugs. Other companies did the same. Switching gears quickly, they were beginning to manufacture more and better stoves, washing machines, refrigerators, and automobiles for less money.

Social change filled the air. The war ushered in a new age for the women left behind. With all the strong young men called up, Rosie the Riveter rolled up her sleeves and pitched in. From the pictures in the magazines I got to see these gals in action, working side by side with men in the mills and factories, doing the same jobs.

"Ma, how did you learn to weld, for Pete's sake?" was a frequent question asked by sons when they came back from the war.

Of course, not all of the women got left behind. Many of them also joined the armed services to become partners in the fight. Along with the traditional role of nursing, they became mechanics' apprentices and filled communication and administrative posts.

I found my WAC in my own backyard and married her in 1946 after she was discharged. Inez kids me (even after fifty years) by telling me that, working in the central payroll division at Camp Shelby in Mississippi, she had access to everyone's records. When she went down the list and got to my name, she said, "Hey, this joker hasn't been paid in four years. Look at all the money he's got coming from the army. He's the one for me!"

Actually, I had gone to high school with Inez. She always seemed like the ideal girl to me, but she didn't seem interested. When I got home, I decided to give her one more chance. On our very first date, I told her I planned to marry her. She laughed—just like the nurse in San Francisco. But just like the nurse, she didn't argue.

Aunt Lena, understanding the needs of the inner man, saved the records that were popular while I was gone. People might think they don't need music, but they're wrong. I spent long hours listening to some of the most beautiful music written during those years of turmoil.

POW Girocho's artifacts: a bento basket for rice, a dog tag made by a Japanese soldier from a copper lantern's reflector, and a samurai doll and fan given to John Henry Poncio by a Japanese sergeant.

Lyrics that spoke of love, hope, dreams, tenderness, and idealism. Not surprisingly, I learned that "Lili Marlene" was sung by American and German soldiers alike.

On Bataan, when Tokyo Rose spun records, we heard her limited selection night after night. Rose failed to understand that we discounted the crap she dispensed and just concentrated on the brand of music, distinctly ours, and it gave us a psychological lift.

In Japan, the Japs played the "Flower Song" in camp, but the notes and the wailing that went with it were so foreign to our ears, it didn't come close to filling the void we felt.

Coming home on the ships, all I can remember hearing over the loudspeakers was, "Sweepers, man your brooms! Sweep her down fore and aft!" Not exactly music to my ears. Not until 'Frisco did I get to hear the latest tunes.

Swing was in, and one of my favorites was Glenn Miller's "In the Mood." It was all wonderful—lively, romantic, easy to dance to, dis-

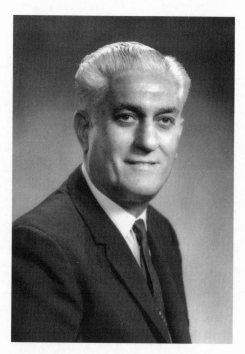

John Henry Poncio in 1970.

tinctly American, and unbeatable therapy. It made you want to go out and just live! "Let's went" became my theme song for that first year back home. I also like to say, "When I got home, I 'lit' running." I know the music played a big part in making it a true statement.

One week later, thanks to Aunt Lena's invaluable gift of time—time to catch up and time to heal—I emerged from my cocoon refreshed, relaxed, and ready to tackle life again. After two more trips to San Antonio, and one to Camp Shelby to reenlist in the air force (just missing Inez, who had returned home), I reported back for duty nine months later.

In many ways, I was older than my twenty-seven years. My hair was turning gray here and there. I would have to learn to live with the medical problems inflicted by years of deprivation, disease, and malnutrition. The sight in my left eye was gone (couldn't hit a baseball anymore!), but I could still see well enough to know that, although the last four years had taken a permanent toll on my body, they had made me stronger, too.

I realized there was no room in my life for bitterness. While I could say "I love you" in five different languages, I only knew one for hate. If I was going to get on with the business of living, I couldn't waste my time on sadness or tears; all that was in the past.

A brand-new world lay ahead. Not a perfect world, to be sure. There would be more challenges to meet—and no doubt my share of heartaches—but with faith, love, hope, and laughter, I knew I could make it.